**THE
COMPASS
OF
NAIVETY**

CLIVE CHABRIER

Copyright Clive Chabrier © 2008

All rights reserved. No part of this book may be reproduced, stored in a retrieval system or utilized in any form by any means, electronic or mechanical, including photocopying, recording, or otherwise without written permission from the copyright owner.

Written by Clive Chabrier
Illustrations by Clive Chabrier
Cover and book design by Matine Chabrier

First edition May 2013

ACKNOWLEDGEMENTS

A huge thanks to Denny Ellis for laboriously typing my tape-recorded story on to the computer in the early stages. To Susanne Templer for endless cups of tea, hospitality and encouragement, and to her recently passed away sister, Marianne, who kindly read and corrected my first tentative hard copy.

To friends and associates that have reviewed, read, or just dipped into the story and been supportive, but who may or may not wish to have their full names included. Some of these are Dr A T. (deceased), Kim A., Andy S., Cath C., Peter H., Glenis P., Peter K., and his mother and friends (in Australia), Marianne L., Albert T., Nancy S., Kendall G., and finally Mike C. who sadly has recently passed away.

To Myrna and Matine for always responding to my many calls of help around computer issues.

To Ruti and Kyene for consistent support and fortitude throughout the crazy series of technical and practical mishaps that resulted in most of the story being lost and re-written several times. And very special thanks to Kyene for her invaluable help in piecing together the shattered jigsaw and for staying with it right to the end.

Also thanks to Trish C. and Caroline K. who read, corrected and commented helpfully on the pre-final manuscript, and Sarah D. for listening while I read the whole story to her in instalments.

My special appreciation to Kendall G. for comments, questions and editorial suggestions.

Finally, I again thank Matine for adjusting the images and manuscript before taking them through the mysterious process of turning them into a book.

CONTENTS

		PAGES
	Prologue	9
1	'Six Eggs'	15
2	'Entrapped by La Legion'	22
3	'Glimpse of a Fantasy'	29
4	'One Small Victory'	38
5	'Whispers of Leaving'	41
6	'Worked Over by Professionals'	46
7	'To North Africa'	53
8	'Avoiding the Square Head'	62
9	'The Shock'	69
10	'Dans la Merde!'	76
11	'Close Combat'	84
12	'Hope is to Bounce'	92
13	'Transition'	100
14	'The Real Thing'	105
15	'I'm made of Jelly?'	116
16	'Tea for Two'	122
17	'It is Fear, Oh Little Hunter…'	125
18	'Sacrifices to a Sacred Order'	129
19	'Paris, Almost!'	133
20	'Time to Leave'	137
21	'A Smokey Freedom'	142
22	'Sod's Law'	150
23	'Algerie Encore'	158
24	'North Africa Receding'	162
25	'A Future Beckons'	165
26	'A Cell with a Stone Pillow'	170
27	'Negative Headway'	177
28	'When Girls Ain't Girls!'	182
29	'Headin' for Paradise'	187
30	'The Great North West'	196
31	'Roo Tail and Damper'	204
32	'Magnetising Ants'	209
33	'Islands in the Sky'	218

34	'The Old Ghan'	229
35	'Reunion Achieved'	234
36	'Ghost in a Ghost Town'	240
37	'Snakes Don't Chase?'	247
38	'Good as Any White Man' and 'The Tree of Healing'	252
39	'On a Barge Among the Islands'	258
40	'Nip of the Red Back'	269
41	'Pearl Shells and Testicles'	277
42	'The Rot Sets In'	291
43	'End of An Era'	295
44	'France too close for Comfort'	302
45	'The Compass Flickers'	306

IMAGES

1	Saharienne Legionnaires	30
2	Fort St Nicholas	33
3	Code	44
4	1st REP Badge	60
5	Map of Algeria	61
6	Clive with beer bottle	89
7	Brevets (wings)	97
8	Clive in 2éme REP uniform	99
9	2nd REP Badge	99
10	Green Beret	105
11	Dangling Prisoners	114
12	Map of Escape	167
13	Map of Western Australia	185
14	Overtaking a road train	193
15	Whim Creek	197
16	Broome	215
17	Boab trees	216
18	Map of Buccaneer Archipelago	219
19	Islands in the sky	223
20	Picture of Ken and Clive with car	235
21	Our house in Broome	279
22	View from our Window	279

NOTE TO READER: This is a true story based on memories of over 50 years ago. Many names and incidents have been adjusted to avoid unnecessary discomfort to anybody. Short discussions and overheard comments have, in places, been attributed to various individual conversations.

PROLOGUE

I have just seen a film *"Beau Travail"*, a brilliant piece of artistic conversion that cleverly micro-echoes that same indoctrination which still stirs somewhere within me, raising its head at odd moments.

Some fifty years later I get a bizarre satisfaction out of singing those melancholy French Foreign Legion songs in my bath, soaking away, capturing old images, a sort of nostalgic daydreaming of a period of my life that was in fact horrific.

Now three days after seeing the film for the second time, I am going through a curious mixture of feelings, observations and questions. Why? How? What actually is memory? What is recall? And just how much of it is repetition of particular events, times and places?

Eastern Algeria 1960

There is a cold blue sky framed by a snow clad mountainous landscape, an eagle soars overhead. I am very deliberately eating my serving of donkey and lentils, standing with other men so together in action, yet so separate inside. Impassively we watch a fellow legionnaire taunting the two wretches, our so-called enemy, who stand trembling miserably and tied back to back. Their long ordeal of torture is over as they are of no further use to us.

I remember little of the faces or clothing of anyone, sure I can piece together obvious facts, our 'macho' camouflage combat clothes, our tight green slanted berets, with the winged dagger insignia of the 2nd Foreign Legion Parachute Regiment' (2^e REP) and the snow clad mountains and rocks ahead of me and to either side, but those are not memories.

The cold blue sky I remember, with the eagle or whatever bird that was overhead, and those awful sickening feelings inside. I remember the general terrain of mountains and valleys, with our relative positions to each other, standing before our self-built hill fort. I could draw a diagram with each thing and person in relation to the others, but not actually remember. I do have an image of the *'djellaba'* worn by one of the prisoners, although to me at that time it was just a white robe.

I recall that we stood about six feet in front of the rock and log defence wall that shielded our otherwise canvas encampment. That same wall we had built with our own hands some weeks before. But there is no memory of actually building it. Wait! ... Yes ... here it comes...

Long, exhausting days of endlessly climbing that hill in all conceivable weather, struggling with trunks of trees and huge often bitterly cold, jagged unwieldy rocks, at all times driven on by our over zealous corporals while ever-vigilant sentries continually scanned our surroundings in piercing sunlight, or peered intensely into the blanket of mist for signs of *'La Fell'* (Fellagha) our ever elusive, yet ominously present foe.

It was at the bottom of this same hill, and many others like it, that I so often believed I was at my last tether. Faint, sore, utterly exhausted, having tramped day or night at seemingly impossible pace for weeks at a time with an over-laden pack, through relentless Algerian mountains, with their valleys, rocks and streams, that we simply referred to as *'La Djebel'*. Only on arrival to be shoved, kicked and punched about by our mainly German corporals and sergeants, screaming at us in their mixed Franco German legion language to,

"Shut the f*** up you good for nothing cadavers!"
"Get your f***ing shit together!"
"Ferme toi la geulle du mensch!"
"Demerdez-vous alors du scheise mensch!"
"Kommst hier du scheise mensch, putain de merde du scheise alors!"

Followed by more punches, shoves and kicks aimed at resurrecting some life and fresh order out of our sinking apathy.

Then came the preparation orders. *"Garde-à-vous! Repos! G'da-vous! R'po! G'vous! 'Po! 'Vous!"* Once satisfied, there came that slow, elongated, count, which signalled our marching orders.

"Section . . . En avant . . . Marche! . . . . . . Deux . . . Trois . . . Et Quatre! . . ."

As we paced our slow, elongated stride in the traditional style of *'La Légion Etrangère'* resolutely climbing the steep slope of our hill in that cold or hot mountain air, it was to prove to any enemy within earshot, that 'we' were in charge of that terrain.

On the order, *"La Tone!"* we matched our stride to one of the slow, resounding, melancholy songs, a dirge about homesickness, duty, sacrifice and death, which is one of the songs that I still sing some fifty years later with mournful pleasure in my bath –

"En Afrique . . . Malgré le vent, la pluie . . . Guettez le sentinel, sur le piton. . . ."

Any belief that I was in fact 'at my last tether' would be brutally cleansed on arrival, along with such fantasies I might have harboured regarding a well-earned rest. For once 'at home' on our rock and log fortified hill top fort, we were immediately brought to attention to be duly screeched at, knocked into shape and presented for inspection by yet another dedicated corporal, who more than likely had not even been on the march with us.

With that ritual complete, damaged equipment, missing items like bullets, grenades and torn clothes were recorded and duly signed for, to be more often than not, deducted from our meagre pay. Just one of the many rackets that I discovered worked upon we newcomers known as *'Les Bleus'* by the longer serving veterans known as *'Les Anciens'*.

Next there came orders for a whole series of urgent tasks to be carried out in the legion's intensely pressurised, thorough and disciplined manner.

"Come on, get your shit together!" (*"Allez-vous en, putain dis-donc! Demerdez vous!"*)

And so, as always, hidden reserves were leached out of us.

Yet, when the long awaited time finally came for sleep, it was in the knowledge that it would be interrupted at some ungodly hour for a lonely stint of guard duty, which would be carried out some hundred yards away beside an isolated rock or bush. Only to rise at four thirty to a couple of hours disciplined activity, followed by the prescribed 'part mug' of sweet black coffee and meagre compliment of bread and bacon.

And then, another day of harsh and often brutal activity would begin.

The sixth code of Legion honour states,
"A mission once given to you becomes sacred and you will accomplish it to the end at all costs."

As we stand chewing our helping of donkey and lentils, the swarthy legionnaire in charge of the pair of bound together prisoners, casually pulls out his sheathed blade and slits the first man's throat, he then proceeds with the deft skill of a professional butcher, to probe and slice until he holds the severed head by its hair, thrusting it into the face of the shaking, staggering, terrified second prisoner.

Following more pointless taunting and laughter, supposedly for the benefit of us on-lookers, the head is heaved out over the cliff, spinning and whirling blood like some macabre Catherine wheel.

While still tied to and therefore staggering to support both himself and the headless collapsing body of his comrade, the second man is frog-marched to the precipice where in absolute terror he is almost indifferently shoved out into the abyss by his executing tormenter, who then calmly wipes the bloodied blade on the snowy ground, replacing the knife into its sheath before casually returning to join us in eating from our mess tins *('gamells')* the donkey and lentils which most of us had finished, or now finish impassively.

Memory moves on to melting snow in sunshine, accompanied by the sickening stench of rotting bodies over an ensuing period of sweltering hot days and freezing nights, which was due to some prisoners' corpses that were left burning within the vicinity of our camp. Standing out on watch alone among the boulders and scrub during the dead of night with that un-holy smoke silently wafting on the breeze was not particularly pleasant, and for me at least, hauntingly upsetting.

This was to be reaffirmed some twenty years later when during a walk through similar terrain in England, a peaceful combination of bubbling streams from leftover snows, silent winter trees and wood smoke wafting on the breeze, re-awakened dormant sensations of horror.

Part of the seventh code of Legion honour states,
"In combat you will act without relish of your task or hatred of your enemy"

Prologue

Certainly the execution that I witnessed beneath that cold blue sky was carried out with both relish and hatred. Sometime later I was expressing my judgemental horror of those awful incidents to a fellow legionnaire who I found to be approachable. The story he told me about the man who carried out that atrocity was at least as bad, if not even more horrible.

I will call that executioner *'Carlos'*, as I thought he was Spanish. Before becoming a legionnaire, *Carlos* had been living with his wife and their two children in Algeria. Returning to his house one night he discovered that a metal wardrobe had been dragged outside into the garden, covered with brushwood and set on fire. When he opened the door of the wardrobe, to his utter horror he discovered inside that the whole of his family had been cooked alive by so called 'freedom fighters'.

A couple of days after the cliff top execution of the two men, we set off in early morning darkness, on one of those gruelling marches, the point of which I never quite understood. They inevitably involved miles of rushing through difficult terrain laden with heavy packs, arms and ammunition, often along tracks that sometimes were obvious though more often than not, only apparent to the owl-eyed *'ancient'* whose job it was to lead us, a man clearly chosen for his amazing ability to follow barely visible tracks, even in the dark. As for me, I just followed struggling with every breath to keep up, convinced as always that I was about to collapse, while I guess the guy behind me was doing just the same.

On this particular occasion, we took a circuitous route that eventually brought us around beneath the same precipice that dropped away a couple of hundred yards from the front of our hill fort. This route meant passing close to the rotting bodies of the earlier disposed of prisoners. As our line of men rapidly paced along, seemingly oblivious of the awful reality now clearly visible in the snowy morning light, *Carlos*, who was ahead of me in line, suddenly broke rank to race over and begin handling the now stinking cadavers.

I was sickened and horrified to see him sit astride the putrid, headless corpse, eagerly fumbling with and tearing away the belt that he had evidently coveted during his cruel macabre activities of the days before. Then obviously very pleased with this trophy, he immediately buckled it around his waist before bounding enthusiastically back to his position in line.

As we raced on to god knows where, all I found myself bizarrely wondering was where the hell did he get all that extra energy, as I just struggled to keep up throughout the whole episode. It was effort, which thankfully served to numb some of the dread that might have consumed me under less pressurised circumstances, in that sense, the intense pace that we were always forced to maintain definitely had psychological benefits.

Certainly on the first occasion that I found myself potentially facing action, I was relieved to discover that rather than feeling petrified as I had expected, I was actually glad of the opportunity to have a break from that endless, relentless marching.

Throughout those times of pressurised tramping about that harsh mountainous terrain both days and nights with the legion, it seemed to me that whenever I felt I only had a few paces left to give, some other poor bugger would drop. On more than one occasion, I saw the guy who carried the medical kit ordered to give a fallen legionnaire who had failed to respond to a barrage of kicks and punches, some sort of injection to get him back on his feet. Much as I pitied him, particularly as *'les caporaux'* began brutally setting about him, I somewhat shamefully thanked my good fortune, knowing that I had once more been reprieved by gaining a desperately needed few moments to recover.

It is only now, beginning to write about all this, that I realise how successful the training had been in toughening us up and making us fit. However, as much as it temporarily numbed me, it failed to totally knock out real feelings and dreams, so that although I had been manipulated against my will into a violent yet mythical world, it would be the school boy promise of visiting my friend in Australia that would guide me out and beyond.

....

CHAPTER ONE
'Six Eggs'

Aldershot, England. Winter/Spring 1958/9

I wasn't a typical teddy boy, nor did the phase last very long as I hadn't been living an average life or having the usual experiences. Following a long spell of several uncomfortably cold months of 'roughing it' on the road, I'd finally got enough work over the Christmas period with Chipperfields Circus at Bingley Hall in Birmingham, to once more get on my feet.

Circus pay was poor, but I received food and a straw lined space to sleep alongside the elephants that I was looking after, which meant I could save what little money I earned. Plus three times a day I got ten shillings a go for the somewhat painful process of riding and being thrown off by the circus's 'un-rideable mule'. Sometimes when the creature was feeling particularly docile, his keeper fed him raw oats and then I knew I was in for a rough ride, as on occasions I had been thrown out of the ring, straight into the seats! This income meant I was able to turn up at my mum and step-dad's house in North Camp, Farnborough with, symbolically at least, enough money in my pocket to satisfy my need to feel independent.

The timing of my arrival had been just right as my French stepfather was in need of a landscape garden labourer for a while. When work with him finished, I soon replaced it with other labouring jobs among the many building sites around the military town of Aldershot. Meanwhile, my long awaited and overdue passport had arrived.

When I was fourteen years old, I worked a while at handling dogs alongside a pipe-smoking man called Owen Jones. I arrived at work one day enthusing about a film I had just seen called 'West of Zanzibar'.

Owen removed his pipe very slowly, looked straight at me and said, "You don't want to be wasting your time seeing it on the cinema boy. You need to get out there and see it for yourself."

And in that moment I thought, yes I will!

Owen went on to say, "Don't talk about religion or politics boy and you should manage to keep out of trouble."

Consequently, by the time I was eighteen I had hitched, worked, stowed away and even been deported to the tune of a couple of trips around the globe, all without passport, contacts or money!

Now at last I had that small, crisp, much wanted book, which had been really hard to come by, due mainly to my being of no fixed abode, living a hand-to-mouth existence and having no reliable or stable contacts. From that kind of position all things to do with officialdom and documents were longwinded and tricky. Acquiring that document had been no exception, beside which my mother (not unreasonably) had somewhat misguidedly been sabotaging the process, in the vain hope that I might become more sensible.

A passport was, and still is, for me a most highly valued possession. Today, due to the unusual circumstances of my journey I have two passports, one British one Australian, and I treasure them both.

Back then I carried my new acquisition everywhere, feeling that it was some kind of status symbol, I was so chuffed with it. Now at last I felt I had 'proof' that I was a 'real traveller'.

Soon, financially better off than I had ever been, I discovered 'Micks', a juke-box cafe near Aldershot bus station where I hung out with the lads, although it was the girls I was really interested in. Hanging out with the lads was the way to the girls! Girls liked jiving, and the 'Aldershot Palais' was then the place to jive.

So I bought all the gear, had my hair done with sideburns and in the D.A. swept back style of the time, complete with a 'Tony Curtis' tumble forward quiff at the front which was always combed with 'panache' not just before going out, but at five-minute intervals, even while, or especially while, jiving and preferably while chewing gum!

The long thin comb was indispensable to the Teddy boy, always readily accessible in the hip pocket of those drainpipe jeans that body-hugged all the way down from beneath the knee length drape jacket, with its 'Wyatt Earp boot lace tie', to the fluorescent pink socks that graced the all important thick black 'crepe soled Brothel Creepers'.

Aldershot for teenagers in the late fifties was not a particularly gentle town, being home to the Parachute Regiment (recently returned from *Cyprus*) and for natural though absurd reasons, punch-ups between the Teds and Paras were a regular event.

I wasn't a hard case Teddy boy, no razor blades stitched in to my lapels as protection against head-butting, no sharpened handle to my comb or flick-knife hidden up the sleeve of my suede drape jacket, but I did have an extremely tough friend, Greg, who was an 'Elvis Presley' look alike.

Greg had been reared for much of his early life on the *gaff* or travelling fairgrounds, which was where I'd met him. He looked and was very strong, putting his strength down to baked beans, which he told me the *gaff's* owners had mostly fed him. His toughness no doubt came from having been used as a 'Take On All Comers Boxer' for the fairground. Now he was my mate and we knocked around together quite a bit.

It was clearly a combination that worked well for picking up girls, unfortunately it was also a situation that attracted a lot of trouble with not only the Paras, but also both local and visiting Teds from other towns.

I never actually avoided getting involved in fights when they came, but it was inevitably Greg, with his Elvis looks and fearless attitude, who drew the trouble and would enthusiastically throw himself into the brunt of it, while I attempted to hold him back. Mostly, we both seemed to come off fairly unhurt.

I only hung around Aldershot for two or three months, managing to upgrade myself from labourer, only to get the sack after a couple of weeks from a job as life-saver at the large open-air swimming pool, a job that involved walking around in whites, while keeping an eye on the bathers.

I had no hesitation in saying at the interview, "Yes, I can life-save." As I noticed there was no water in the pool for them to test me.

They just took my word for it.

Later when I was on shift, and the one-acre area was covered with water and bathers, a teenage girl did get into trouble. Enthusiastically I dived in, only to realise then that I wasn't at all sure of what the heck I was supposed to do.

Luckily I was good at holding my breath, so basically I walked along the concrete bottom of the pool keeping the quite large girl afloat with my up-stretched arms, while heading for what I trusted was the side of the pool where concerned onlookers clamoured to help her out, and where in spite of my messy antics I was thanked, cheered and patted on the back.

Getting sacked had nothing to do with that incident, I was actually a good swimmer and possibly could have saved her more impressively, or maybe not? The dismissal was fair enough, as it was for constantly chatting up girls instead of watching over the swimmers.

Late one afternoon with my mum in North Camp, following the third or fourth slick of the comb through my D.A. and Tony Curtis quiff, she asked,

"Clive, if for some reason, you come back early this evening, could you bring back six eggs from the late night shop?"

"Sure mum." I said, not realising that when I walked out of the front door, it would be the last we would see of each other for nearly five years!

Later, heading for Aldershot Palais via Mick's café, out of long habit, even though the distance was only a mile, I stuck my thumb out for a lift. Within moments, perhaps symbolically, a large black Daimler hearse pulled up for me and I got in.

"Where are you going?" I asked the driver, who was looking pasty enough to have climbed in from the back of his own vehicle.

"Dover." He said, unsmiling.

"Sound's great. Think I'll come with you!" I said, picturing the crisp new passport in my pocket. "I'll go and visit Ken my old school friend in Western Australia."

"And just how do you intend doing that from Dover?" asked the driver, in a patronising voice.

"Oh I don't know," I said trying not to sound ruffled, "I suppose I'll turn right when I get to Calais."

There was an awkward silence, in fact come to think about it, pasty never spoke to me for the rest of the journey, not altogether surprising I guess considering my comment. But the hearse was under way and right there and then in my Teddy boy outfit, with little more than the money for six eggs, coffees and juke box tunes at Mick's, plus the entry fee to the Palais, my passport and comb in pocket and without so much as a toothbrush, I was heading on a 'compass of naivety' for Perth on the other side of the world in Western Australia to keep my schoolboy promise.

Several miles later, sitting next to that silent expressionless driver in black, whilst watching the English countryside roll by, the two uppermost thoughts that made me smile were, what will Ken say when I turn up at his door in Australia? And, wow, I'm travelling at over 90 miles an hour with Dracula in a hearse!

On arrival at Dover in the early evening, having thanked the driver, while discreetly avoiding what I feared would be a clammy handshake, I headed straight off to buy a cheap one-way ticket to France. For various reasons it was better to take the ferry out of Folkestone at around midnight. So I hitched there, bought a ticket, chatted up a nice girl and moved into the back row of the local cinema.

Early next morning as I waited on the outside deck of the channel car ferry watching it dock, I overheard some interesting bits of parting conversation between a young ginger-haired guy with a Liverpool accent wearing a dark blue suit and a couple of loud American girls, they were wishing him luck in finding his brother in the 'French Foreign Legion'. That very name was real fantasy stuff in those days, all sorts of Hollywood and comic strip images came up of men in white *képis* with hankies down the back of their necks, beneath a blazing hot sun, desperately defending themselves among sand dunes or at some lonely desert fort against hoards of Saharan horsemen. I was very impressed, like many English boys of my era who were fed their facts from Hollywood and comics.
 I was seriously out of touch.

When we got around to talking, he told me his name was Nick, though often people called him 'Scouse', and that he was planning to get into the French Foreign Legion to find his brother, who had left home to join the Legion some months prior to this conversation. Apparently, no one had heard anything of or from him since.

While chatting about his plans, Nick said he would be heading for the Foreign Legion recruiting office at *Lille*. I thought we had agreed to travel together, but somehow during disembarkation we became separated. I assumed he had taken the offer of a good lift but now when I think about it, he probably hadn't wanted to travel with such a 'weirdo'. Anyway, by the time the last car had rolled off the ferry it was clear that I was on my own, so I just started thumbing the early morning traffic towards *Lille*, for no other reason than it being the last place I'd been heading for.

Lifts were pathetically slow and by lunchtime I hadn't made much progress. So, finding myself in a small French town and hungry, I bought a bar of chocolate, a small baguette and a bottle of soft drink which I had to haggle over as I didn't have quite enough money to pay for the lot. From that moment, I didn't have a penny in the world, it was a very familiar feeling and I loved it.

Going to Australia now, was promising to become an exciting adventure!

The slow pace continued and after lots of waiting between many lifts, I arrived very late in the town of *Lille* where I made my first mistake, which was to creep into a disused building after dark and find a nice cosy heap of soft material to sleep in. The result was, that I spent the whole night without light, scratching frantically, worried about what creatures were biting me, until daylight revealed that I had been sleeping in a bed of something like fibreglass.

All kinds of thoughts and survival ideas came pouring in, as teeth were frantically torn out of my precious comb in an attempt to rid my Teddy boy hair of imaginary fleas. First thought was, what a let down it would be to fail so early in the adventure defeated by a bloody itch!

Then it occurred, that if I could find where my Liverpudlian contact of the previous day was joining the Legion, I could look him up to wish him luck. After all, I figured, he must be in some kind of camp with facilities where I could clean the itchy stuff out of my clothes, get a shower and some coffee.

Who knows, may be even some breakfast to help me on my journey to Australia.

It was a case of walking around in the early dawn scratching, until I came across a *Gendarme*, that I could ask in broken French,

"If you please *Monsieur le Gendarme*, where is the *Bureau d'Engagement de La Légion Étrangère?*"

The friendly cloaked *Gendarme* understood and was immediately helpful, calling over a somewhat disinterested passing soldier who had been peacefully sleepwalking to his barracks.

Following the *Gendarme's* instructions, the soldier led me in silence half a mile or so to (what was probably) *La Citadelle*, inside of which was a disappointingly ordinary looking military barracks. Not at all what my fantasies had built up for a French Foreign Legion place to look like. But once inside the camp, it became more interesting when my soldier guide, pointing to a small white blockhouse, said something along the lines of *"Voila!* Over there my friend is the Recruitment Office of *La Légion Étrangère."*

Sure enough, there, standing guard outside the door, was an actual legionnaire in a real uniform complete with big hairy red *épaulettes*, wide belt over a broad, blue waist-sash, a heavy looking rifle and wearing that so familiar white cap (referred to as *'le képi blanc'*). It didn't have a hanky down the back but it was my first sighting of a real live legionnaire, this was really something to write home about!

....

CHAPTER TWO
'Entrapped by La Legion'

Grinning enthusiastically, I approached the legionnaire using sign language with a bit of English and broken French thrown in. The very big, seemingly German, guy turned out to be really jovial and friendly as, with much guttural laughing and joking, he took me inside the block house to see what I took to be at the time, some sort of desk sergeant who was another heavily built rugged man sitting behind a wooden table and wearing a dark *képi*. He struck me as of a higher rank and looking more like a *Gendarme* than a legionnaire. He also had a booming voice but his accent was less guttural.

As I tried to get across, with considerable difficulty, that my reason for coming was to find the ginger-haired 'Englander' called Nick, that I'd met on the ferry coming to France.

I held out my precious new crisp passport to support my sign language in emphasising my point and carried on to explain that, *'Das Englander'* had been coming to *Lille* to look for his brother, who had joined the Foreign Legion some time ago.

We seemed to be getting on all right as there were a lot of hearty good natured exchanges between the three of us, which included the first legionnaire thumping me heavily on the back with great bellows of laughter, while making admiring comments about various aspects of my Teddy boy outfit, then mysteriously attempting, but failing, to roll up the skin tight leg of my drainpipes for the purpose I gathered, of feeling my calf muscle!

It appeared that when he did finally locate the muscle through the fabric it was a good one, because I received an even heartier clout on the back as they both once again bellowed with laughter while exchanging what sounded to me like a flood of half recognisable, but good natured, obscenities.

The good natured mood continued as the original white capped legionnaire, still laughing though clutching his gun, led me to a door which he opened to reveal a group of sullen looking men and among them was Nick, the very guy from the ferry that I'd come to find.

Still grinning, I stepped forward to greet him but was immediately thrown into confusion, firstly by his refusal to even acknowledge me and secondly by realising that the door was being locked behind me. Confusion quickly became unease as I became aware of the heavily laden mood in this dark room where eye contact was avoided and where no one smiled or spoke, and it wasn't just Nick that was totally ignoring me.

Later, as I somewhat nervously tried asking other men what was happening, I just got inaudible mutterings with avoidance of eye contact, followed by dismissive silence.

While waiting uneasily in that foreboding atmosphere for something to make sense, I remembered that the desk guy still had my passport. I also realised that the only other possession I had owned - my prize comb - lay toothless, lonely and lost somewhere near the pile of itchy, scratchy stuff I'd slept in. Considering that I was heading for Australia, even by my own standards, I was now travelling very light.

We were in a long dim scruffy room, with a small heavily barred window. The space was furnished with a badly stained long solid old wooden table, accompanied by two equally stained wooden benches at either side and with a few similar chairs. A lone, naked, dusty light bulb dangled from the grubby ceiling, attracting a few slowly circulating flies that seemed to emphasise the solitary atmosphere of the eight or nine men, either sitting in withdrawn silence on the available seats, or standing gloomily staring through grimy glass into an empty courtyard.

As it had slowly dawned on me that I was a prisoner, so too I had realised I was rapidly increasing in itchiness and mostly in embarrassing places. Unfortunately, the longer the brooding silence the worse the itch was getting, and I knew that if these hostile men got the idea I was all 'loused up', it would really 'louse' things up for me!

Every attempt to find out what was going on, or what to expect, proved futile. Questions continued to get the same 'grunt treatment' leaving me with little choice than to become part of that heavy brooding atmosphere, while wondering why I was being ignored.

Of course it just hadn't occurred to the self-absorbed teenager that I was, at that time, just how my outlandish appearance outside of England in 1959 might have contributed to the responses I'd been getting. Nor had the idea even occurred that my solitary hitch from the ferry might have been down to the simple fact that Nick may have thought it a bad idea to be seen with such an oddball.

After time had dragged on, someone opened the door from the outside for a couple of unfriendly, greasy-looking, lean, shaven-headed men wearing dirty torn army pants and filthy (once khaki) vests, to slam a large soot blackened metal pot of mashed potato onto the wooden table. This was followed by a big round chunk of crusty bread, tin mugs and a tin wash jug that turned out to be full of a rough red wine that I later learned, was referred to as *'Pinard'*.

No plates or eating tools, just every man grab for himself. I say every man, but in that oppressive, serious, tense, macho atmosphere, with men who clearly did not want to be there, I was feeling less manly by the minute and all the other guys seemed so much older. It all felt like we were waiting for some kind of punishment and we were so obviously prisoners, which didn't quite add up.

Yet the door was continually locked day and night and even the men who brought food were aggressively unapproachable, refusing point blank to give any of us information or answer any questions. That was probably because they were always accompanied by a blank-looking 'armed' guard.

I only remember that room. We were there for several days but I don't remember sleeping or where we slept, I don't even remember using a toilet.

Sometime, possibly during the second day, we were put out into a strong mesh wire compound, which was set among other similar compounds. In one of those cages, because that's what they were, was a lone French soldier, the other cages were empty. One of our men got talking to the soldier.

That night someone quietly whispered to me, *"Soldat"* pointing outside, I indicated that I understood. He made a sleeping gesture with his hands, followed by a pistol shooting gesture with his fingers, *"Mort"*.

I looked at him quizzically, but he just turned the sides of his mouth down and then turned away.

It was my first bit of communication since being locked in that room and I was being told that the soldier we had seen in the cage was to be shot.

Next day we were put in the same compound again, all the others were empty and the soldier had gone. I got no answers about him, but it sure put the fear up me about my whole situation, as did the arrival of an aggressive English guy later that day, who clearly intended to come across as 'Mr Tough Guy'.

He looked about my stepfather's age, forty plus, but he was I discovered later, a well-worn, weathered twenty seven year old, with overgrown black coarse hair, beard and moustache. His fading black leather cap, flying jacket and boots were even more weathered.

This guy had come specifically to join the Legion, carrying a canvas army pack, and some kind of rifle. Much to his annoyance the rifle had been confiscated, as I gather, had everyone's possessions on arrival. My precious passport included! He just wouldn't shut up about his gun, continually pacing around while threatening all kinds of violent action, until he saw through the barred window a couple of our keepers messing about with it. Totally incensed, he made the big mistake of hurling abuse at them, then moments later three of them came in, dragged him out and spent a leisurely time roughing him over.

This was all within earshot, another event which substantially added to my fear, as well as to the general mounting tension within the group.

Because the Brit had presented himself as tough and in spite of language difficulties, succeeded in boasting about being ex-SAS and having recently fought the *Mau-Mau* in *Kenya*.

The fact that we all knew he'd been done over, and able to see his black eye and bruises, really must have put his nose out even more than the beating. It sent him initially into pacing around the room seething and threatening revenge.

As no one took any notice, he eventually sank into an even darker angry silence than the rest of us, even ignoring the red wine, mashed potato and bread when we all fell onto it like a pack of wild animals.

On two occasions a couple of armed legionnaires had marched into our room, picked seemingly at random an obviously scared individual and half marched, half carted him off. All I could find out when each of them had been more or less deposited back, was that it had to do with questioning. Then they came for me.

I was suddenly grabbed, half pushed, escorted between two lots of crunching boots to another building, then left standing, anxiously wondering what the hell was about to happen to me. Scared, I reassured myself somewhat that the other two men had been returned intact. At some point, a voice from behind a door called out and I was promptly shoved into the presence of a tight looking, hatless, balding official, wearing dark framed spectacles and no smile.

From behind his desk, he fired broken English questions at me in some accent that reminded me of my childhood doctor who was a Czechoslovakian.

"Are you having any second thoughts about joining the Legion?" He asked.

I was stunned and said nothing. He demanded I answer his question and repeated it. What's he on about I wondered? I never had any first thoughts, never mind second ones! But feeling scared and intimidated by what had happened so far, ever mindful of the heavy rifles that my cold-eyed guards were carrying and picturing the missing French soldier from the compound, I decided to nod and mutter a sort of non descript sound.

"**Speak up Englander!**" He shouted, and I sensed the menace.

"No." I said speaking up loudly, fearing what might happen if I answered otherwise. He wrote something down, spoke to my escorts and as I was marched out to be unceremoniously, shoved back into the now familiar room, I wondered, does this mean I'm now in the Foreign Legion? I was certainly 'in' something, and that something was becoming very scary!

As I stood looking through the bars to avoid everyone's eyes, especially 'Mau-Mau's,' and with no one to discuss my predicament, I told myself it's all an obvious mistake, there's bound to be an opportunity to sort it out.

But it wasn't going to be long before I would be much less certain about that!

A couple of mashed potato days later, ten of us, including 'Mau-Mau' and Nick, totally without warning, were ordered abruptly outside and on to a waiting army lorry *(camion)*. It was canvas covered with a bench or wooden seats down its length.

If there had been any illusions about our freedom so far they were to be jolted now, as we were carefully guarded by two expressionless soldiers in camouflage gear, wielding sub-machine-guns who took up their positions at each end of our lorry. They told us indifferently, that we were going to Paris and I got a distinct feeling that it wouldn't be to *Le Moulin Rouge!*

In fact we were taken to what may have been *Chateau Vincennes*, although I'd always thought it was *Fort de Nogent*. In either event, just like other prisons I've had the honour, or misfortune, to find myself in, I never did get to see the outside. Here we arrived blind to our destination, carefully guarded in the back of our covered lorry. Once inside the building and down from the truck, we were made to exchange our by then smelly civilian clothes, for some old worn torn rags and showered before being released into a community, which at first encounter had the appearance of a courtyard full of prisoners of war.

There was a big crowd of bedraggled looking men of various nationalities apparently brought in from recruiting centres all over France. A lot were Germans who had come via a big recruiting centre at Strasbourg.

Most men were hanging around in small scruffy groups, some looked sullen, dazed or shocked while others were earnestly or furtively talking, and I saw a couple of guys playing at some street type game.

Two German guys with very dead looking eyes were begging, intercepting anyone that walked by, including me, with a demanding, **"Man, come here you!"** *("Mensch, komm her du!")*

Followed by, "Have you bread?" *("Hast du brot?")*

"Have you food?" *("Hast du essen?")* or,

"Have you a light?" *("Hast du feuer?")* or,

"Have you cigarettes?" *("Hast du zigaretten?")*

Meanwhile, a few animated Mediterranean looking types were scurrying about wheeling and dealing god knows what.

Our small group of new arrivals cautiously began circulating, on the look out for familiar faces, or in my case looking for someone, anyone, who would actually speak to me, and preferably in English so I could ask some questions.

Our ex-SAS tough guy 'Mau-Mau', perked up once he had met a small wiry, sun-dried Brit with the darkest, bushiest eyebrows I'd ever seen, who, in a real military style, shook hands firmly introducing himself.

"John *Stanton*, ex-Palestine Police."

To which 'Mau-Mau' could reply in similar vein, "Fred Durham, ex-SAS, *Mau-Mau* fighting *Kenya*."

By the time they had met a couple of other Brits with a satisfactory attitude and acceptable credentials Mau-Mau was in his element. I tried talking to them with limited success, but those guys were above interacting with anyone as 'un-military' as me. As all of us were by then dressed in rags, their avoidance obviously wasn't just down to my Teddy boy outfit.

Bizarrely, I still hadn't got anywhere with Nick who by then had sunk into a deep depression and as far as I could see, wasn't talking to anyone.

Over the following days 'Mau-Mau' somehow managed to set himself up as a sort of Brits group leader, deciding that we lot (which unfortunately included me, and a new Scottish arrival called Johnny) must all stick together. He further dictated that we were all to go for the toughest, most élite outfit, which he knew was the Parachute Regiment, nothing less would do. I didn't like the idea at all.

Firstly I was, and still am, morbidly terrified of heights and secondly, the paratroopers with their army-style camouflage outfits and green berets didn't fit my fantasy of the Foreign Legion at all. White *képis* with hankies down the back, galloping on horses or camels across virgin sand dunes, with long cloaks flying in the wind and rescuing damsels in distress was much more my fantasy.

Also, by that time I had seen a wonderful photograph in a copy of the Legion's in-house magazine, `Le Képi Blanc`. It was a centre spread of `La Compagnie Saharienne` showing this magnificent outfit presenting their colours in a scene that was just like something straight out of the 'Arabian Nights'.

....

CHAPTER THREE
'Glimpse of a Fantasy'

The scene was of a white fort at night set in its sea of desert sand, floodlit for an occasion, with legionnaires illuminated as they stood guard high up on the turrets and at each side of the huge, arched entrance door. Men were dressed in the flamboyant uniform of that seemingly exotic desert company, and what a uniform it was!

They all wore white or black *képis* in accordance with their rank, with white or black billowing trousers having thirty-two pleats to each leg that narrowed at the ankles. There were large embroidered symbols on their outer sides representing, I was told, the star constellation of the Southern Cross.

They were worn with complementing white or black drill tunics accompanied by dark blue waist sashes over which lay whitened leather belts attached to diagonally crossed bandolier cartridge holders with the bullet tops clearly visible.

Below the pleated trousers could be seen some kind of crafted leather desert sandals, but what really set them off, were the rich full-length capes in pure white, sweeping across their front neckline and back over each shoulder to reveal rich coloured linings which contrasted with the bright red epaulettes.

There were several men wearing white gauntlets to hold huge elaborate regimental banners supported by polished leather waist or hip harnesses. Some of the men sported magnificent full beards.

I thought they looked incredible and in that moment of intoxication saw myself sending a photograph to my mum and little brother of me wearing that fantastic outfit.

A compilation of Saharienne Legionnaires from memory.

I had shared my excitement of that *Saharienne* fantasy with Johnny, the only person I had met up to that time that I could share anything with. He had come directly to Paris with the intention of joining up and was seriously regretting it. We met on my second day there. He was a short guy, bowlegged and stocky, with coarse sandy hair and a permanent earnest frown.

The Legion had already labelled him Johnny in spite of his thick Glaswegian accent that was so broad I had trouble in understanding it, that name is usually bestowed on all Englishmen although they seemed to miss me!

I soon gathered that Johnny had been brought up in various Barnardo's homes. He never told me actual details of the gut wrenching events that had led to him joining the Legion, but I gathered that it was something that had involved fatalities to his recently acquired family in a road accident in which he might have been the driver. Although we were an extremely unlikely match, we were nonetheless, destined to spend a lot of time with each other and it wouldn't be too long before I would discover just how messed up Johnny was from his tragic experiences.

Like me, he too had been finding it just as hard to get to know anything and having no luck in communicating with anyone, so we were both pretty much in the dark about most things.

'Mau-Mau's' clique, which we had inevitably become part of, continued to treat us both as third-rate members, regularly passing us off with the now familiar yes/no grunts, often not even those. As there was such a big mob of Germans, Italians and Spaniards present, the less represented nationalities felt under threat and tended to keep to themselves. The result was that hardly anyone risked speaking English to Johnny or me, a situation that automatically threw us even closer together.

After some days the ancient fort's tannoy system was used to inform us prisoners, or potential recruits, of the rules and conditions of enlistment. We were of course eager, even excited, that at last we would learn something.

However, by the time the information had been broadcast in German, Italian, Spanish and French, the frenzied gabbling of the various races in the old echoing stone castle, meant that we less represented nationalities got to hear very little and understand even less. The outcome for me and Johnny was finding out nothing.

So from then on, it would be a case of discovering reality as and where we found it, which in many ways was probably for the best, because somehow it brought out a survival sense of fun that continued to develop between us for the duration of our time together.

In the midst of that babble of noise and confusion, for the fourth time I was put through the grab-march-shove routine, into a small bare room to await my fate. Again two yobbish guards half accompanied, half pushed me into yet another room where various questions were rapidly fired at me by the younger of two officials sat behind a desk, via a very tall, rigid sounding interpreter.

It wasn't particularly unfriendly until the older, grey-haired official suddenly shouted angrily that I wasn't coming up with definite names, dates and places. He screamed that I was messing him about and got really aggressive for a while. Then for some reason best known to himself, he calmed down, even making a couple of not very funny attempts at joking, until the younger man went back to asking the questions.

Then out of the blue, the big question of enlisting came up again. It came via the interpreter from the younger official. I hesitated, trying to weigh up the situation. I saw the grey-haired official smiling, a sort of patronising, all-is-forgiven type of smile.

I thought maybe there actually was a choice, perhaps now I could simply say no. Then came a shock as the grey-haired guy spoke directly to me in loud, clear, flawless English,

"Do you still want to join the French Foreign Legion?"

I froze!

Somehow in that on-going environment of intimidation, the sheer unexpectedness of my interrogator speaking English, having all that time questioned me through an interpreter, felt chilling and really unnerved me, it was like suddenly being stripped naked, in that instant I felt even more vulnerable. It was as though I could no longer hide even behind language!

As I stood before those unpredictable officials, helpless between expressionless armed escorts, knowing I was captive in a hostile environment, it seemed once again safer to simply say loudly and clearly "Yes, sir!"

As I was escorted out, I kicked myself that I'd been too scared of the imagined consequences to say no, as once again the same question occupied my thoughts, had I just committed myself to five years of god knows what?

The developing mood in that ancient fort accurately reflected the atmosphere of the harsh stone building, becoming mainly one of heavy brooding. Worried men, who had been stripped of all contact with the outside world, were scared angry men who hung about in furtive sometimes threatening groups.

Meanwhile, the diet of rough red wine and starch kept coming, different nationalities kept drinking, inevitably arguments developed, then more often than not actual fights. Apart from just a few men being allocated minimal chores or *corvée*, we had nothing physical to let off our frustration, fear, pain or explosive anger.

Plates and utensils were still not supplied, so eating had become a free-for-all, with men brutalised into fighting each other over a fist full of mashed potato.

After what seemed an age of languishing in that filthy threat-laden, dehumanising atmosphere, a large bunch of us one evening were issued coarse nondescript old khaki uniforms and 'greatcoats', in order to be transported under guard in what appeared to be a civilian train that had been specifically laid on for us. Although we were never officially told, everyone seemed to know that we were heading on this overnight train for *Fort St Nicholas*, a grim stone on rock, chateau type fort that supposedly guards the south side of the old seaport harbour of *Marseille*.

I say supposedly, because I read somewhere that the guns originally faced inwards, trained on the citizens of *Marseille*.

An image of Fort St Nicholas overlooking Marseille Harbour, where holiday makers were oblivious of what went on in that ancient chateau.

From the start it was a tense volatile train journey when we were left to our own devices as our guards travelled in a separate carriage. Men were already half pissed on wine when beer somehow got into our possession. So that before long, angry, frightened, men were alarmingly drunk and aggressive which was fast becoming the norm.

Johnny rapidly became drunk and potentially violent, suffering from some ferocious insecurity in the close proximity of that raucous explosion of foreign languages, he was totally convinced that everyone was talking about and taking the piss out of us, especially the Germans who he had a real thing about. The result was me spending that stinking and unnerving journey keeping both him and myself out of fights.

Like it or not, Johnny was after all my companion, even if he was argumentative and reeking of both vomit and urine, having unsuccessfully pissed into a beer bottle and successfully spewed out of a window into a strong back draft as we passed under some bridge or tunnel.

Finally, I found myself at some risk struggling to prevent him from throwing himself out of the speeding train in a fit of drink-fuelled desperation.

I think we must have completed the final morning leg of the journey under armed guard, in the familiar covered-in military trucks, eventually arriving as a wretched rabble to be herded aggressively by our escorts once we were inside the 'apparently' very impressive looking *Fort St Nicholas.*

Little of interest happened to us newcomers on the first day beyond getting hosed down, deloused and having our scratchy woollen uniforms swapped for tattered, torn garments, much like the rags we had been relieved of in Paris. Then, like so many sheep, we were released into the central courtyard, which was for all intents and purposes, another movie style prison set-up not very different from the situation we had left in Paris.

Most men quickly found and expanded their own groups, huddled less and were more animated than they had been at the previous fort as they discovered fresh contacts.

In this prison more exchanges of information were likely, fresh possibilities of even the slightest, but so desperately wanted, news from the outside world might be found! Soon the same half dozen Latin types, bartered intently with new found punters, though what they bartered for was still a mystery to me. In the midst of all this, the same pair of dead-eyed German zombies scuffed around begging for anything they could smoke, eat or drink.

Penned up together in that old stone cage as we all were, the territorial nature of the various gatherings was off-putting enough, but it was also a situation that wasn't being helped by Johnny's angry challenging stance towards some Germans that he had maintained ever since the train journey.

Consequently, in order to keep out of trouble I figured it necessary to stay by Johnny while hanging awkwardly around our group, which by then comprised of 'Mau-Mau', very much acting his boss part; the bushy eye-browed ex-police guy *Stanton*; *Ryan* a red-faced Irishman; two other ex-military Brits; plus a couple of English speakers, *Vince* and *Roald*, who both seemed to have travelled with an earlier group from Paris. *Roald* was a massive booming Anglo-Dutch mercenary recently from South Africa. As for *Vince*, other than his being quiet and hanging like a shadow round *Roald*, I don't remember much about him.

[34]

There was also a quiet Norwegian guy who had attached himself to our group, his English was very limited but he must have felt that it gave us something in common as he hadn't managed to locate one single fellow countrymen among the whole population.

Then of course, there was Johnny.

There had been a couple of other men with language connections on the edge of our clique at *Paris*, but once we reached *St Nicholas* they discovered more of their own kind and joined them.

Since leaving *Paris* there had been no sign whatsoever of Nick. Johnny heard our military lot saying that under questioning Security *(Sureté)* would have picked up that Nick was a mental case and automatically evicted him. Whatever the truth, that was the last I ever heard of the ginger-haired scouse I had met on the ferry and later looked up in *Lille* hoping for a wash and a cup of coffee. The coffee hadn't happened so far, and it sure wasn't going to be free.

Somehow, I doubt that Nick ever discovered anything about his missing brother.

The first toilet facilities I managed to locate at *Fort St Nicholas* turned out to be an absolute mess, inadequate and filthy with one tap providing ice cold water over a dirty trough inside a dingy, dark, windowless stone alcove.

This was the wash place for scores of men. While the few disgusting bluebottle-infested, hosed out once a day, hole-in-the-ground toilets had human excrement encroaching the stone floor for over a foot around each hole and were, if possible, made even more disgusting by poor lighting and the liberal use of glossy non-absorbent magazines that were the only available toilet paper.

That night to my surprise, we were issued fairly new prison-style pyjamas and straw-filled palliasses before being ordered to bed-down on bunk beds in the dungeons. They were echoing, shadowy spaces deep in the bowels of the sinister stone fortress, where unyielding structures resounded to the general cacophony of shouting prisoners and barking, screeching Legion guards, whose studded boots crashed down on ancient stone slabs, while huge iron gates groaned and clanged with their chunky metal locks rasping and grating.

It all added to an atmosphere of fear and urgent expectation, as did the general aggressive, often guttural sometimes-screechy sounds of our multi-lingual rabble, many of whom added throat clearing, coughing, spitting and using the sides of their hands to blast snot onto the stone floor. Even the actual layout of the huge number of narrow bunks seemed sinister, being set up three high, with only a narrow gap between sleeping platforms with the sheer concentration of numbers leaving very limited space for the aisles.

Maybe I'd seen too many Hollywood films, but the overall image, especially with the prison-style pyjamas, looked to me just like some concentration camp straight from the movies.

In that archaic prison, several hundred men carried on much the same as we had at the fort in *Paris*, but the atmosphere was rapidly deteriorating. Time was passing in idleness with absolutely no communication to, or from, the outside world. More threats and intimidation were present, continuous wine and starch was fuelling fights, there was much more being shoved around in an atmosphere of mounting fear that was being disguised and expressed as aggression.

Bouts of heavy interrogation, interspersed with medicals and questionable inoculations that had already begun in *Paris*, were becoming more frequent and adding to the pressure. It was bad enough for all of us, but it must have been hell for those guys who actually did have something to hide, hell also for those poor suffering men who received no news and who knew nothing of their families and loved ones left in politically unsafe war-torn regions.

As 'Mau-Mau' put it, "There were bound to be more than a few of those poor bastards!"

The upper battlements looked out over the harbour where holidaymakers and tourists in the sunshine mingled with locals among the cafes, fishing boats, yachts, pleasure boats and other general waterside activities. It was a gut wrenching sensation to look out at that scene that was so close, literally just over there, and to realise that no one knew what was going on up here in the fort. None knew that we were prisoners, life just went on as if we didn't exist.

I still find it hard to believe that all those unlikely events were happening to me in France so close to the beginning of the 1960's.

It was up on those battlements, in bright sunshine, overlooking that same scene that several of us were ordered to strip to the waist. A couple of our screaming hard-case keepers bullied us into some semblance of attention, then the superior barked an order to someone behind us, a few moments later I felt a searing stab at the inside edge of my shoulder blade. Furtively glancing back, I saw the next guy in line had a hypodermic needle sticking out of his back.

Further orders were given and it appeared that with bizarre military precision and in stages responding to orders, we were delivered our inoculations.

It must have gone along the line something like:- needle in; syringe screw on; plunger in; syringe remove. Then, followed the order to fall out, a couple of men did just that, literally falling straight on to the stone floor, where they were just left! Although somewhat furtively, a few of us later assisted them to somewhere a little more comfortable.

....

CHAPTER FOUR
'One Small Victory'

On another occasion, on those same battlements willingly, or unwillingly, ten of us were to some measure brought to attention by a loud, *"Garde-à-vous!"*

Which by now though untrained, we recognised and responded to by standing stiff and staring ahead.

The Italian sounding corporal ordered the first man in line, also an Italian, **"Recruit, remove the cap!"** *(Recrue, enlever le capot!)*

The man complied, clumsily removing the upturned green and red pod-like item from his head, awkwardly snapping it sharply beneath his arm, as had now become the custom, remaining stiff and impassive, eyes staring straight ahead.

A legionnaire given the role of 'barber' was ordered something along the lines of, *"Legionnaire Schmidt* – **hair regulation – cut!"**

As clippers mowed closely up the sides and back of the young man's head, handfuls of what must have been prized black Italian hair, fell to the ground. Next, with scissors, the top hair was clipped down to a quarter of an inch, leaving an absurd tuft the size of a fried egg, which certainly wasn't the fashionable style for young men at the end of the fifties and most definitely not young Italian men.

The acting barber then stood to attention and shouted, **"At your service,**

Corporal!" *(Á vos ordres, caporal!)*

Then came the order, "**Recruit - replace the cap!**" *(Recrue - mettez le capot!)*

All along the line of waiting men the actions were repeated, until it was my turn and the order was delivered. *"Recrue - enlever le capot!"*

I obeyed and waited, face impassive, eyes staring ahead. But I was, all be it fearfully, concealing a silent pleasure. My head was totally bald, smooth shiny bald, not as much as a shadow!

"**Legionnaire Schmidt, hair regulation cut!**" ordered the corporal.

Legionnaire Schmidt hesitated, the corporal stiffened and practically screeched the order, "**Legionnaire Schmidt. Hair regulation cut!**"

Then, bizarre as it may seem, ten men were kept standing to attention while another grown man, a professionally trained corporal at that, ordered and oversaw yet another trained man, absurdly and in regimental style, run his clippers impotently up the sides and back of my hairless head.

To top it all his scissors actually snipped at the vacant 'air' above my head to leave an imaginary regulation tuft.

Then with the task fulfilled, Legionnaire Schmidt stepped back to attention and with audible desperation shouted, "Regulation haircut complete. *Á vos ordres caporal!*"

Meanwhile, still at attention showing no expression and with eyes still staring straight ahead, I waited expectantly, as did the other men and yes, I was fearful. Yet as the order came to replace that stupid pod of a hat, for the first time since I had been so unexpectedly imprisoned at *Lille*, I actually felt elation, for I knew that tables had been turned and a small victory won against overwhelming odds.

Not only had two of our keepers been cornered into exposing their own silly game, but there was also the satisfaction of having denied them the theft, of my Teddy boy hairstyle!

Armies all over the world have long used the 'haircut' as an effective demeaning tactic on young men. So having already seen a few bald heads, I had figured what might be coming and had time to prepare. By managing with some difficulty to get hold of a razor, I had asked Johnny to shave every hair from my head so they couldn't cut it.

That incident was a tremendous confidence boost, and an important turning point just when I needed it. They could bully, intimidate and frighten, but on that occasion I reclaimed something of myself discovering in the process that there would always be a means of maintaining personal identity, so I watched and it soon became apparent that my dislike of alcohol was really a godsend.

Not drinking from the liberal daily supply of red wine was playing an important part in preventing their system from breaking me down as quickly or as effectively as it seemed to be breaking down some of the other men.

....

CHAPTER FIVE
'Whispers of Leaving'

After what must have been around 14 days from my arrival at *Lille*, escape was being whispered among the few guys I was in touch with. Now writing about it, I actually find it reassuring in a curious sort of way. I've long had nagging doubts about my perception of the manner in which I found my self actually in the Legion, particularly in relation to the repetitive questions regarding my wanting or not wanting to join.

Given that I was locked up, under guard and felt intimidated whenever the question was asked and considering it was inevitably accompanied by aggressive questioning, I always feared physical violence if I'd said 'no'. I'm now fairly sure that my experience wasn't unique, yet no one seemed to comment on feeling at the very 'least' that they were being aggressively coaxed into joining. After all, the fact that people were talking about 'escaping' must have implied a belief that they were captives rather than volunteer recruits or surely they would have used the word 'deserting'.

  Interestingly, I've since read comments by military-inclined men who around that period applied with full intention to join the Legion, express confusion about the repetitive question, "Do you still want to join the Legion?" They repeatedly said 'yes' and couldn't understand why that same question was being asked over and over and some said, "It was as though they were trying to scare me off!"

For those men who came wanting to join, the only intimidating thing about the repetitive questioning was fear of rejection.

It was that same eager group of military-inclined enthusiasts intent on proving themselves, and keen not to let what they perceived as 'the side' down, who would gradually, within that unreal environment, convert those men with no hope or tangible future into their own military brand of thinking and values. A world in which the word 'escape' would soon be replaced with that dirty word 'desertion'.

With the benefit of hindsight it's easy to see that well before the act of enlisting we were, over a prolonged period, systematically threatened and brainwashed. The endless supply of starch and wine, together with the emerging influence of those military enthusiasts all contributed towards inevitable enlistment.

Much as I don't like the word 'victim', the truth is, that any individual who came to enquire about the Legion with no definite intention of joining yet who, without clear choice, ended up enlisted was, I believe, a subject of more than just underhanded brutal persuasion!

As mind conditioning continued to take effect, many of these men would several months later have survived the harsh bonding journey through brutality, pain, sleep deprivation and belittlement. By the time they had received the 'yearned for' 'parental approval', recognition and rewards from the 'fatherly' perpetrators of their abuse, they were well and truly 'set up' to buy wholeheartedly into the Legion package.

The whole journey would have provided a powerful experience of acceptance and belonging to a family whose sense of identity would become inflated through symbolic tokens of achievement and recognition, until a passionate spirit of belonging, *'Esprite de Corps'*, was established.

By which time, a man having first been 'assisted to lose his identity', then helped to 'rediscover himself' within 'the family' would be unlikely to harp back on such an irrelevant question as, "Did I really choose to enlist in the Legion of my own free-will?"

For to doubt it would be to risk separation from his new family, render his painful investment, his new found purpose and his very well-being, null-and-void.

The mythical aspect of the Legion and its very deserved reputation attracted successful soldiers wishing to be a part of an elite, along with ex-soldiers who were still drawn to a military life, plus a fair share of young men eager to prove themselves. It also attracted failed soldiers hoping to make good and I believe some came seeking punishment, desperate to pay off a burdening sense of guilt.

Quite a few individuals said they joined in an attempt to avoid recrimination or possible prison.

Of course many came escaping from a variety of circumstances, such as war, politics, legal, and relationship issues.

It was a natural magnet for men looking for adventure as well as misguided men who joined on a whim.

Some men were just homeless and hungry.

That same reputation unfortunately attracted deluded types who seemed to be in love with their own hard man image, or men who, for whatever reason, just seemed to enjoy the darker side of war. The result was a Foreign Legion in the late fifties, made up of some thirty thousand both ordinary and extraordinary men, sons, fathers and brothers from over fifty-two countries, individuals from all walks of life, dentists, accountants, lorry drivers, seamen, labourer's and others.

Of these men that had found their various ways to France and been directed to a recruiting centre, many could not have suspected that without warning they would enter an aggressive hostile environment that immediately severed their freedom along with all their connections to the outside world.

Consequently, men that arrived bitter, frightened or vengeful, were driven even deeper into their own darkness creating a poisonous atmosphere that radiated outwards absorbing every negative influence until it contributed to one big, frightened, unhappy mix that within the all male environment, sought its expression through hostility and aggression.

This was a fermenting place and these were men who would soon be willing to kill people they never knew, or die themselves for an employer or a cause of which they had previously known nothing! It was an institution that paid a pittance, neither a religion nor a nation. Simply a mixture of men brought to order in the service of marching, fighting, killing and dying, all with the conviction 'THE LEGION IS OUR COUNTRY' (*LEGIO PATRIA NOSTRA*).

> **CODE OF HONOUR**
>
> Legionnaire, you are a volunteer serving France with honour and fidelity.
>
> Each Legionnaire is your brother in arms whatever his nationality, his race or his religion might be. You show him the same close solidarity that links the members of the same family.
>
> Respectful of traditions, devoted to your leaders, discipline and comradeship are your strengths, courage and loyalty your virtues.
>
> Proud of your status as Legionnaire, you display this in your always impeccable uniform, your always dignified but modest behaviour, and your clean living quarters.
>
> An elite soldier, you train rigorously, you maintain your weapon as your most precious possession, and you take constant care of your physical form.
>
> The mission is sacred, you carry it out until the end and, if necessary in the field, at the risk of your life.
>
> In combat, you act without passion and without hate, you respect defeated enemies, and you never abandon your dead, your wounded, or your arms.

Updated version of the 'Code of Honour'.

As more time passed within the old castle walls, many men, although still not signed up, whispered about desertion as though they were already committed legionnaires, even discussing the likely punishment for their potential crime should they be caught. Consequently, an unhealthy secrecy permeated until not only did we have the brutality of our guards to contend with, but also the watchful judgmental ears and eyes of the many 'Mau-Mau' and *Stanton* types who were disgusted by what they saw as cowardly cop-out behaviour.

And so we unwittingly contributed to our own programming, becoming our own jailers and jailers to our fellow inmates. Even Johnny confided, well out of the earshot of 'Mau-Mau', about the possibility of us deserting. I reasoned that as we had reluctantly come this far and put up with so much, we might just as well stay with it until we had experienced the Foreign Legion proper in Africa. I said I'd give it a year then escape.

Interestingly enough, when I did choose to escape some fourteen months after having arrived at *Lille*, Johnny and one or two of the others guys that I confided in, all wished me well, but for themselves they seemed to have lost all motivation to escape, even though they acknowledged not really wanting to remain.

Escape would have been very difficult from the Fort especially being bald headed, dressed in rags, with silly caps and little knowledge of *Marseille, France*, or the language. During that period I heard of men being kicked out because of various health issues.

According to 'Mau-Mau', some men might be found unsuitable during one of the many interrogations by Interpol, *Deuxième Bureau*, or the Legion's own security service (*La Sûreté*) for having connections to suspect political organisations and that they might dig up 'wanted persons' and hand them to the 'appropriate authorities'. He said that if a 'wanted man' managed to slip through the interrogation gauntlet undiscovered he would be protected by the Legion, but at the end of his service he would be given an opportunity to re-enlist and if he hesitated they'd make sure he'd know that the Legion's protection would not extend beyond the garrison gates.

CHAPTER SIX
'Worked over by professionals'

Something sinister was happening in the dungeons at night-time, adding more sleep deprivation to our general discomfort and more than a few of us were extremely frightened by it.

As we attempted sleep in our claustrophobic bunks amidst the coughing, farting, spitting, hoarse whisperings and international yells to shut up, throughout the night at various times, an individual was noisily ousted from his bunk, seemingly at random, under a bright light and then with much banging and shouting brutishly man-handled by several thuggish legionnaires who physically escorted him out through crashing iron gates, shocked, bare footed and hanging onto his pyjamas for dear life.

They were last seen as a shrinking pool of light that vanished into the eerie darkness of the fort, it was the last we saw or heard of them, no one knowing what it was about or where these men were being taken, at least no one within the limited circle that either me or Johnny were in communication with.

As I had dreaded, eventually my turn came. I too was subjected to blinding light, punches and screamed obscenities as they encouraged me out of bed, instinctively struggling to hold up my regulation issue pyjama trousers as I was dragged from between bunks and frog-marched through the iron gates, my bare feet menaced by boots on either side crunching heavily on the cold stone slabs.

As with the other men, I was whisked away in a pool of light through the surrounding darkness of the medieval fortress to some unforeseeable fate.

This event brought up all the fear that I had experienced as a child when my violent stepfather would yank me out of bed in the night shouting, shoving and generally interrogating me. Those and other reverberating images were not lost to me years later when I trained to become a 'Healing Breath Facilitator' and learned that we recreate our unresolved experiences over and over until we heal them.

I was forty years old when, during one of those profound sessions, I encountered the primal experience of this persecution pattern. The process involves a specific form of breathing, which is normally carried out while lying down. The facilitator monitors and guides the recipient's breathing pattern over a prolonged period, simultaneously encouraging relaxation at all levels. This has the effect of releasing the charge of formerly suppressed energy, in the form of images, feelings or sensations. During the peak of one particularly powerful session, I encountered terror when I experienced myself lying in a grave amidst frenzied activity, as figures with white tall cone-shaped hats threw dry earth down onto me. I knew they were Klu Klux Klansmen burying me alive, I could feel my arms folded across my chest, I could see, hear and smell the flames of their burning torches and feel the dust.

Thankfully the scene abruptly changed as I found myself in some kind of procession being fussed over by several people, I felt the weight of my arms still folded across my chest and I seemed to be ritualistically laid out in some kind of container which was bumping about as we all moved purposefully along.

As if from a dream, I came round to the sounds of my facilitator making tea and was aware of lying on the mat back in the room. I could still feel the weight of my arms crossed over my chest, yet when I opened my eyes I discovered that it was only the residual sensation from the experience. My arms were in fact, at my sides.

Later while working with these breath-evoked images, I was able to unravel a combination of both factual and likely events that exposed the cause of many irrational fears and victim tendencies.

As an infant I had lived in my grandparent's house near the sea, they lived a predict-

able lifestyle with an orderly timetable. Subject to weather, the likely daily ritual would have been that following breakfast the table would have been cleared, while I was put into one of those deep-hooded black prams so typical of that time, tucked snugly in with my arms crossed over my chest to avoid draughts. I would have then been pushed into the yard to be placed at an angle that avoided direct sunlight, yet maximised the sun's beneficial rays, while I got a healthy dose of morning air. Each morning the tablecloth would probably have been shaken out into the same yard as a daily event without mishap, until one morning possibly a young cousin might have shaken the cloth with exuberance, resulting in scattered crumbs landing on and in my pram.

This would likely have attracted large, screeching seagulls to swoop in, vying with each other for the new supply of food. Their 'klu klux klan-like' wings would have flapped 'dust' and crumbs into my face, as I lay terrified in the 'grave-like' depths of my pram. As the competing birds, tussled and squawked in their 'white pointed gowns', they would have rocked the pram so that glimpses of 'fiery' sunlight completed a pre-verbal picture that would be fuelled by my imagination, to be resurrected by images and countless events in later life.

My anguished cries would have alerted the adults and concerned family members would have gathered around me to wheel me bumpily back into the house. A procession with me contained in my carrier, arms still crossed over my chest, the centre of concern and attention, as experienced in the breathwork session.

Following that powerful session with the memories it evoked and the subsequent processes, I never again experienced those unhealthy patterns that I had continued to recreate throughout my life until that healing session.

Still vulnerably clinging to my pyjama trousers 'like it really mattered', I was coaxed on through more corridors and iron gates until we came out of the building under a heavy clouded night sky, to then cross a very ordinary looking road passing into what must have been the ruins of an older part of the castle. There my captors left me in the open, standing expectantly among sparse scrub close to an old crumbling stone wall. Some distance away was a long wooden hut, with light rays streaming from a door to expose a legionnaire standing guard.

Common sense told me there was no point in running, anyway where would

I go? Where does a man run in just a pair of unsupported, very identifiable, pyjama trousers?

Gradually as my eyes became accustomed to the semi-darkness, there was an uncomfortable realisation that the crumbling stone was an ancient execution wall with plants growing in holes where once gunshot had smashed into the stone and around the area were a number of old rusting items. It may, or may not have been the case, but it wasn't long before my agitated mind saw those objects as ancient torture devices.

It is pretty obvious that being left there with no explanation was intended to scare the living shits out of me and, it did.

After presumably sufficient time had passed to unnerve me, the guard I had seen at the hut door, abruptly marched over and took me to be interrogated inside the hut by a Hollywood version of a middle aged, pince-nez, Gestapo type. As I waited clinging to my pyjama trousers with bright light shining in my eyes, just like in the movies, 'pince-nez' slowly, methodically, fingered his way through a thick file of papers which were all about me!

In such an un-informed naive state, it never occurred to me that the pack of information might have been an interrogation bluff, or even that he may or may not have been a *Deuxième Bureau* interrogator. I now know they really couldn't have known much about me, especially given the already widespread vagaries of my past. But at that time I assumed they knew everything.

Fingers paused from time to time between the pages, as if to consider something or to ask me in English in a slow matter-of-fact tone, questions such as where, when and why?

As I was genuinely unable to remember many dates, sequences or even places, his manner became progressively more demanding. Once, we had attempted a brief history of my short life, i.e. French step-father, schooling in both France and England, various assumed names, multiple employments (which included ships, circuses, fairgrounds plus periods of detainment and deportations from the Channel Islands, New Zealand and the West Indies), interspersed with a down-and-out existence on the road.

He got very angry, convinced I was lying about heading for Australia without belongings, tickets, visas or money and demanding to know why my British passport was so new.

He repeatedly shouted, **"Why did you destroy your old passport?"**

At one point he said something to the guard, who promptly took me outside forcing me to stand beyond arms reach of the wall, so I would have to lean my weight forward on fingertips (nice!). Although this was carried out under threat, after all it was him who had the nasty pointed thing at the end of his gun and he had his job to do, but this man didn't seem to have the same brutish devotion to his work as all our other captors. He might have got the angles wrong, or maybe he was just a decent guy, because the truth is that it didn't actually cause much pain, although the process was clearly meant to.

After a prolonged period of finger leaning in mild discomfort while remembering nothing new, I was again back in the hut facing the bright light for a second round of intense verbal bombardment, while I attempted unsuccessfully to explain why I was unable to answer the same questions he'd already asked me. Then for reasons completely mysterious to me, he softened as though satisfied with my responses, even though I had said nothing new.

The guard promptly marched me out and I assumed it was for more finger persuasion, but I needn't have worried, as deliberately avoiding my questions the guard amiably walked me back through the iron gates and on through more gates to an unfamiliar area, where I was released into a group, some of whom I recognised as the men that had similarly been dragged from their bunks. And so, the mystery was solved.

As for the reason? Well, it gradually became apparent that many men were missing, including Ryan.

Following those bizarre events there was a sense of release with a noticeable improvement in atmosphere. Several of us were put into small groups *(equipes)*, to be sent for long days of working in the outskirts of *Marseille*. It felt better than doing nothing, promised much but gave little as there was no pleasure in being driven through the back streets of that great city in a covered-in army lorry, feeling, looking and being treated like shit, plus being issued tattered old army clothes with battered tin helmets. We sure didn't look or feel happy being escorted by armed tormentors to oversee us shovelling rubble at a demolition site in the middle of nowhere.

Meanwhile, mini interrogations, medical examinations, tests and inoculations continued, with more faces noticeably disappearing. Desertions, expulsions, even suicides were rumoured, all to be confirmed, of course as absolute facts by 'Mau-Mau'.

I was disturbed when one test revealed a broken tooth that I'd not wanted them to know about, as I imagined their dental treatment would be somewhat nasty, but when it came to it, the Swiss Foreign Legion dentist turned out to be really gentle, even apologising for the fact that he could only fit a temporary filling. That temporary filling has lasted to this day!

Then right out of the blue first me, then Johnny, found ourselves enrolled. I was called into an office and given yet another sheet of paper to sign, which I assumed was probably for the tatty old uniform.

I had just begun writing my name when the blank-faced official surprised me with a big smile, stating in heavily accented English, "No, you don't sign like that." He then scrawled something for me to copy where his finger pointed. "You must know who you are *Rutand*. Now take this information and memorise it well. Off you go *Rutand, Michel!*"

Why the hell was he calling me *Rutand, Michel?* As I walked out I was confused until I saw what was written and I realised I was looking at my new identity!

Name:- *Legionnaire Rutand, Michele; Matricule:-* 128,2…, Born:- April 12th 1939, Belgium, Ghent; Mother's maiden name:- *de Flores, Emile;* Father's name:- *Rutand, Renné.*

This was so totally unexpected that it caught me off guard. I'd obviously been living from day to day believing somehow that sooner or later there would be a way out of my situation. But this event, though less intimidating that others, had left no room for response and it hadn't matched the picture that both me and Johnny had formed where there would be some official enrolment process with a final opportunity for release before signing up.

But all feelings of injustice were soon brushed aside when Johnny turned up practically beside himself with rage, I thought it was because he too had been enrolled without consent, but no, for Johnny it was something far worse.

On his form it stated that he Johnny, was now *'Mûller, Hans',* born in *Dûsseldorf.* Johnny wasn't upset about enlistment, he was raging because he had just become a German!

Suddenly my feelings were replaced with outright laughter which of course fuelled Johnny's anger even further, but even our focus on that couldn't last, as all around us excited voices began to get louder and we soon joined in as we picked up that we were about to be paid and receive an enlistment handout.

Of course each man had a different version of how much we'd actually be paid so for a while there was little room for any other conversation.

Then just as suddenly and probably just as orchestrated, it was announced that we were up to capacity and would be leaving for *Algeria* first thing in the morning. At which point, all concern of how we'd become enlisted began to fade as we both got plugged into the excitement of moving. Neither of us had been to *North Africa*, in fact, Johnny hadn't even been out of the U.K. until his unfortunate enrolment trip to *Paris*.

With so much movement in the air, my travel bug was awake with dreams taking place in the deep *Sahara*, vividly fulfilling all sorts of fantasies on horseback in that fantastic uniform of the Saharan company, not that I'd ever ridden a horse and somehow in those dreams I always looked so much taller!

########## **CHAPTER SEVEN** ##########
'To North Africa'

From *Marseille* the sea journey was meant to be a full day and a half. Three lorries took us to the docks for shipping to the port of *Oran* on the North African coast.

It would be nice to write a romanticised description of that beautiful old harbour receding with the impressive Fort St. Nicolas beneath an early morning Mediterranean sun, but I can't.

I saw nothing as we were all battened down with the animals, deep in the poorly lit stinking hold of the five thousand tonne *'Sidi-bel-Abbès'*, a ship that was used to carry humans and god knows what else, all with a minimal attempt to clean up between sailings.

We, the two-legged beasts, were provided filthy, stained, damaged deck chairs for what turned out to be, a rough sea crossing and utterly disgusting experience.

Our promised first 'pay out' although only equivalent to a few quid per man had been sufficient for the acquisition of some beers on the black market, which from earlier experience on the train, when it was combined with our supply of wine, produced some nasty results.

Consequently, from the start our uncontrolled rabble was once again drunk, arguing, fighting, pissing and vomiting, with some men eventually lying in their own and other's putrid mess. The crowded space below deck, that had been airless and stinking when we first arrived, quickly became indescribable.

The provided swill that they called food, if not immediately cast a side, was eaten only to be thrown up all over the heaving deck later, adding to the kaleidoscope of colourful slime that oozed as a moving tide, accompanying the rolling and pitching of the ship and leaving nowhere safe from its foul encroachment.

The one saving grace was that eventually men became too sick for fighting, or too disgusted to bother.

I felt awful and very sorry for myself, yet even sorrier for the few North African women and children who seemed fated to share our demise. I am not sure whether they had freedom to come and go from the hold, we certainly did not and before long I just felt too wretched to care and to sick to move even though I had noticed with horror that some men unable to get either out from the hold, or into the toilets, were just crapping wherever they could.

One memorable incident that stood out because of its contrast happened when we were leaving the hold and entering into brighter light. Johnny, being very short, rounded a corner to find his nose momentarily within an inch of the deep cleavage of an extremely large woman's breast and within the context of the whole degrading journey, that incident seemed extremely funny, providing a release of laughter for a long time after the event.

Eventually, we emerged as from a bad dream relieved and many hours behind schedule into a drizzling North African evening where, in view of our disgusting state, I was glad that we walked hidden by darkness from the quay, to waiting covered-in trucks that took us to a Military reception centre somewhere among the back streets of the city. The short night we spent there was wonderful in contrast to all we had experienced until then and given our stinking condition, the occupying French soldiers were quite friendly although, not unsurprisingly, they kept a little distant.

For the first time since being in captivity I was able to clean up with hot water and soap and use utensils to eat good food without fighting for it, although some men clearly either didn't care to, or didn't know how to, use cutlery.

Then we got to sleep on actual beds with real mattresses and clean bedding, unfortunately it was to be a night cut short, as well before daylight, without so much as a good-bye, we were rudely coerced into the confines of our three canvas backed lorries for the two or three hour drive inland towards *Sidi-bel-Abbes*. That garrison town is traditionally known as the spiritual home of the French Foreign Legion in *North Africa*, it is obviously also the town that spawned the name of the proud ship in whose hold we had just had such an 'enlightening' experience.

For those of us deep inside the canvas it was an un-eventful journey punctuated only by gear changes and the adjusted sounds of our roaring engines.

I mostly dreamed of coffee or food until we were dumped on arrival at our destination and immediately confined to barracks having seen nothing of either the countryside or the town. But for we enlisted volunteers, or prisoners that we still seemed to be, the place was a colossal improvement on anything we'd known so far other than the reception centre where we had spent that short night.

It was far more what I imagined a normal military barracks should be - clean, well lit, orderly and with all its amenities intact.

It was still early morning when following cold showers, even though hot water was available, we were firmly coaxed into a sort of order and herded past a series of counters beneath overhead lights, where a legionnaire visually assessed each of us before throwing from his side of the counter, items of clothing and kit which included greatcoats, tin helmets, pyjamas, plus other things such as towels, bedding and toiletries and considering I'd been using my finger as a toothbrush since leaving home, it was good to find one in my pack. Then, still based on a visual assessment, he proceeded to chuck boots at us that hopefully would fit.

The activities that followed were mostly to do with sorting and packing the ill-fitting clothes that our new keepers assured us were fine.

Even wrong size boots didn't seem to matter, in fact when one brave guy with a boot that didn't resemble his foot risked asking if he could change his pair, the shouted reply was, **"In the Legion we don't change boots, we change feet. Démerdez-vous."**

A comment we would all quickly get used to, roughly translating as 'de-shit yourself'. It was the most often used piece of legion jargon meaning 'sort it out for yourself'.

Once organised, we lined up to receive a miniature slice of that dried sausage referred to as *'la saussison'* on a matching sized chunk of bread that was placed in each of our newly acquired mess tins, followed by hot sweet black coffee poured into our tin mugs, 'bliss.'

I had months ago, naively walked into that recruitment office at *Lille* hoping for a coffee and now finally in *North Africa* had got one!

That evening we enjoyed a really good meal at long tables with benches and there was plenty of it, along with the usual red wine.

Spirits began rising fast.

In a surprisingly short space of time a semblance of order began to emerge, men began to act reasonably and there was a definite sense of optimism, based in no small part on the rumour we would soon move on to training.

Johnny got really excited and called me every time he heard a group of legionnaires loudly singing as they passed the outside of our enclosure. There was a real sense of power as they marched along at a curious slow drawn out pace.

I thought it looked and sounded like some kind of dynamic funeral march, which in retrospect was not unperceptive, as most Legion marching tunes are about celebrating honour, courage, suffering and death. Musically many were German Military tunes with at least one having recognisable German words.

I had always been puzzled as to why legionnaires marched like that until recently when I took a trip to the Tunisian Sahara to experience sleeping among the sand dunes under a full moon, a pleasure, which oddly enough had eluded me while I was in the Legion. Out on a camel trek, I was taking a break from riding the beast by walking behind it, when I noticed that although the nonchalant creature appeared to move very slowly, it was in fact moving at quite a fast pace, especially for a man walking in sand. So I tried matching the movements of the camel's back legs when I noticed that both of us were proceeding at Legion marching pace. So it seems possible that the slow extended marching pace, along with those melancholy drawn out marching songs, might just be based on the limited notes of a bugle and the slow ambling back legs of a camel. Eighty-eight paces per minute - the pace of Kings, Emperors and camels?

Bel-Abbès was the centre through which all recruits had to pass on their way into the Legion and presumably also out. I'd got out of the idea of a few men in white *képis* playing Hollywood style games with impressive robed Arabs in the desert, having learned that the Foreign Legion was a large modern army.

Ronaldo, a Spanish sounding guy who seemed to be 'in the know', confirmed that the Legion currently fielded over '30,000' men in *Algeria* alone, with a couple of thousand more scattered throughout France's Colonies.

Yet during the couple of weeks we spent in the clean modern amenities of *Bel-Abbés*, though I saw two or three covered-in lorries arrive on three occasions, indifferently depositing their cargo of drab new arrivals, I never saw anyone leave. In fact, throughout my fourteen months in the Legion I never actually met anyone whose release was imminent. I met men due to leave in a matter of months, or very occasionally weeks, but usually this information would come out as they were being transferred to another unit.

Later whenever I met men who had served longer than the minimum five-year period and asked "Why?"

I got sheepish replies such as, "Oh I don't know, I must have drunk too much and signed something." Or,

"Well, I probably signed one of those bits of paper somewhere along the line."

When I pursued the subject further I met with irritation, so dropped it, but I always wondered just where all those men went?

Ronaldo also told me there was a distinct impression among some legionnaires, that men were recruited or released as the supply and demand situation dictated. He reckoned there was an absence of departing men at this time because the Algerian situation was requiring more and more trained legionnaires following that hell-hole of Indo-China, where the battle of *'Dien Bien Phu'* had swallowed so many of the Legion's best.

He went on to say there was a practice of grooming a particular type of guy for release into the community as a recruiting magnet. It would always be a man who had been an excellent legionnaire, devoted, tough and who wholeheartedly believed in all that the Legion stood for. But he would also be a man that had developed a punch drunk mentality, probably suffering from a mental state known as *'le cafard'*, brought about by too much drink and sun.

This selected man, would be prepared, or additionally brainwashed, by giving him a glorious farewell that followed a wonderful period at *Bel-Abbès* of drinking and eating, with access to brothels, bars and cafes, a sort of freedom of the town with regular pay. Only this last period of his otherwise hard brutal years would be remembered and that with sublime pleasure.

This tough ex-legionnaire when liberated into the community would talk to, then enthuse, young men around the streets and bars of *Paris* or *Marseille*, encouraging, even bringing them to join the wonderful *Légion Etrangère*. But he himself would never again be admitted.

"That kind of man," *Ronaldo* continued, "is much more valuable to the Legion on the outside."

Near to the end of our relative comfort and minor activities that we were enjoying at *Bel-Abbès*, we were all, including men who had arrived both before and after us, called to attention on the parade ground, for some top brass to address us.

Among them there was a tall, impressive looking, highly decorated French General who wore with his many other decorations the oversized silver parachute wings that would soon become familiar to us. The gist of his speech was that the 'Glorious France' had recently suffered great losses in Indo-China where nearly all of the French Foreign Legion Paratroopers had been wiped out, mostly at a place called *'Dien Bien Phu'*.

"It is a matter of absolute urgency" he boomed, "**that we continue to rebuild an Elite Paratroop Force for immediate rapid action in *Algeria*.**"

He went on to stress that no man could be made to join the Para's so volunteers were needed right now. He continued waving his hands while appealing to our macho fantasies by listing off the many heroic attributes required for such a glorious cause.

Just as I was wondering if *Rutand, Michel,* or *Muller, Hans* could possibly be recycled names of men that had died at *Dien Bien Phu*, a whole bunch of our assembled men stepped forward, including the six remaining Brits, more than enthusiastically encouraged by 'Mau-Mau'. Then to my horror, I realised I would have to become one of them.

I have to say, that as I volunteered it was in the belief that I would be on safe ground. I reasoned that I could both appease 'Mau-Mau' and the Brits by really appearing keen, safe in the knowledge that as my mum had told me many times, I was not fit and strong like other boys, so I would naturally fail both the medical and fitness tests. Then taking my stepfather's low opinion of me into account that I would probably be too thick to do much at all, I'd fail the intelligence test as well.

But, it seemed the gods of cussedness were out for a joke. As following various medical, fitness, and intelligence tests as well as contrived ability tests, which included keeping up with escalating Morse Code sentences, which I couldn't, a surprisingly small number of us were finally accepted. Neither 'Mau-Mau', nor any of the Brits got through successfully, with two exceptions however.

Ironically those exceptions were *Rutand, Michel* and *Muller, Hans!*

We both could hardly believe our ears. What the hell had we two got ourselves into now?

Later, on the same day that we got our results, I saw 'Mau-Mau' for the last time in the shower block. Somehow, seeing the tough man that I had for months been intimidated by, naked, shorn, deflated, very disappointed and standing in such an out of character pose of vulnerability, yet still managing what must have been for him a brave grin, brought up in me a kind of sadness.

It was a relief to know, that he'd no longer be an uncomfortable threat in a world that was already threatening enough, but I could take no pleasure from that last image of the man we called 'Mau-Mau'.

In summing up, I reckoned I had been damn lucky so far. I was for now, admittedly in the Foreign Legion, but I was in Africa, which is after all closer to Australia than Aldershot! I had received more than enough inoculations and injections to see me through the journey, whichever way it unfolded.

The barrage of tests showed I was in good health and surprisingly fit and it seems that I had a modicum of intelligence. Yeah well, okay, if that last bit were true then what the hell was I doing there?

What felt very important to me was that I had survived a period of forced confinement in a unique violent anarchy, all without getting my head kicked in, or worse. What was even more important now that I had become coerced into enlisting, was the fact that I hadn't made any enemies. Even the uncomfortable presence of 'Mau-Mau' had after all only been potentially threatening and I'd probably magnified the threat in my head anyway.

Although not comparable to the above events, I had once in the past been in a confined situation where I'd made an enemy and been stuck with him, so was very glad that I hadn't repeated the experience here. That particular occasion had been as a boy in the Merchant Navy, on board a twenty-eight thousand tonne passenger-cargo ship, travelling out of Southampton via France, Spain and the Canaries then up and down the 'sea ports' of the East coast of South America. We were four sixteen year old 'boy ratings' sharing a four-berth cabin. One lad, a city 'hard kid', had set himself up as the bully-boss, arrogantly ordering the three of us kids about. The longer the journey lasted, the more intense his demands got and the more threatening he became. It had reached the stage of him throwing his cigarette butts on the floor and demanding that I stamp them out. On a particular occasion I reacted in spite of my fear and it wasn't at all heroic. He was sitting arrogantly on a chair when he goaded me once too often and got my fist straight in his face. The punch was reactive, uncalculated and therefore weak and from somewhere he produced a knife and forced me on my back across one of the bunks. Struggling to prevent him stabbing me I desperately held both his wrists as he lunged at me over and over, redirecting the back of one of his wrists with each lunge onto the sharp edge of a metal locker, until his knife hand gave way and the weapon dropped out of his probably paralysed hand. We were still rolling about fighting when a couple of senior crew members passed by and gave us both a good rollicking. Nothing else came of the incident but we three boys were never bullied by him again. However, I never really relaxed while we were both on that same ship and it was through those type of situations that I learned early in my travels a degree of keeping to myself and avoiding the sort of behaviour that might make enemies.

1st REP Badge.

Once accepted for Legion Para training, there was no time wasted. In fact we left *Siddi-bel-Abbès*, of which we'd still seen nothing, the following morning to begin our training at the hands, knees, fists and boots of the 1st Foreign Legion Parachute Regiment *(Premier Regiment Etranger de Parachutistes or 1er REP)* at 'Camp Zeralda'.

Their Camp was near a village of the same name situated east along the coast from the city of *Algiers*. Apparently we were lucky to be going there, as the barracks were very modern having actually been purpose built by men of the *1st REP.*

As we set off, blind to the outside world in our now familiar canvas-backed lorries, there was a feeling of apprehension, somewhat intensified by the fact that we no longer recognised any faces from *Lille, Paris, Marseilles* or *Bel-Abbès*, at least not in our vehicle. Yet we were curiously optimistic and pleased to be on the move, agreeing that maybe there were familiar faces on one of the other lorries.

At the end of the long journey, which looks on the map to be some two to three hundred miles, and of which I remember nothing, we sleepy, unfit, unprepared men rumbled in darkness up to the gates of *'Camp Zeralda'*, naively looking forward to getting our heads down in nice comfortable beds.

I guess by then we should have known better!

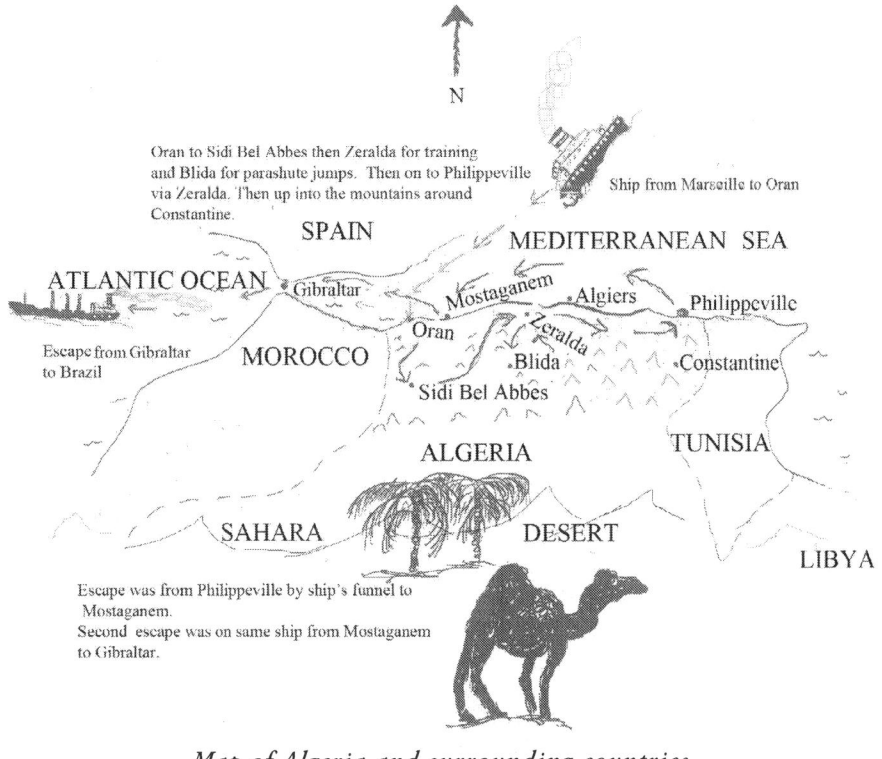

Map of Algeria and surrounding countries.

CHAPTER EIGHT
'Avoiding The Square Head'

No sooner had we pulled up before the camp gates, than we were either yanked, pushed, kicked or shocked out of our vehicles with more abuse and kicks aimed at us until we could form some resemblance of a group.

From that first blur of events the image I most remember was of a short, tight, vital looking guy who was dressed in the now familiar camouflage combat gear and green *berét* of the Legion Paras. Even just standing there watching us through sunglasses in that headlight glare, he came across as every inch the fighter with an impressive sheathed knife or dagger with its leather braid thong, strapped low around his muscular thigh adding mystery to the already tough image.

I was quickly wrenched from my fascination by the menacing delivery of a message in high-pitched syllables that was French, but with an accent and connotation that made it sound Italian. Words poured from this other man's mouth like so much sewage.

Each high-pitched sentence was screamed and punctuated by an 'a' sound, as in ant.

"I am not a man to be fucked about-a. Here you will all shit flames-a!" *(Ici tu vas tout shiet les flames-a!)*

A voice near my ear was muttering disdainfully, "The bastard's Corsican." *(Corse.)*

His obscene creative tirade of punctuated sentences continued, with few of us comprehending the words, but all of us getting the message.

As if to add irritation, he terminated nearly every sentence with "You understand-a?" *(Tu comprends-a?)*

To which we were being persuaded by surrounding corporals *(caporaux)* to shout *"Oui, sergent chef!"* louder and louder.

Unfortunately, one of our group got a bit flash and added a mimicking 'a' to his response, a big mistake, which caused an uneasy silence. There was a shout from somewhere, then like a wildcat the guy with the sheath-knife was across the few yards and into our group. I didn't see the punch, but I heard it! A man went down and I heard that!

The screechy delivery just carried on as though nothing had happened. "**From now you will only stand at ease when told to, perhaps when receiving instruction or learning terms in French-a!**" "*Comprends-a?*"

This time when we all called out *"Oui, sergent chef!"* It was immediate and loud, we were learning fast.

"**At all other times,**" the voice went on, "**you will run at the double!** *Comprends-a?*"

"Oui, sergent chef!" The shout was even louder.

"**You will run to your place of instruction, you will run to your place of eating and to your place of sleeping-a. If you go for a piss or a shit-a you will run at the double!** *Comprends-a* **you slimey shits?**"

"Oui, sergent chef!"

"**Meanwhile on command-a, you will run on the spot while you are prepared for a ten kilometre run with full pack, so that each of you slimey shits will understand what running is-a and also to understand that you are all shit!** *(merde) Comprends-a?*"

"Oui, sergent chef!"

Not one man disagreed whatever language he spoke, we all got it, we were 'shit'!

After the rigmarole of orders being passed from rank to rank, all hell broke loose as we were screamed at, punched, shoved and kicked, while running and stumbling around unable to believe what was happening to us. Half a dozen legion tormenters had us strip down to underpants, empty our rucksacks and throw the lot into one big heap, then bizarrely we were all encouraged to play a game in which they joined. They were laughing and enjoying so we all nervously laughed too, as together we heaved, separated and spread the heap of gear all over a wide area.

Then there was utter pandemonium as the mood changed and we were ordered under threat that each man was to find his own individual gear and place it before him, all within five minutes. The 'boot-assisted guidance' that followed ensured that each man ended up with a heap of gear before him, unlikely to be his own but nonetheless determinedly claiming that it was.

There was an instruction given that in five minutes we would begin the run, every single item was to be worn or carried and we were told that a nasty punishment awaited a man who lost so much as one single item. *"Demerdez-vous!"*

The circus that followed might have been funny under other circumstances, but for us then it was deadly serious. Early efforts to work a system were abandoned under the threat of a punch as we resorted to cramming rucksacks and piling on masses of clothes which bulged out from under unfasten-able greatcoats. On heads, tin helmets were forced down over hats, while water bottles, mess tins and other crap dangled from our clothing or were precariously attached to our damned heavy rucksacks.

The run, though possibly nothing like ten kilometres was nonetheless nightmarish in our decrepit condition, especially having vegetated for weeks on starch and wine to now suddenly find that we were being treated as though we were fit. It began in the dark with screaming, swearing, pushing and shoving until we were all staggering forwards, whilst being monitored and encouraged along dirt roads and then narrow lanes that skirted the edges of vineyards.

Feet suffered ill-fitting boots as we struggled beneath weight and sheer heat generated by such heavy layers of clothing.

From the onset I was flagging, gasping and overheating, even though it was a cold early morning. Yet somehow in my numb state I was able to let the constant wave of shoves and threats carry me forward passing desperate stragglers until I was through the camp gates, by which time the North African sun was beginning to gain strength. I didn't understand the order that was given on my arrival, but immediately copied the other men by stripping off and throwing everything on to one central pile.

Still running on the spot I followed the line of men working their way through the cold showers and then still wet, passed along familiar counters collecting fresh kit. After which those of us who had completed the run were issued sweet black coffee with a match-boxed sized snack that we were ordered to, "take ten minutes standing easy and enjoy". Bliss!

The next orders were for tending to our blood stained and blistered feet for which we could sit when necessary, but on no account to be caught resting. During those activities I was able to speak to Johnny and we both realised we didn't recognise a single face and felt very concerned that we had no allies.

After a few hours of packing our kit under instruction, we were ordered to queue up, wash our hands then queue up again, still running of course, for *'la soupe'*, a word that turned out to be Legion talk for any meal, one of the many words used as a multilingual compromise.

What followed was a demeaning kindegarten type 'hand check' at the door where we were ordered to hold out our hands and show backs, fronts then nails before entering the canteen *(refectoire)*. All similarity to kindegarten ceased when some men were kicked, punched, kneed in the guts or worse then turned away. While those of us lucky enough to get in to eat were made to stand behind benches at long tables until ordered to be seated (*'asseyez-vous'*).

Then came a real surprise as we first saw and then relished the first of the excellent meals that would accompany us for the duration of our training. They included steak, salad, artichokes with mayonnaise and, though I still didn't drink it, red wine.

Somewhat revived after eating, we were kept on our toes by a corporal for several more hours while a sergeant instructed us how to precisely prepare our kit for the regular evening inspection ordeal known as *'appel'*.

Along with the obvious stuff such as order, cleanliness, polished boots bed making etc., they seemed to be focused around a square parcel known as *'un paquetage carre'* which was an eighteen inch cube to be assembled correctly with the help of cut-out cardboard squares and the use of long dark blue waist sashes from our dress uniforms. When completed these formed dark blue cubes to be filled with specific items upon the top of which our *képi blanc* would sit proudly between large red epaulettes, various other items were added to complete the overall display.

The sergeant seemed to take great pleasure in emphasising that these *paquetage carrés* that would live on a shelf at the head of our beds for the duration of our training would become for some of us the cause of a lot of misery!

When it came, *appel* turned out to be ferocious as we stood rigid at the foot of our bed quickly learning what to expect from our three heavy-duty *caporaux* and our *Caporal-Chef Bergenbach*, who, not only from his accent, but also from his tattoos was unmistakably German.

During the *appel, Bergenbach* was followed around by the small weasely, arse-licking *Caporal Ruesler*, a prowling guy who had a fixed smile that did nothing to help his sly appearance.

Standing strategically was *Caporal De Groot*, a big Dutch speaking white African with a tight mouth that always seems to spit contempt through barred teeth the moment its thin line of lips were parted.

Rumour was that all three men had survived *Dien Bien Phu* and I got a distinct feeling they wanted us to pay for it.

The biggest but quietest man was *Caporal Krajevic*. He was around six foot six, pockmarked and with ears that looked as though, if he hadn't spent many hours fighting in the ring, then he must have been dragged feet first through a tight *Viet Minh* tunnel.

As we waited it was forcefully made clear to us by *Bergenbach*, with nods of agreement from *Ruesler*, **"You have all failed to be precise and will now pay for your carelessness."** Speaking French with a lot of German punctuation he went from man to man eye-balling and muttering threats into every man's ear.

In response, each man shouted, *"Non, caporal-chef!"*

When he got to me he whispered right into my ear. "Do you think your Queen Elizabeth will help you here?"

"Dit, non caporal-chef." Encouraged *Ruesler*, poking me none too gently in the ribs, *"Non, caporal-chef!"* I shouted, feeling slightly amused but mostly uneasy at the same time.

As they progressed to the next man, suddenly there was violent punching and frightened shouts, I glanced but *Ruesler* quickly screeched me back into my rigid position as *De Groot* and *Krajevic* started pacing around. There was a commotion somewhere behind me but I didn't risk looking again.

"Resistance, in case anyone has such thoughts will be met," said *Bergenbach*, **"with a square head!"** *(avec une tête carré!)*

We had no idea what *'un tête carré'* was, but between them the brutes made it sound very ominous and none of us wanted one, so we continued to stand rigid as each man's *paquetage* was dramatically slung through the nearest window. A minute of silence passed and I began to think maybe *appel* is over, but suddenly it was like being in the middle of a thunderstorm as thirty metal lockers crashed to the floor, accompanied by demonic screams as rolls of bedding and anything movable was heaved out through the windows, then silence.

One unfortunate guy flinched as *Bergenbach* passed him and consequently yelped as he received a knee to the thigh. *Bergenbach* then passed us over to *Ruesler* and left with his fellow corporals.

We were then given an impossibly short time to get all our stuff back in perfect order as *Ruesler* announced, "**Lights out in fifteen minutes, there will be an inspection at six a.m. Anything not spot on will have an owner and that owner will be made to shit flames and just remember that not even god will be able to protect any thief *(voleur)* found with an item of someone else's in their kit. Believe me, we have very severe ways of dealing with thieves in La Legion.**"

We had all heard nasty descriptions of *'crucifixion par la bayonnette'* and even if that didn't happen, I was already panicking about *une tête carré*, whatever that was.

Six a.m. saw us practically falling from our bunks and standing erect to a loud, "***Debout. Schnell, dépêche toi alors!***" from *Krajevic,* who was not so quiet after all.

His shouts were quickly supported by the other corporals as they too screamed obscenities, while hounding us through the showers.

Still wet, we began dressing in preparation for the promised inspection, only to be told a few minutes later, "**You have three minutes to be out on the parade ground dressed in sports gear or you will 'all' be shitting flames!**"

This of course meant a whole upheaval of our belongings that would require re-organising before the evening *appel*.

But moments later we were on the parade ground thankful there was no inspection, but quickly brought to reality by a good dose of screaming abuse and threats, before receiving instructions for the morning run which involved several miles of shoves and kicks through vineyard tracks to the beach, then over sand dunes and back to camp. We showered again and made another change of clothes prior to standing gratefully 'at ease' *(au respos)*, gulping down our sweet black coffee with its meagre snack before trotting behind corporal *Ruesler* to our place of instruction, which was a black-board and table some yards from our barrack room.

Upon a few quick *"Gard-à-vous"* and *"Respos"* from *Ruesler*, which finished on one loud *"Gard-à-vous"*, we remained at attention for the following twenty minutes.

I can't speak for everyone but I was trembling and hoped it didn't show, still haunted by the threat of the unknown *tête carré*.

A *Sergent Perez* arrived to begin our very basic instruction in learning how to stand, how to respond and some relevant French words. Both me and Johnny found the 'standing to attention' *(garde-à-vous)* very odd.

It involved slamming feet together, shoulders back, chin in and placing the outer edges of slightly bent arms against an imaginary trouser seam, with cupped palms facing forward. The order was often shortened to a loud *'vous'*. 'At ease' *(au repos)* on the other hand was sometimes shortened to *'po'*, and involved a relatively comfortable position where the left arm and leg were respectively relaxed at the elbow and knee, while the palm of the right hand rested with the thumb on the belt buckle.

We learned to say "yes" *(oui)* to lower ranks, as in *"Oui, sergent"* but to higher ranks it was to be "yes, my" *(oui, mon)* as in *"Oui, mon capitaine"*. So, "At your service, my captain" became *"À vos ordres, mon capitaine"*.

By this process we were learning not only correct forms of address and relevant French words, (we never had French lessons), but also several forms of painful punishment, or 'exercise' as they called it, whenever we failed to get a word immediately right!

....

CHAPTER NINE
'The Shock'

Three days into instruction we had our first real shock as we stood to attention, attempting to master the mechanics and French terms of the bolt action *MAS.36*, a rifle with a thin bayonet commonly known as the 'tooth pick'. Every few minutes someone made a mistake and was kicked or punched by our ever-grinning *Carporal Ruesler* into doing 'press-ups', accompanied by screams of "Up" *(En haut)*, or "Down" *(En bas)*, or "Duck walks" *(Marcher à la canard)*.

The latter involved a squatting walk, carrying a rifle across forward outstretched arms while at the same time shouting **"Quack! Quack!"**

It must have looked and sounded particularly funny when we all had to do it at once in order to suffer for an individual's mistake, it was good for balance and developing arms and legs but sheer hell and not amusing for most of us in those early days.

As we stood focused on the dissected rifle parts, we heard aggressive shouting, whistles and awful wailing sounds that sounded like men or animals screaming. Inquisitive tendencies were bluntly brought back to task by *Ruesler*.

Meanwhile the sounds got disturbingly louder, until eventually they were close and practically behind us. At a nod from the Sergeant, *Ruesler,* ordered us to turn about and stand to attention in order to witness, what was for me, one of the most awful scenes I'd encountered until that time.

Two utterly devastated young men, barely looking human, were coming towards us dragging their outstretched, agonised bodies along by their bleeding elbows. It was as though their hollow staring eyes could not see us.

On their backs were rucksacks that some bastard had filled with rocks and as if that weren't cruel enough, the straps of the rucksacks had been deliberately removed and replaced with wire. On their heads, beneath the North African sun, each wore a tin helmet from which the protective inner padding had been removed and on their feet were what appeared to be ill-fitting, old, dried out boots, lacking the normal protection of either socks or laces.

This so called 'punishment' was being dished out by an indifferent looking brute with cold blue eyes who was wearing the dark *képi* of rank, carrying a sort of sten gun casually rested over one arm and wielding a solid chunk of timber in the other.

A silver whistle hung from his lips, and when either wretch failed to immediately respond to the brute's whistle blast by painfully rising to his feet and stumbling forward, he received what, in that heat, must have been a craze-inducing, reverberating crack across his unpadded helmet, then mere seconds later on a double whistle blast, the wretches had to trip themselves and launch their agonised bodies full length on the hard sand, to continue the dragging by blood stained elbows. Both men were already out of their minds with terror and pain, having endured this torment for some time.

My heart was pounding at the sight of it, I honestly couldn't see how it was possible for them to go on and I was hearing our sergeant's words like they were in some distant dream.

"**These lower than the lowest of shits that you see here before you deserted last night. Look carefully, this punishment is called** *'la pelote'*. **Luckily for these pathetic specimens who are both as soft as their mother's bellies, it will only go on till midnight as they are new to the Legion. They don't realise how fortunate they are, because if they had been caught by the** *Fell* **instead of the French army, they would have been sent back here with their pricks dangling out of their mouths, unable to even squeal like the couple of pathetic pigs that they both are. Let this be a lesson to each and everyone of you who might even so much as think of deserting** *la Legion*. **Now** *Carporal Ruesler*, **if you will…**"

"**About turn!**" ordered *Ruesler*, seizing the opportunity to poke the ribs of a couple of slow responders.

I caught the same look of utter shock and horror that I was feeling on some of my companions' faces, as we deliberately tried to re-focus on the *MAS 36* rifle parts, all trying desperately, all be it unsuccessfully, to push out the horrendous images we had just witnessed. But because the sounds of agonising screams, shouts, whistles and crack's of wood on helmets were unavoidable as the punishment continued around us, holding out those images was impossible. I stood there stiffly 'at attention', but horribly conscious that I was trembling.

Hardly surprising we still got names of parts wrong, and were duly ordered to do more press ups and 'duck marching' by corporal *Ruesler*, as for an hour or more those horrifying sounds continued in the background. This was curiously made even more disturbing by the constant self-satisfied leering smile on the face of our corporal.

I exchanged a look of horror with Johnny as men furtively grimaced at each other while the Italians amongst us made gestures by squeezing together their upturned fingers, which I quickly recognised from my own sensations was representing our pulsating sphincter muscles.

Then came the call for *'la soupe'* and as instructed we all ran at the double to the taps to wash our hands, then on to the *réfectoire* for the demeaning clean hands ritual. The guy in front of me got a knee to his stomach and was still writhing on the ground as, holding my breath, I gratefully passed the inspecting corporal.

In spite of what I'd seen, like everyone else I was suddenly ravenously hungry!

On command, we marched to stand at attention behind our allocated stools. We passed the two Italian wretches who, too weak to stand of their own accord, had been secured back to back to the upright supports of the building. They looked to me like victims of some awful death camp, with their blood stained shaven heads drooping, staring down from hollow eye sockets, limp, broken and without food or water.

At our stools the duty sergeant shouted, *"Bon appétit!"*
To which we replied, *"Merci, et bon appétit sergent!"*
Then a corporal called, *"Repos! Asseyez-vous!"*
We all tore enthusiastically into the excellent meal with periodic shouts from our corporal to keep the noise down.

As we devoured and drank our fill in full view of those two wretches, the poor bastards were being tormented by our mocking corporal yobs, splashing and drinking water that those poor men were denied, just inches from their faces and when we left our tables there was a lot of coaxing from those bastards to make us taunt and mock the victims even further.

This whole dark pantomime was clearly aimed at causing hatred for deserters and what was really sick was that some men were already buying into it, why I just could not understand, as France wasn't even their country, there was no reason why they should feel loyal to the legion or anyone in it, and there had been no other way for those two poor young boys to get out.

Later that evening, I saw them in a drainage ditch for one of the off periods of their 'two hours on/two hours off routine'. They lay as they had last fallen, either too exhausted or maybe too scared to move. Not surprisingly, the legion took on a whole new meaning after that and I reminded myself that I was only a legionnaire because 'they' had decided to call me one.

That wasn't the only time I saw *la pelote* dished out, but it was the most upsetting, partly because we were so new, but also because it involved raw boys who had not yet had the benefit of toughening up. Those unfortunate young men were, from what I heard, simply two normal Italian lads that had wandered into a situation, found it was bad and tried to get out. I don't know anyone that ever saw them again, word was they'd been transferred and I shudder to think what really did happen to them, I never even found out their names. Johnny was told about another victim of *la pelote*, who out of sheer desperation attacked his tormentor only to be shot dead 'in self-defence'.

Watered down variations of *la pelote*, using rucksacks with normal straps, filled to bursting point with everything we owned either worn, or somehow attached and dangling, was common practice. It was ridiculous, demeaning and exhausting with everything ending up crumpled and filthy to be washed, ironed and perfect for an inspection at some ungodly hour. This meant staying up and competing for one of the few available irons, which I definitely wasn't very good at.
Meanwhile our four loving guardians would amuse themselves by turning lights on and off to create more confusion and to ensure even more sleep deprivation.

Throughout those long months of training, *appel* remained a frightening ordeal. It was always carried out by our same four bullies and supposedly overseen by a sergeant who wasn't there during the first few days. I think several of us mistakenly imagined that when Sergeant *Wagner* arrived he would naturally curb our over-zealous corporals, but that wasn't to be the case.

We had our first experience of the sergeant one evening as we stood rigid at the foot of our beds, following the usual physical threats by *Bergenbach* and an actual violent attack to the face of one of our men, when suddenly *Ruesler* called, **"Section, Repos!"** followed quickly by, **"Debout!"** as Sergeant *Wagner* entered the room.

Without a word he slowly walked up to each man and for several seconds looked him straight in the face. When he finally reached me it was a shock to realise that I was being scrutinised by the cold blue eyes I'd seen on the face of that vicious sergeant we had all witnessed putting the two Italian boys through their nightmare ordeal.

As he concluded his inspection he made absolutely no mention of the man's bruised face. He simply accepted his *caporal chef's* presentation of 'all present and correct' before exchanging goodnights and leaving the room.

If anyone of us had been hoping the sergeant would temper our keepers' excesses, we now knew we could certainly forget that.

If fear was one aim of the indoctrination process and sleep deprivation another, they both worked well, because practically every man there functioned between fear and exhaustion for most of the time, with each overwhelming day progressing with a vitality sucking unease towards that doomed, time-consuming preparation of our kit and that stupid immaculate blue cube.

It was inevitable that they would find something wrong, such as one of the thirteen creases of a shirt ironed off centre or a speck of dirt on the lace of a boot.

So at *appel*, we stood as thirty-two upright statue's practically shitting our pants, while the three or four predators prowled back and forth amusing themselves by intimidating us and taking their time before each launched into his personal sadistic pleasure.

De Groot liked to whisper threats while kneeing a man in the thigh so that standing to attention would be painful.

Krajevic was so potentially threatening that he could just stand in front of a man enjoying the effect.

The savage *Bergenbach* might floor a man with a punch in the guts for not responding immediately to a screamed question such as, **"Why are you lower than your mother's shit?"** Or he might stare closely into a man's face and knee him in the balls.

Ruesler would usually follow up *Bergenbach's* attacks by a sharp elbow poke in the ribs.

For me the first few weeks of dreading *un tête carré* consumed any moments of potential relief. I had begun to hope that the speciality of *Bergenbach's* might be some reference to his own head, which was a big square thing sitting on a bullish neck. In fact, *Bergenbach* was a bull of a man. But sadly that hope was dissolved when a well meaning guy told me that *'un tête carré'* referred to what *Bergenbach* could do to a man's head in a particularly nasty way!

Knowing that to show fear would guarantee attack from *Bergenbach*, I tried desperately not to flinch as he thunderously heaved my metal locker to the floor, then screamed Franco-German obscenities down my ear, along with nasty threats that mercifully were never carried out, although the expectation felt nearly as bad.

At the time unfortunately I had no way of knowing that Johnny being Scottish and me English probably protected us from excessive brutality. I found out years later about a code instilled at Corporal school, 'Never to be seen picking on another nationality too often'. There was actually an advantage to being a minority of one. I guess if there had been a Scottish or English corporal in our section one of us might not have been so blessed.

Legionnaire *Klaus* was not so lucky, I couldn't believe the beatings that man could take and still bounce back.

During one particular *appel*, *Klaus* was unfortunate enough to flinch and raise a hand as *Bergenbach* came near, hardly surprising considering the boorish thug with his grinning side-kick had assaulted him on several previous occasions. Well that was it, we all excelled at staring ahead as our *caporal chef* set about him, he beat him for ages and the sounds were awful.

We weren't exactly able to see what happened but could guess and we all knew *Ruesler* would be putting his elbow in as he was always close to *Bergen-*

bach's arse. In the middle of the ordeal *Krajevic* boomed a loud **"Gdz vous!"** which was kind of pointless as we were already very much 'at attention' anyway, if only from fear.

Then we heard *Wagner* strolling purposefully into the room and once more I thought this time *Bergenbach's* in for it, but no. When the sergeant slowly passed the suffering *Klaus* there wasn't even a pause.

At the end of his round *Bergenbach* presented us, *Wagner* acknowledged him, we all shouted our goodnights and *Ruesler* dismissed us announcing, **"Lights out in two minutes."**

That experience confirmed what I had heard, namely that the Legion invested irrational power to a rank that was just above corporal, we were truly at the mercy of these pigs. Later in darkness I wrapped myself in a miserable ball, withdrew from life and plunged into the merciful arms of oblivion until my guard duty stint at three in the morning.

The next time I saw *Klaus,* I couldn't believe or understand quite what I was seeing, both of his eyes were sunken folds and all the flesh of his face, head and neck were swollen in such a way that he actually did have a large 'square head'.

Days later I saw him together with his persecutors, they were each patting him on the back, all laughing, including him.

"You *Klaus,*" they were telling him, "are privileged to be first to receive *'un tête carré'.*" They continued, "You are a fine chap. You took it like a man, passed the test and are now really well on the way to becoming a true legionnaire."

At all following *appels Klaus* was to suffer the tragic indignity of having to please those bastards by supporting their sick humour as they regularly poked him about taunting him with mock threats of repetition, during which *Klaus* had to keep smiling and laughing, after all, they were all good fellows together.

It was then I began to wonder whether *Ruesler's* fixed smile might just have been as a result of a *'un tête carré'* received from *Bergenbach* at some earlier time. It could certainly be one explanation of the master/dog like nature of their relationship.

CHAPTER TEN
'Dans la Merde!'

Midway through training at *Zeralda*, the whole of our section underwent an experience that was probably unusual by legion or even para standards, and not an experience to uphold the popular fantasies or macho images of the foreign legion or the 1st REP.

Each morning, crack of dawn and before dreaded close combat training, we did our pre-coffee gallop to the beach and back, which meant passing along the sides of vineyards where tantalising grapes hung, ripening, as it was the end of July.

We were of course ordered, with appropriate threats, not to pick any of them but we were hot and thirsty while the grapes were cool, juicy, easily available and even though they had a white dust on them, far too good for most of us to miss. Handfuls were snatched and stuffed into eager mouths as we ran past.

It should have been obvious to us that the farmer had sprayed them with something pretty nasty and might well have had us in mind, and who could have blamed him. By then although the legion did our thinking, thirst got the better of us, and the miserable outcome was that those of our section who hadn't already been hospitalised by the close combat training, got a really bad dose of the shits *(la chiasse)*.

'*Dans la Merde!*'

Our solidly built by 1st REP toilets at the camp, modern enough by French standards, comprised of an oblong brick building with a door at each of its four corners. It had a long dividing wall so creating two sections and there was a row of about eight crapping holes along each side of that wall. Opposite the crap holes in each section a pissing trough ran the inside length of the outer wall.

North African summer meant water rationing, so these toilets, whether they needed it or not, were thoroughly hosed and scrubbed out only once a day and that was in the dark early hours while it was still relatively cool.

Absence of toilet paper resulted in glossy magazines and the like being used, which without constant water led to blocked holes with their repulsive contents oozing freely. As no man wanted to squat near a hole and put his parts at risk from emerging shit, he crapped further away as did each man that followed him.

Consequently, by the time the sun rose there was a thick, warm fly-skating rink formed by human excrement across both concrete floors and so, after our morning grape-eating gallops to the beach and back, the excrement was particularly rich.

Following the usual nerve-racking *appel*, while desperate for sleep, an extra inspection was sprung upon us. In various states of undress, ***"Debout!"*** had us as frozen statues at the foot of our beds, even our corporals stood rigid.

Sergent chef Angelos, known by us until then as a quiet and fair guy, strode purposefully to the front of our room, announcing simply to *Caporal chef Bergenbach*, "My shirt is missing and I want it returned."

"**Oui, Sergent Chef!**" Snapped *Bergenbach*.

Then there was total silence during which no man, not even our corporal chef uttered a word. The *sergent chef* quietly did the round, inspecting each of our shirts in turn, then indicated something towards *Bergenbach* and left the room. *Bergenbach* nodded to his corporals and he also left.

This allowed our three vultures the opportunity to apply some individual questioning, a situation which they threw themselves into with relish each closing to within an inch of a man's face, eyeballing him and screaming, **"Are you the snake-bellied thief that has taken the Sergeant's f.....g shirt?"**

It was all extremely threatening, as we each waited for a knee in the balls, fist in the gut or punch in the face, none of which ever came.

At sometime during the onslaught *Bergenbach* returned, bellowing **"Prosti-**

tutes of shit, *(putain de merde)* you are all fucking me about. So, you shitting thieves *(du scheister voleurs)* will 'all' shit flames and we 'will' discover the thief that stole the Sergent Chef's fucking shirt."

An explosive frenzy of activity followed with three repeats of the unnerving locker crashing, heaving out the window of bedding etc., but compared with my fantasies of crucifixion by bayonet those were the least of my worries.

As the third avalanche of kicks and punches pursued us into the night, we found our bedding and belongings being sprayed with water by *De Groot*, while *Krajevic* was kicking it all around in the sand.

Then we were given five minutes to put on as many wet clothes as possible from the common pile and stuff the remainder into our rucksacks ready for carrying out *la pelote*. Had not the sheer weight of sand and water made it impossible it would have included every item, so I guess we got off light!

However, we were soon miserably dragging our limp bodies by the elbows, running, duck-walking and even making pathetic attempts at press-ups, all of which of course was around the stinking toilet block.

It was then that the smiley-faced weasel had his great brainwave! "**You are all like shit** *(vous êtes tous comme la merde).*" He said. "**And where does shit belong? There** *(voila)* **with the real shit.**"

He pointed gleefully, giggling like some warped school-kid at the layer of filth on the shit house floor, then drawing himself up to his full five foot-five inches he masterfully ordered us to elbow-drag ourselves full length through that stinking slime. It meant literally crawling around through human diarrhoea as the other two corporals and *Bergenbach* joined the fun by each guarding a door to ensure that we all co-operated in acting out *Ruesler's* big joke.

It was the first time I'd seen that man, with his permanent frozen smile, look truly happy and it wasn't down to his usual petty sadism. I believe *Ruesler* was happy because he had actually had a thought all by himself, carried it out and was being appreciated and supported for it!

It's strange to think that as I crawled around in human diarrhoea I was observing what motivated that boot-licking sod!

Not surprisingly men were keeping their faces as far above the floor as possible, which merely added to our tormentors resolve to degrade us, so as each man reached a door he felt a boot ease his face into the slime.

I made a conscious show of 'appearing' to press my face into that muck by keeping as low as possible and it worked, because as I passed *Bergenbach* I heard him murmur, "Ah, English, good, very good, your Queen Elizabeth would be very proud of you." As I made it, unassisted by boot through each door, my biggest concern was not to graze my face and have it go septic.

Their game continued, until every man had surrendered to the stinking ordeal when, other than for *Ruesler* who had felt himself to be the centre of attraction, the novelty must have worn off or maybe the smell had got too much, because with raucous laughter, which believe it or not included us laughing, they duck-marched us back to our bedding and hosed us down. *Ruesler,* enjoying it so much, was the last corporal to go, leaving the hose for a free-for-all and told us to expect a five a.m. inspection.

For some time we took turns desperately trying to rid ourselves of the awful stink, but then remembering the punishment for stealing we began frantically working together, especially in identifying and locating our own shirts.

For the remainder of the night we worked painstakingly towards the promised inspection that never came. We all figured that those tough buggers couldn't cope with our stench and that as no more was said about the missing shirt, *Angelos* probably didn't want it back anyway, or hadn't even lost it in the first place.

For the remaining days and nights that the smell lingered, *appel* was a doddle and we actually caught up on some sleep.

Not one man got ill as a result of that ordeal, in fact it was a way of life that didn't seem to permit it and I never saw anyone actually get sick. There were of course men new to Africa who needed treatment for boils and skin rashes and most men got at least one dose of the shits.

Our resistance to disease was probably because we were never still, always running or marching for twenty, thirty or more miles through the hills with heavy packs or singing our hearts out as we marched to some legion song.

When we were learning theory we still stood easy or at attention, and the constant punishments still ensured rope climbs, press-ups, duck-marching or whatever was requested, so long as it required effort.

Although food was excellent we were hungry as guard dogs and always deprived of sleep.

So the infirmary mostly dealt with injuries acquired on the assault course or during close combat drill or from those mysteriously frequent self-inflicted accidents, which of course were never put down to incidents at the evening *appel*.

The French language or *argot* spoken in the legion was by men with a variety of foreign accents and so was not always easy to follow, and although our training period wasn't a time exactly filled with laughter, there were some absurd moments brought about because of it.

For example, even though it was directed at me with a certain amount of menace I couldn't help but see the funny side of being reprimanded by our original welcoming host to *Camp Zeralda*, the *Corsican Sergent Chef Franzuni*, or *Franzuni-a*, as everyone out of earshot called him. In the Legion I was referred to variously as *'Rutan' 'Rutand'* or *'Rutang'* and this is the gist of what *Sergent Chef Franzuni* piercingly screamed at me.

Loosely interpreted it went, **"You, Rutand-a, you are more stupid-a, than my prick is precious-a!** *(Twa, Rutand-a, twa, tu es plus fool-a que ma bite est mignon-a!)"* What could a man say to that but scream back? *"Merci, Sergent Chef!"*

It was during such brief snatches of 'endearment' that our German corporals, knowing I was English, would repeatedly make comments such as, "What would your Queen Elizabeth think of you now?"

Yet at no point was I ever discriminated against for my nationality.

The following funny incident, though not amusing for Johnny at the time, happened when he was having great difficulty in getting his tongue around the French language and shouting louder and louder in the vain hope of being understood. He so often painfully struggled with a particular word that he urgently needed. Johnny was a determined man, far less afraid of the background threat of violence than I was, but the big fear for him was the thought of making a fool of himself in front of other people.

At one point during instruction, because we had been making good progress in dissecting, assembling, identifying and shooting the *M.A.T.49 Pistolet Mitraillete* (a sort of French equivalent of the Sten gun), an officer came to view our progress. He was a Lieutenant, who was to be addressed as *'Mon Lieutenant'* which sounded to us at the time something like *'Mong Loit-n-ong'*.

We were each to respond to this officer in the prescribed manner, by first slamming to attention with a sharp salute, while shouting as loud as possible our rank, followed by our full legion name, our six-digit serial number or 'matricule' and finish with "At your service *Mon Lieutenant"*. Then a further salute, and give a full answer to the question he asked followed up by more 'attention' 'acknowledgment' and salute'.

It wasn't easy for most of us and the French way of pronouncing the letter *'r'* seems to thwart most British speaking people, so Johnny was in a real sweat about having to give an answer in case it had any of the dreaded *'r's* in it.

Of course when the time came, sod's law took a hand and the poor bugger got the worse tongue twister possible.

The complete sentence that Johnny had to scream out, contained loads of r's and his many desperate attempts to pronounce them had us all falling about with laughter, including the Lieutenant and all the NCOs, which was just as well!

It took three attempts of Johnny shooting to attention and saluting before he managed to scream at the top of his voice, *"***Legionnaire deuxième-classe, Muller Heinz, matricule, cent-vingt-huit-mille, trois-cent, quatre vingt ….….***"* Then sharply salute and scream, *"***A vos ordres mon lieutenant!***"*

He waited stoney-faced as the Lieutenant pointed out an object on the table and while trying to look serious asked, *"Legionnaire Muller,* what is this item?" *("Qu'est-ce que ce cette truc?")*

It took another three attempts before Johnny could answer valiantly, *"***Cette truc est un ressort récupérator***".*

Then totally oblivious to the rising amusement around him, he once again saluted and screamed, *"***A vos ordres, mon lieutenant!***"*

This third attempt satisfied the officer's good mood and brought a wide grin to his face.

Needless to say that inspection went very well and although it was at the expense of Johnny's painful experience, we all had a fairly relaxed time.

For a man with such a thick Glaswegian accent and no natural flair for language, this example was extreme, yet whatever was difficult enough for all of us seemed to be made that much harder for Johnny. His early life must have conditioned him to have things even tougher for himself than they already were and somehow in spite of the fears and pressures we were all experiencing, I found myself feeling protective towards my unlikely colleague, though certainly he never asked for it and probably wouldn't have want it anyway.

Our experience on the train journey to *Marseille,* showed that he was no pushover and in fact the harder things got, the more Johnny threw himself in to it.

The legion's cultivated 'father role' meant that as soon as training had begun, his survival as a small kid in a Barnado's home had resulted in tendencies that the legion training could bring out and exploit. Johnny was exhibiting a desire to not only succeed and prove himself, but to also show total unswerving loyalty. I got the sense that I was beginning to glimpse the image of a typical evolving legionnaire, rapidly emerging as tough, willing, determined and loyal.

An example of this took place one day when we were out on a road march and someone turned, accidentally bringing their rifle into contact with Johnny's eyebrow. The knock caused him a bleeding gash over one eye which he ignored just marching on, with blood pouring from the wound and not saying a word. As we proceeded along the commonly used dirt road, *Caporal Ruesler* commented on the wound. Johnny just pointed to it saying, *"Accident caporal, accident."*

Then the weasel suggested Johnny pack some dirt into the wound. "That will stop it bleeding Johnny."

"Dirt?" asked Johnny, pointing to the ground.

"Mais oui, alors." Replied the weasel, indicating that Johnny scoop some dirt off the road and pack it into the open wound.

"Ah oui, caporal." said Johnny as he understood, promptly taking up a handful of road dirt which he packed into the gash while continuing to march.

"Very good, Johnny," said the weasle, *"La Reine Elizabeth* will be very proud of you!"

And the fine dust did stop the bleeding.

Naturally, Johnny's wound went septic, almost costing him an eye, but luckily, whatever he couldn't make right with a handful of dirt, the medics did with a large dose of penicillin and Johnny was another step on the way to becoming a true legionnaire.

For Johnny the legion was already fulfilling its parental role, even before our officers had ritualised that role by giving us presents at Christmas and serving us at the table, a practice that has long been legion tradition, both at Christmas and at the all important legion celebration of *'Camerone'*.

....

CHAPTER ELEVEN
'Close Combat'

I hated close combat, because it hurt. Our instructor turned out to be a lean angular looking Brit of average height and with a curious accent that permeated his legion French, and I wondered if it might have been Scottish.

Sergent Roland certainly knew how to hold his own in the presence of some very tough characters, especially considering there was nothing between him and them should one or more of them get out of hand. He never even seemed to bother with the backup of a corporal as security. I had never seen anyone so completely sure of himself.

As he apparently spoke English I would have liked to talk to him, but during our training there was simply never any time.

Although I am neither fat, nor a beer drinker, I've got a big belly these days, which I put down to muscle misuse due to some particular close combat drill that we regularly practiced. It was carried out as a sort of leap-frog progression in a circle.

First, the group lay flat on their backs about three feet apart, and a man would get up and run stepping from belly to belly around the whole ring, then lie back in his place. Number two would follow suit and all others would take turns, until told to stop.

We were taught to shout **"Arrgh!"** on the exhale, while pressing our bellies out each time a foot landed. It was manageable, until personality and national irritations flared up, which quickly happened as say, an Italian might stomp enthusiastically on a Spaniard, or a Belgian too heavily on a German. Then the whole game became painfully vicious, as we all, like idiots, strived to get even.

The second version, following a similar progression, involved us kneeling with hands behind our backs and bellies thrust forward in a circle. We then all took turns at running around the circle, kicking each man in the guts to the same resounding mixture of yells that were desperate attempts at **'Arrgh'** until *Roland* called, "**Stop!**"

In the beginning when it was carried out wearing only canvas shoes, several of the men were hurt or injured during each morning's activity, but as we toughened up I think we must have 'wised up', because as we moved on to wearing proper boots, the injury incidents actually became less. Johnny reckoned close combat was really good. I couldn't believe what he was saying as I thought it was really bad, although a couple of impressive techniques did catch both our imaginations.

For some close combat trainings we each carried the *MAS 36* rifle with its skinny bayonet which *Roland* taught us to use by stepping forward, planting the rifle-butt to the side of the foot while rolling over one shoulder in a partial somersault, and there was a back roll version.

Carried out correctly, these quick flips could result in avoiding an enemy's aim, while assuming a perfect kneeling, lying or standing position for firing. On the other hand, if an assailant came on too fast, the planted rifle made for perfect impalement.

The second technique involved two types of grenade, the familiar 'pineapple type' as seen in films that spreads deadly cast iron missiles all over the place, and the relatively harmless, aluminium type that just hisses and explodes - though not totally harmless as one of our men found out when one exploded sending its handle into the poor guy's neck.

Both types are on a time fuse and hiss once the pin is pulled. Soldiers the world over are conditioned to flatten themselves at that sound, knowing the explosion will send shrapnel outwards and upwards. We were shown how to gain advantage when ambushed, by lobbing aluminium grenades and getting on top of the enemy while they were still lying flat responding to that hiss.

Some months later, south of *Philippeville* when I was with my *2ème REP* combat section, I heard how one of our sections was ambushed on a mountain road. Although outnumbered, they instantly poured from their open lorries lobbing those aluminium grenades and completely turning the tables by succeeding in killing all the Fell attackers before they could realise what had hit them.

The fearful environment in which, both day and night, we experienced our training was an atmosphere that would remain constant until our long period of concentrated instruction, preparation and conditioning were over, with brutality and sadism being the order of the day. With hindsight, it would seem that timing had a lot to do with it. That great French General at *Bel-Abbès* had spoken of the huge losses in Indo-China and of the urgent need for a parachute regiment to be trained for an Algeria that was bubbling over.

Many of our trainers and minders were recently returned from that nightmare *Dien-Bien-Phu* massacre, so the pool of available men as trainers in Algeria must have been limited and their preparation for training recruits might well have been rushed. I suspect that these tough, loyal and brave fighting men, having only recently experienced the dark face of humanity, were suddenly with little de-briefing, given 'us lot' to speedily beat into shape.

They would have had every reason to ensure that we would become tough and able to be relied on absolutely in the face of adversity, because they had first hand knowledge and knew that the work we were being prepared for would demand exactly that.

It seems inevitable therefore, that some were going to just 'take it out on us' or misguidedly try to get their own back in some perverse way, and not surprisingly, there were men who just gave way to their sadistic tendencies.

Also from what little I have now gathered, both previous and later recruits to the legion normally passed through a considerable selection process and then went on to legion training. Following that, certain men were selected for the para's and would be sent for an even more demanding version, which if completed successfully, led to being sent for actual parachuting instruction at the French centre in *Blida*.

But our 1959 rabble seemed to be more or less unselected raw recruits and we were rushed straight into a combined full-on training in the hands of those heavy duty *1er R.E.P* instructors.

Eventually came the day for our final tests. Preparation included a massive, painful day and night of forced marching through the hills with really heavy kit, and I struggled desperately the whole way. My relief at not having arrived back last was short lived when I found that we were expected to complete the dreaded assault course *(le parcours de combatant)* in double quick time. Luck and fear pulled me through as my body slithered like an angry viper beneath the wire, keeping ahead of the live rounds that I was convinced were following me.

Redeeming marks came my way at the shooting range as we fired rapid shots from the shoulder with the *MAS 36* while standing, trembling and panting from previous exertions. I even did a half decent job firing the *MAT 49* in short bursts from the hip. Fortunately, I remembered that evaluation would include controlled use of ammunition, an easy thing to forget while sweating, gasping and shaking like a leaf. Believe it or not, we'd been taught to control our firing rhythm by screaming *"mama-papa, mama-papa, mama-papa!"*

How's that for ensuring we cut off any family loyalties outside of the legion!

I lost track of time as, mostly under duress, we carried out numerous tasks with specific objectives while encountering contrived and nasty obstructions. This was in order to demonstrate our expertise in handling the variety of guns and equipment with which we had now become familiar.

Day became night as we continued in pitch-blackness to elbow-drag our bodies through some sort of man-made quagmire where, mucky, cold, shivering and blind we dismantled our guns and re-assembled them as ordered. Before first light, we washed in a passing stream then smartened up for an inspection.

By sunrise we were marching back to camp in traditional style, powerfully striding the slow pace to our rousing version of *'Westerwald'* empowered by our German colleagues. That was followed in French by *'Contre les Viet'* our REP song. Then we finished with my personal favourite slow melancholy legion song, *'En Afrique'*.

Back at camp, coffee was served with its portion of cheese. Then pressure was once more applied as we were told in the usual manner to make our kit perfect for a special morning inspection, when we could once again expect our dedicated corporals to give us hell, even though we'd had no sleep for three days.

When it came, we were told in colourful legion language that we had all failed and how, to a man, we were utter crap and good for nothing. We had disgraced the honour, history and sacrifices of 'La Legion' and furthermore we had shown them, i.e. our instructors, up personally with our abysmal and pathetic efforts, all of which was totally unforgivable.

They would now have the despicable task of training us all over again, as we could not even be considered good enough for legion infantry, never mind the para's. "We" they said, "**have all been far too soft on you, but you can all be assured that it will be remedied!**"

We should have all felt dejected having failed after all the flack we'd taken, plus the prospect of a re-run only to be demoted at the end, but we were all just too tired to feel anything.

After the inspection we joined other sections on the parade ground for an address by an officer who in serious tones informed us that, "**As it is too late for changing earlier arrangements, some of you will be going to** *Blida* **for jump training, even though you had clearly wasted our training and everyone's time. But if any man among you should disgrace the legion in front of those French instructors or in front of representative groups from all the elite services, by failing the entry tests, you will not be coming back here with everyone else to be sent to the common infantry, you will be kept here and made to regret your very birth. That much I am promising you!**"

Following the standard rituals of dismissal, we staggered and limped back to our blocks, numb to this latest knowledge that even harder times were to come. By that point we were existing in a meaningless void, only able to respond to the immediate tasks at hand. We were to wash, iron and prepare our kit for *appel*, which luckily when it did come that evening was brief and uneventful.

In fact, the anticipated miserable time didn't materialise and we had a couple of the easiest days ever, during which it felt almost wrong not to run everywhere, but none of our corporals were there to enforce it, as they were all required elsewhere.

A *sergent Clément* from the stores was given the job of guiding us through the cleaning and returning of gear, as well as the collection and organising of the clothes and equipment required for *Blida*. Although we were all concerned about the re-training threat to follow *Blida*, several guys talked of a short sharp instruction period for adjusting us to the infantry that wouldn't happen at *Zeralda*, or even be in the hands of the 1st REP. Some of us were not so sure about that but we were all optimistic about the forthcoming instruction, believing for certain that *Blida* couldn't possibly be as bad as *Camp Zeralda*.

Strange as it may seem, that unexpected leisure period and change of pace quickly led to boredom. There wasn't much we could do in the camp and although we weren't far from *Algiers* we weren't allowed out.

The camp brothel was out of bounds to the likes of us and the few francs that were handed out, about ten pounds, were quickly swallowed in *le foyer*, mostly spent badly through lack of experience. Johnny suggested we pool our money with other guys to buy a camera and film, hence the only two photographs of me in the legion.

In one picture I'm holding a bottle of *Kronenbourg* which considering I didn't drink at that time was bloody silly. I remember buying a pack of razor blades, as we were fed up with endlessly sharpening our shrinking blades around the inside of a smashed bottle.

Clive during a lull at the end of training with 1st REP at Camp Zeralda.

On the final evening we got to watch a film, which funnily enough featured in English the Chipperfield family with their Circus at Bingley Hall, the very place where I had worked for them looking after elephants and painfully riding the unrideable mule. 'Poor pay for pain' I had thought at the time, but it was a lot more pay for a lot less pain than I'd managed to get in the legion.

I had been with the circus only months before setting off for Australia. What a strange feeling, in that environment so cut off from everything normal, to see and hear them so close on that screen, yet so far from home.

I lay awake that night after an uneventful *appel*, with a curious sensation as it occurred to me that I might never see home again. There hadn't been time for such ideas, or to think about what a hopeless situation I'd got into since *Sidi bel-Abbès*. It was sod's law that just when I didn't need time to think, here it was, but not for long, as suddenly we were being delivered the final address before leaving *Zeralda*.

The only thing I remember about it was being told of some operational reason why we would all be armed and taking an alternative route to *Blida*.

As we prepared to leave the training camp, there was a real sense of escape knowing we were getting away from *Zeralda*. It soon turned to enthusiasm and joy as we began to experience a genuine feeling of purpose, smartly turned out in our new issue combat gear and fully operational. The powerful sense of well-being was symbolically mirrored in the fact that our old heavy government surplus issue boots had been replaced and we now stepped lightly in our soft, brand new, American feather-light rangers, with their special shock resistant goose-down sole linings.

The whole *buzz* of activity, including the arrival of men and trucks of the motorised convoy that would take us to our next destination, was a keen energy liberating experience. Unlike previous journeys where we had been roughly herded, hidden and guarded like guilty non-descript vagaries of humanity, this time was so different. We now mattered, were going somewhere and were now clearly part of an event. We were sitting up in the open trucks, on show, with our *MAT 49s* facing outwards, ready for action. I think we all felt in some way powerfully connected to the roar of the engines.

It was all optimism and macho as our trucks thundered through the North African countryside, past flat areas of grapevines, up and down between cork tree hills, crunching gears and screaming the revs, before finally streaming out on to an open plain beneath a clear blue sky. Then to my horror, I saw dozens of parachutes pouring out of aeroplanes in clusters. Due to my fear of heights a cold sweat immediately gripped me, so consequently I remember nothing whatsoever of our arrival at *Blida*.

....

CHAPTER TWELVE
'Hope is to Bounce'

The threatened programme of tough exercises and tests by the French Military at *Blida* turned out to be a piece of cake for each and every one of us. It was then that I began to realise how well prepared and incredibly fit we all were and it was also when I woke up to the fact that those buggers at *Zeralda* had been bluffing us because, in terms of comparison, the facts spoke for themselves.

There were several small groups of just a few carefully selected men from various Colonial and French Elite units at *Blida* for the same purpose that we were. Apparently, at the outcome of the physical program there had been at least one failure from each of those groups, yet not one man from our lot experienced the slightest difficulty in getting through.

Apart from my personal mounting anxiety and terror of heights that made my mind decide that the mere thought of jumping out of an aeroplane was a death sentence, the overall experience of Blida was really very good and if I hadn't been so morbidly scared of heights I might have enjoyed it.

Our French instructors known as *Moniteurs,* were so calm and respectful compared with our screaming 1st REP bullyboys that it all felt like some wonderful holiday. We were actually treated as guests and the guys there, knowing we were broke, insisted on buying our drinks, coffees, snacks, or whatever from their well-appointed *foyer.* What was particularly nice for us, on top of the civilised experience of not being bullied and the obvious friendliness, was the realisation that we would be directly under their command for the next six weeks, with the added bonus of plenty of sleep and an opportunity to write home.

It was obvious that those men held us in very high regard, one guy told me that if I were in the French army I would have had at least a couple of promotions by now, I think he was probably referring to all of us.

Jump training was just that, all about jumping, learning to fall, leaving the plane, guiding the 'chute, etc. We dropped from land-based fuselages, learning to roll on the ground correctly, then progressed to high platforms where in a harness we each leapt and dropped, all sharing the unpleasant experience of 'crotch panic', a fear of the sudden jolt between legs at the end of the line. I think we all enjoyed zipping along wires to practise coming in fast at different angles and landing in high winds.

When we were shown how parachutes were folded, a subject I had been prepared to study particularly well, my fear wasn't laid to rest when it turned out that we didn't fold our own 'chutes but that they were actually folded by local Arab women who worked for the French Military. I'm sure they all did a wonderful job, but I found it really difficult not to slide into thoughts of sabotage and the reassurance that these were top quality USA government 'surplus' parachutes didn't help.

When the dreaded day finally came and I naively thought my nights of panic would soon be over. I wrote a letter to my mum giving it to Johnny for posting in the event that I should die of heart failure and I wasn't kidding, I honestly believed there was a good chance that I might die of shock. Johnny didn't seem to find my letter that crazy, maybe he was more preoccupied with his own fears than I had realised.

The day of our first jump was curiously quiet so maybe I wasn't the only one in a daze. I remember eating a slow breakfast and everything else taking on the same dream-like quality, until thirty of us were standing by our parachutes, facing our *moniteurs*, at some distance from the noisy planes that would shortly carry us into the blue.

The repeated orders "Get your kit on." (*équipez-vous*) may have been given crisply, but our carrying them out was definitely not crisp, in fact it was a shambles in spite of our many hours of practice. I don't think there was a man there who didn't require a *moniteur* to re-adjust his straps.

When our 'stick' finally did take off, it was in one of those military type aeroplanes where jumping is done from side doors, except that we all noticed that there were no side doors! Inside they were like incredibly noisy tin boxes.

We all sat along the sides of our plane on benches (*banquettes*) and were immediately ordered to sing our legion para marching song, which from its words clearly drew its origins from Indo-China. I've no doubt that singing that macho song at full pitch did help steady nerves, even mine.

Ten to fifteen minutes later our plane was at the right height and levelled off for the drop run.

We all stopped singing as orders were given, "**Stand!**" "***Debout!***" "***Accrochez!***" ("Hook up.")

Meanwhile a larger than life 'rubber man' '*l'homme caoutchouc*', complete with its own parachute, was thrown out to test wind-drift so we could have a reasonable chance of landing in roughly the right area.

Moments later, there was obvious concern among our *moniteurs* who suddenly ordered us all to sit right down on the floor as the plane banked steeply away from its course.

There was suddenly a lot of 'pulsating anus' hand gestures that we had learned from our Italian colleagues. The reason for concern was that the fourteen stone rubber man's parachute had simply not opened!

Oh-Shit, I thought, one of those second hand 'chutes that could easily have been mine, at least the rubber man could bounce!

The pilot kept circling the plane in readiness for another possible run and after a lot of time wasting indecision, we were once more heading along the drop zone. Again came the commands, "***Debout!***", "***Accrochez!***" when suddenly a self-invited pushy bugger legion sergeant, who was from another section, let out a 'loud scream' and took a running 'gung ho' leap straight out of the open door.

That drama prompted immediate action and we were all suddenly, with hearts pounding, moving forward. Upon reaching the door, each man turned less smartly than he should have, in order to position himself with hands outside the fuselage for added leverage. A slap on the back, the international word 'Go' and each man before me leapt vigorously into space.

Sooner than expected, and much sooner than I wanted my turn came, but with wind noise and my own pulse pounding in my ears, I didn't hear the *moniteur,* but I did feel him re-arrange my reluctant hands from the inside edge of the door to the outside so I could potentially at least, use leverage. By the time the hard slap on my back came, I was ready and leapt as hard as I bloody well could.

It wasn't heroics, I was determined not to get caught up in the tail plane, we were taught to leap far out for just that reason, and it had been one lesson I had no trouble in absorbing as I had read prior to these events of just such an experience in 'Wide World Magazine'.

In that article, a pilot, having been unable to shake a snagged parachutist free of his tail-plane was running low on fuel and forced to land. Luckily, firemen at the last moment were able to spray the runway with a thick layer of foam and miraculously the man survived by being dragged along it instead of the runway's hard surface.

I've often heard peoples' description of how wonderful the whole experience of jumping out of an aeroplane is. Well, for me it wasn't. When I jumped my eyes were tightly closed until I felt the sudden sensation of buoyancy and opened them, only to see other parachutes going up, which could only mean one thing - my parachute was going down much too fast.

There was momentary relief as it slowed down which was quickly followed by the odd feeling of sitting up there on nothing, only to realise that the tiny cross 'way over there in the wrong place' was the drop target, and there were things I should have been doing. Like spreading open the straps for a 'canopy check' to ensure I hadn't a cord looped over to form *'un braziere'* where pendulum friction of silk on silk might burn through and separate the two domes.

In that split second of looking up, I was initially shocked to see hundreds of small holes in my canopy. I happened to have the only parachute with a fine camouflage design like thousands of green leaves, which, in my agitated state, for a moment looked just like holes.

Next came the horizon check *(le tour de l' horizon)* to ensure I had space and wasn't starving anyone else's chute of air, or about to starve my own. By which time the earth was rushing up as I came in much too fast on the forward swing of the pendulum, slamming the earth like a sack of potatoes to the sweet sight and sound of that pushy legion sergeant waving his arms and screaming at me that I had hesitated, and would now be well and truly in the shit.

As I collapsed my dome that was already dragging me in the wind, I was taken well away from him and much relieved to be on the ground with my bundle of silk, as was an Italian nearby who was picking up handfuls of earth and kissing it. I had, under considerable legion threat, been forced to confront my greatest fear.

Unfortunately, I was to face it over and over as I remained just as terrified before each and every jump.

Legion parachutists held a unique record for emptying a plane full of men fast at very low altitude, a useful skill that has often given them the edge when it mattered most. Inside the plane it felt like a rugby scrum, as we were chaotically funnelled towards the open door, anxious not to get fouled-up in each other's equipment as we left the plane in a tangled mass.

Low altitude jumping, results in a sky full of parachutes for a very short time as within moments men are deployed on the ground ready for action, even able to fire at the enemy as they descend. On leaving the plane quick responses are required to spread out and avoid anyone getting air starvation. The kind of leap-frogging that can be brought about between 'chutes through air loss, is bad news generally, but with long parachutes and short distances the ground comes up much too fast.

Even a good jump allows no time to activate an emergency parachute and there is much to do, like releasing the heavy kit bag with its long attached cord so it can reach the ground first, and getting weapons organised for instant action. Also, one hopes for a few seconds to guide the landing, which is crucial when there's limited choice. Even more so in a combat situation.

Our whole company completed the course of instruction and qualifying jumps with no serious incidents outside of a few sprains and bruises. Our *moniteurs* who were delighted with us set out eagerly to prove it to us in the *foyer* and it turned out to be quite a night.

On our last day with some pomp and ceremony, we were awarded our oversized silver wings (*les brevets*), which for many of our North European friends including Johnny, was an awkward experience that caused considerable discomfort. For not only did we have to present arms, stand to attention, salute, scream our names, serial numbers, ranks etc, but on top of that, once the wings were pinned to our chests, we had to shake hands with a highly decorated, magnificent French Officer, scream **"*Merci, mon General!*"** and receive a smacking great kiss on the cheek before stepping back and giving the final salute.

There were naturally a lot of jokes and we all left the place in high spirits feeling that *Blida*, the training and all the guys there had been a great experience.

Brevet parachutiste militaire

Back at *Zeralda* our moods hit rock bottom as our corporals dived straight into us with that same diabolical pressure. However this period was spent in uniform, marching and singing legion songs to ever-greater proficiency, which actually brought us back from the depths. Eventually it all came together as a grand final ritual, involving lots of ceremonial marching and singing, with bands on mass.

It was all part of becoming a French Foreign Legion Paratrooper, and our day-to-day uniform would from now on be the camouflage combat gear and green *béret* of the paras.

The white *képi*, dark blue waist sash, and red *épaulettes*, complete with legion and regimental insignia would now only be worn for dress occasions, or on leave.

The huge *épaulettes* looked O.K. worn on the darker heavy winter uniforms, but dreadful on the lightweight khaki summer shirts where they dangled down the front of the shoulders like two limp red hairy fish.

I joked with Johnny that after all we had gone through, we still weren't going to wear a white *képi* with a hankie down the back. It was all a bit disappointing, as definitely the white legion *képi* meant far more to me and Johnny than the coveted 'green *béret*', and somehow we'd missed out on the ritualistic *képi* presentation that we'd heard about, simply receiving them along with our initial kit, only to discover with disgust that they weren't white anyway, they just had white washable cotton covers. Ah well, there you go!

Apparently with the olden day legionnaires, the original *képi* was khaki and it was a matter of pride to own one that had been bleached white by the sun as indication of long service. Trouble was, that white made an easy target, so owners were required to soak their *képis* in coffee grains to make them less conspicuous.

As we marched so tightly in unison as a vigorous body of incredibly proud and fit men, pent up with a seething energy, in our unique, slow, deliberate style, we powerfully blasted out our distinctive legion songs, smartly turned out in our fine crisp uniforms, and backed by our regimental band.
 I am sure that in those few hours, we all felt proud, powerful, and unstoppable. There is no doubt that marching and singing with such disciplined resonance was an empowering experience that brought out feelings of invincibility.
 It is hardly surprising that the legion has always placed such emphasis on its very unique style of singing and marching.

Indoctrination or not, on that day I felt it too, and there was reason for a little self-pride. I had more than survived, in spite of the odds, inadvertently achieving what I never, for one moment in my life, suspected I was capable of. For a few hours I felt proudly that I was one of those 'mythical elite' that I had heard and read about through my childhood and teens. I had actually, albeit unintentionally, fulfilled a childhood fantasy.

At the time, in the midst of our experience of self-approval, jubilation, congratulation and unbelievably, the palpable love and approval of our corporals and sergeants, those same brutes that had violated and punished us, it didn't occur to me how close I had been to becoming a victim just as any man would be who had survived beatings from a beloved father, continuing to serve him and even felt proud of that father for having beaten him and proud of himself for having endured his beatings.
 Similarly, our four fathers in the form of three corporals and that bastard corporal chef were unbelievably proud of us for having taken their beatings.

Now they could feel proud in the knowledge that we, their sons, could take whatever might be dished out to us.

On our last day at *Zeralda*, allocations were made which resulted in half of what remained of our training group, including Johnny and myself, being transferred to The 2nd Foreign Legion Parachute Regiment or *2éme R.E.P.*, which was based at a sea port city called *Philippeville* nearly three hundred miles east along the *Algerian* coast.

Clive in 2nd R.E.P. winter uniform after training and jumps.

2nd REP badge.

Our uniforms remained the same, but we each exchanged our shield-like 1st REP badge for the inverted silver triangle of the 2nd REP, which had its 'number two' above the Legion's seven-flamed grenade on its traditional diagonally-divided green and red background all of which was centred over a winged dragon. As members of the 2nd REP, we all wore at our left shoulder the coveted red Fourragère of the *Légion d'Honneur* awarded to the regiment for courageous actions.

CHAPTER THIRTEEN
'Transition'

Although packed into rattling old box-cars that were cold at night, we were all glad to benefit from the generated body warmth, even if it was at the expense of putting up with generated 'body gas'.

While the long hot days, which could have been stifling, were eased by hauling back the huge sliding sections to allow welcome breezes for those fortunate enough to get near the opening.

Whenever the train stopped, as it frequently did, the breezes disappeared as Arab children clamoured around attempting to sell us food, usually a sort of pancake made without eggs. Others asked for loose change, not realising that we were the wrong soldiers to ask as, apart from those of higher rank, I doubt if there was the price of a decent meal between us.

One real benefit of our six months of hell was that we had become orderly, so behaviour was no longer reminiscent of that awful drunken train journey from *Paris*, or the nauseating experience in the cargo hold of the good ship *'Sidi–bel-Abbès'*.

Whenever the noisy train went silent, there were opportunities to find out odd bits of somewhat questionable information. For example, French Officers volunteered to serve in the legion taking a drop in both rank and pay, not just for the honour and esteem that it accorded them, but also because when they returned to their own regiments, they were generally awarded a higher rank.

I was also told 'in theory' that a man, after having served his five-year term could, if he chose, leave the legion and acquire French nationality, also 'in theory', that if a legionnaire survived long enough, he would get a pension.

When I questioned the word, 'theory', it just caused an outburst of laughter and jokes about 'the blues' (*les bleus*) expecting to live that long! *Les bleus* referred to we newcomers, a sort of French equivalent to being called green or raw.

There was an Arabic looking corporal who spoke a little English and explained to me that over fifty-two nationalities were represented in the legion, but that there had been a time when the number had been well over a hundred.

I was about to ask about the serial number I'd been allocated when I was distracted by Johnny, who had successfully managed to get across to an older looking sergeant chef the question that I really didn't want to hear.

"How soon will we see action Sergeant Chef?"

The reply was curious, as that very serious-looking man that, from his appearance, I had fully expected to have a German accent, shrugged his shoulders, shortened his neck and drooped his mouth in a typically French manner to say in a philosophical tone,

"*Il y a la Fells. Il y a les Djebels. Il y de bon travail à faire.* Et *alors?*" His lengthening neck shortened again for the word '*alors*'. It was a gesture that I thought could only be French.

Johnny was looking puzzled, so the English-speaking corporal interpreted,

"There is La Fell. There are the mountains. There is work to be done. So?"

That explanation seemed to make Johnny happy enough, and he immediately started questioning the corporal, who told him that we were likely to be operating in a mountain terrain of rocks, caves and streams that was particularly difficult for soldiering and really favoured the enemy. I was happy when the noisy train was moving and Johnny couldn't pursue those types of questions any further.

A loud relentless voice was droning, even above the sound of the train, which was unmistakably French and from the occasional sentence that I heard, it was apparent that the owner of the voice was really shooting his mouth off.

"*La bouche.*" (The mouth.) Muttered the corporal in my ear and grinned, as

I nodded in agreement.

Then I was left to thinking for the next few hours. I found myself wondering about that Sergeant Chef having such a German appearance with such a French manner.

I heard much later that French men couldn't sign up as French, so they usually chose to have Belgian nationality.

The legion maintained a definite privacy code to discourage men from asking about another man's past, nationality, religion etc., and we had now been vetted and accepted as part of the legion family. Nevertheless, some private things were discussed and some men, like the owner of that 'mouth', were going to tell everyone everything anyway, whether it was true or not!

That journey seemed to drag on forever as inside the boxcar we couldn't see or do much and there was nowhere to really stretch out. Now and again I heard snatches of conversations from which I gathered that things weren't all well with the military. There was apparently a widespread mistrust around *General De Gaulle's* various public statements along with a real fear that *Algeria* might soon be granted independence, which according to *'la bouche'* could never happen without a military mutiny. I think someone shut *'la bouche'* up because there was a definite silence after that.

I must have dozed off as it was dark when we arrived at *Philippeville,* where covered-in trucks were waiting to drive us to *'Base Camp Pehau',* our *2ème REP* barracks that were situated a short coastal drive east of the city, on a low hill and facing out over a wide expanse of the Mediterranean sea.

Not that we got to see that view because on arrival we promptly got ourselves cleaned up, collected kit, got fed, and got our heads down, as well before dawn we were in our convoy of open trucks rumbling southwards towards our mountain base-camp, from which we would be sent to join various operational units, somewhere up in the *Aurés* mountains.

It was a nerve racking drive for anyone with vertigo, sitting in the back of an open truck full of men, very aware that we were driving like there was no tomorrow around bends that had sheer drops to the rocks below.

The road we were on looked like it was made of wire-mesh parcels of rock, which was pretty much what they were. It, like many other such roads, had been built by former legionnaires and was considered to be very good. As I saw the twists and turns, I was glad we didn't meet anyone coming the other way, in fact we seemed to be the only trucks on the road.

When some guys pointed excitedly at the wreck of a truck like ours, broken on a rock far below, it was a sinister reminder we were in ambush country and although I didn't know it at the time, our very experienced drivers were continually adjusting to the possibility of ambush along the way.

I kept wishing I was on the other side of the truck and not always so near the edge with nowhere to jump, and found myself withdrawing my senses from the dramatic terrain that we might have to operate in. Thankfully, *Sergent Angelos*, who I hadn't noticed on the train but who was nevertheless still with us, ordered me into his space and took mine.

Although he took it to enjoy the thrill and show of sitting precariously where I had hung on uneasily, in spite of feeling relieved, I did have an uneasy thought that I had been tactfully rescued. Shit, was my fear so obvious that he had to protect the other guys from being affected by it? Bugger, I thought, even though I now wore the wings of a paratrooper, nothing much seemed to have changed and I was still scared of heights.

Some years prior to leaving England, I had turned up hungry, homeless and looking for any kind of work in Swindon. It was Easter and arriving just before lunch on a Thursday, I found the employment office about to close until the following Tuesday. They sent me for a job helping a roof mender. When he called me up to the roof, I overcame my fear and climbed the three stories up the ladder, but when trying to climb on to the roof I froze, so the boss then had to waste valuable time coaxing me down. I was sacked before I even began, still hungry!

Kicking up a hell of a storm of dust, our trucks rolled up to what at first sight appeared to be a valley of tents. The layout included dozens of six man tents, several marquee style and a few that looked like canvas prefabs. All were arranged in military style, over a huge flat dirt area, which gave the impression that they were spread out to the distant peaks.

Following arrival formalities, we stretched our legs and received some actual soup before exchanging various kit in preparation for splitting off to our several destinations.

Back in our open truck we were given American-style ration packs and bread for sharing as we headed for our hill-fort that was several hours further up the mountains. Apart from Johnny, *Sergent Angelos* and myself, there were only six of us that I vaguely recognised.

One legionnaire was a very tall impressive Scandinavian looking guy, who I never saw again. Another was a Swiss guy called *Verma,* who actually ended up in my section and a third guy who, due to where he was sitting, I couldn't make out. Also there was the Arab looking corporal chef who had answered Johnny's question on the train and a sergeant who turned out to be from the *Deuxième Bureaux* and was visiting our camp to interview an Arab prisoner.

Plus, there was a man that I couldn't see but could definitely hear, it was the owner of 'the mouth' we had heard droning in our boxcar. His name I would later discover was *Delouche*, and sure enough he would soon be referred to as '*Delouche, la bouche*', or more often than not simply *'la bouche'*.

'La bouche' had been telling everyone how he'd been part of a *Marseille* street gang of black shirts, and had personally sorted out what one of his fellow members had messed up. He claimed that for what he'd done, the authorities would have given him life, and he would probably have been murdered had they put him in prison. His record prevented him from getting into the French army so a deal was done, and now he was here. Not to serve France, but to help kill vermin.

I doubt if anyone actually believed him, but just like the rest of us, *Delouche* had every right to fabricate his own past!

Further into the mountains the terrain became less dramatic, with some areas lightly wooded and with rugged hills, valleys and streams punctuated here and there by large rocky outcrops. I began to think that it was probably quite peaceful as I munched away at my chunk of bread and strip of chocolate from my ration pack.

An hour or two later, we arrived uneventfully to disembark near our rock and log fortified hill top camp.

Then I noticed that *'la bouche'* had somehow talked his way into travelling upfront with our driver.

....

CHAPTER FOURTEEN
'The Real Thing'

From white kepi to green beret.

However uneventful the journey might have been, it suddenly became eventful when we got there. Having marched up our hill, we were just passing through the apprehensive process of being organised for an inspection, when we heard the unmistakable sound of grenades exploding, small arm bursts and light machine gun fire.

Instantly we were storming along a track at an alarming pace, both amazed and invigorated as we rushed along for a few miles, feeling as though we, *les bleus*, had been rapidly and dramatically absorbed into the ranks of those established combatants that we had come to join.

When the radio operator stopped to hurriedly communicate, we were able to snatch a watchful rest on one knee, just long enough for me and Johnny to look at each other with a, 'this was fun', grin. Then we were rushing off over miles of terrain at the same lung searing pace.

Nothing happened, we encountered no one and several hours later we were at the foot of our hill, where we were brought to attention, smartened up and had our first experience of powerfully striding and singing our way back up to what was to become for a while, our new home.

Once the originally intended inspection had taken place, we knew which sections we'd been allocated, and I was pleased to find that I was to be in the same section as Johnny and *Sergent Angelos*. Both me and Johnny agreed that although it didn't compare with the brutal atmosphere of *Zeralda*, we certainly knew we'd arrived, and we knew we had a job to do.

Our section was due to set off for its three weeks in the *djebel* at four a.m. and as the men were mostly engaged in rock collecting activity some distance away, I had a little time to familiarise.

Set above a sheer rock-face with an all round view of woods and mountains under a mostly blue sky, the hill-top fort provided good observation. It was well equipped, mostly under canvas, with fortified hand-built rock and tree-trunk walls, with areas of cover. We slept in comfortable, well-spaced beds, eating good food at long tables while seated on benches beneath a protective awning.

As I looked around, the first thing to really attract my attention was a low cage that had been dug into the hillside, glancing through the wooden stakes I saw it was empty but not far from it were two upright purposeful looking forked posts about six feet apart that looked as though they should support a cross-bar.

Following the experience of *Zeralda* I wondered at how they might be used for punishing legionnaires.

Set into another slope was a dug out kitchen with front and upper sides open and its roof of logs waterproofed by heavy flat stones. Inside, a skinny, bare-footed, dark skinned boy squatted with eyes red and streaming from the constant smoke emitted by the wood fire that he tended. He was at all times watched over or, more accurately, guarded by an armed legionnaire.

Above the boy's fire sat a huge pot of couscous, which was the grain based food that, alternated with gravel-strewn hard lentils was to form our staple diet which I would later find was accompanied mostly by goat, occasionally chicken and on the odd occasion donkey. On one occasion in the future our section brought back a wild boar, but by the time it was cooked we were off storming *la djebel*.

The operational pattern was to work in the hill-top fort one week in four, the other three weeks was out functioning both day and night as a section of thirty-two men. We would quickly discover that meant always marching intensely and always laden with our guns, ammunition, grenades, digging shovels, sleeping bags, water and all-weather equipment. That included for each man a sort of waterproof poncho that could double up with another man's, to form a type of tent-shelter for keeping off the worst weather. But we seldom used them.

During these marches someone might collapse, and I would thankfully enjoy a breather while the victim was non-too-gently encouraged to continue.

Our work consisted of clearing areas of the '*Fell*' and keeping them clear, while simultaneously building hill-forts that would all be within sight of each other. Once that job was done, the forts were handed over to French conscripts that we somewhat disdainfully referred to as '*les reguliaires*'. We would then start the same building work in another region, which was a rhythm that guaranteed us freezing mountains in winter and dry burning summers elsewhere.

Apparently our Company mostly returned to find the hill-forts in a bad state of repair and the '*Fell*' back in evidence.

Our round the clock reality meant long days of scouring mountains, caves, streams and dwellings, while during hours of darkness we marched rapidly to turn up in unexpected places and mount an ambush beside some obscure looking goat track, then an hour or so later had a quick coffee and raced off again.

We marched along tracks in line and in a wide row we combed the sides of rivers, hills and valleys. But unlike the soldiers in films, we continually adjusted our distance from each other as the terrain demanded, so as to offer minimal targets to our invisible enemy.

Our water came from streams, our food was dropped from the air in the form of U.S. ration packs, each intended for two persons, but supplemented with a stale loaf it fed five of us.

Having bounced across the ground each round crusty loaf had cracks that were useful for dividing it, although by the time we actually got to eat, the man carrying the rations would hand out segments that were green and furry, but hunger betrayed eyesight as each man silently retired to his allocated position to quietly munch while keenly focusing on his hostile surroundings.

When sleep came there was precious little of it, so no time was wasted talking, each man simply threw himself into sleep until aroused to replace his colleague for a lonely hour on watch at some distance from the group.

For a long time the only legionnaire I seemed to interact with was legionnaire *Verma* and although I felt a liking for him there was little opportunity for talk. Beyond that I knew no one and saw no familiar faces from *Zeralda* other than Johnny's, who I sometimes glimpsed, but only briefly and at some distance.

During those early stages *Sergent Angelos* seemed to be permanently based at our hill-fort.

As senior ranks always marched with us, we could never really think they were pushing us too hard and even if we did think it, which I did, we certainly knew better than to say it. Only once did I ever see a man hold us up and not get a hard time. It was legionnaire *Oblomov*.

Every one realised, or so the story went, that this middle-aged ex-Infantry corporal had left the legion, then somehow slipped back through the screening system to valiantly make it through to the *2ème R.E.P.* where he became once more a legionnaire second class. He had already established his marching ability for several months.

On this occasion we were passing in sunshine around the foot of the precipice that fell from the front of our hill-fort, it was nearing spring and the worst of the snow had all but gone, but not gone for me the memories of those macabre events carried out by legionnaire *Carlos* some weeks before. There was some sort of hold up, and as I looked back along the line I wondered if it was something to do with those unpleasant earlier events, but it wasn't.

Legionnaire Oblimov was leaning back, resting against a convenient rock among smiles and pleasant exchanges of words, as the whole section seemed to momentarily assume a state of relaxed normality. Men stood easy, some offloaded their gear, though none went as far as actually sitting down. I remember thinking what a nice photograph it would have made. The whole event only lasted minutes, but for that one occasion a man was allowed to lean for just a couple of minutes to take a breather, and get away with it.

It was the only example of that I ever saw, and the whole march that followed was the least pressurised that we ever had.

If there were some specific assignment, we might operate alongside one of our fellow sections or companies or be joined by an *Algerian* 'Harki' unit. Later, big operations would involve co-operating with the French Red Berets (*les Berets Rouges*), or outfits with fancy names like Alpine Hunters (*Les Chasseurs Alpines*) instantly recognisable by their outlandishly large floppy black berets, and the Hunt Commandos (*Commando de la Chasse*) with their military-style black berets, and there were also occasions that we even interacted with *les reguliaires*.

In spite of having shown in training that I was a good marksman with a rifle, I had little practice of firing a *MAT 49*. Yet the role they gave me in section, was that of *Voltigeur*, armed with a *MAT 49* (machine pistol) with lots of bullets in spring loaded magazines, plus a couple of aluminium pretend grenades and two of the cast iron pineapple type.

Whenever we approached a suspicious cave, dwelling, or other potential hiding place, within moments our *52* light machine gun was set up with a broad overview and snipers strategically placed. The V*oltigeurs* would then approach, kick away obstructions such as doors, and cover each other as one went in.

On those occasions that 'the one' was me, I rushed straight into a dwelling, straight through the dark and straight out into the light, saw no one, wanted to see no one, and hoped to hell that no one wanted see me. It was partly due to going in from bright sunlight, but mostly because all I wanted to see was the way out!

I had nothing against those people and wished like hell they would have nothing against me. It wasn't my war, I hadn't chosen to be there, and apart from some loyalty to Johnny, I hadn't been bonded to the legion and most certainly not to France. As far as I could make out, we were foreign pawns being used to tread roughshod over a people we didn't even know in their own land, and I hated it.

Meanwhile, my purpose in life was to survive my journey to Australia and visit Ken.

Soon after joining my section, we were unexpectedly picked up by one of the troop helicopters known as *'les Bananes'* and dropped somewhere cold, dark and mountainous. Following an awful night of unbelievably harsh conditions, first light showed us to be among barren, snow-covered mountains somewhere above a place called *Texanna*. Relentless snow blizzards, hail, sleet and wind had hammered us all night, while a valiant attempt to make camp had proved ultimately futile.

Everything about us was sodden. Sleeping bags, rucksacks and numerous other items had become mounds of frozen mud. Food, drink and the means of heating them, if not lost, were inaccessible, as whatever the wind hadn't ripped away in darkness, mud held tight for morning cold to freeze solid.

A short break in the weather saw us promptly setting off to a lower altitude where we must have made contact with the outer world because following a further march to lower, softer hills one of *les Bananes* brought us much needed supplies to eat on board. Then we were unexpectedly ferried to a dry, sunny location that looked like 'post card' desert.

Unbelievably, we immediately began marching and soon became hot and wet from sweat, where we'd previously been cold and wet from snow. Then much too soon, *les Bananes* returned ferrying us back to where they'd found us, all warmed up and ready to march.

A few miserable hours through howling wind and bitter sleet brought us to our rendezvous with some French conscripts who had been waiting with the engines of their trucks running to keep 'their' cabs nice and warm. But we were ordered into cold comfort beneath canvas, and soon heading for another unknown destination. There was a definite feeling that some French officer with a sense of humour had, from the comfort of his helicopter, taken pity and sent us to dry out a bit before putting us through the next cold ordeal.

We travelled damp and cold through that freezing night, with only badly fitting canvas to offer some small protection against a relentless, following wind of bitter sleet. Survival that night came from communal body warmth that was generated by eagerly blasting out our legion songs.

Back in our familiar sector we continued our clearing work and for the first and only time, I fired my *MAT 49*. We had been with *les béret rouge* paras sweeping a snake-like valley for several hours, and as usual apart from spasmodic bursts of gunfire there seemed little action going on.

Some of us had been told to sit among bushes to watch over similar bushes on the far side of the river, three of our men started firing into them with no effect.

Suddenly, I was being screamed at by a *Sergent Batine*. "**Rutand, *merde alors*, why the hell aren't you shooting?**"

He was angry, threatening me and ordered me to start firing, so I did! I might just have killed a bush!

When that day was over we were congratulated, apparently our section had discovered a small arms cache, killed five *Fell*, taken two prisoners and lost no one. *Les béret rouge* had been less fortunate losing two men, although they had also been successful in killing several *Fell*.

Had I been faced with the prospect of killing anyone, I am not sure that I either would or could have, I definitely wouldn't have wanted to and I suspect my hesitation might have got me killed. But in the heat of real battle, who really knows?

There was one experience that had left me wondering. It happened when, as usual, I was desperately trying to keep up, certain I was about to drop, when we came up over yet another ridge. In the next valley, a small group of men 'assumed to be the enemy' were moving around in a clearing beside a little dwelling. Immediately our *A.A.52* was positioned and adjusted for range.

A command to stand still was shouted at the distant group by our sergeant whose colleague had binoculars trained on them. Naturally enough the men made a run for it.

"**Give it a burst!**" (*tirez un coup*) came the order.

The gunner missed and tell-tale puffs of dirt littered the ground as the figures erratically scrambled.

"*Putain, démerde toi alors!*" The officer shouted.

The next round also missed, and I could see that the gunner was making a complete mess of it. In the excitement I found myself frustrated, and for a few moments I was itching to take over because I knew I couldn't miss those targets at that range!

I would like to think, had it actually come to it, I would have remembered in time that those figures were real humans and not just targets, and hopefully would have fired to miss, but I honestly can't be sure, as the whole process we were involved in was so calculated to numb. That endless forced marching over hills not only exhausted, it mesmerised, it conditioned us to function on automatic, and mostly that's what we did.

I've since wondered at that machine gunner's agenda, I'm pretty sure he aimed to miss. I would like to think so because if I'm right about that, there's still hope for humanity!

In another incident I was guarding three prisoners who were being led somewhere. It was my first experience and I was unaware that the 'somewhere' would be their death. As we were halted in our progress along a fairly defined *piste*, the prisoners were ushered past me, and I was stunned as two of my fellow men let off their 'mama-papa' bursts straight into the backs of two of them.

I was still reeling when Sergeant Batine ordered me, **"Rutand shoot the pig."**

The third prisoner was a shaking jelly as I hesitated.

"*Demerdez vous, alors! Tirez un coup!*" Batine yelled. "*Tirez putain. Un – deux - trois!*" Batine was counting and holding his pistol to my head but I couldn't move. He continued, "*Cinq – six – sept!*"

I was fully conscious of both his steady counting and the violently shaking prisoner. I knew what was happening and never doubted the sergeant's intent but I wouldn't, maybe couldn't, shoot as I waited for the inevitable.

It came as a mighty blow sending me straight for the gully where I landed near the two corpses. In a daze I thought, the bastard never finished counting!

When from somewhere came,

"Rutand come on, get those cadavers into that hollow. Move!"

The same voice was arguing with *Batine*, and I recognised *Sergent Angelos* as 'mama-papa' bursts shook the air and the third prisoner's body landed close by.

On glancing up I caught sight of *Carlos* re-arranging his *MAT 49* as he turned away with obvious satisfaction. Next *Verma* was in the gully with me, pushing and shoving, acting like a corporal and ordering me, to help move the bodies into a deeper section as *Angelos* and *Batine* continued shouting at each other.

Later as we marched, it took me time to realise what had happened. It seemed clear that *Sergent Angelos* had intervened, saving me from *Batine*'s wrath by knocking me into the trench and ordering me to shift the corpses. *Verma*, a Legionnaire 1st class, recognising *Angelos*'s purpose had jumped in, shoving me about to support *Angelos*'s order which was indirectly, to get me out of the situation. *Angelos* had saved me again.

Bizarrely, although the blood-thirsty *Carlos* had shot the prisoner for his own satisfaction, he might also have unwittingly saved my skin, and just possibly, even my life!

After my bush-shooting episode some of our section were given two prisoners for carrying back to camp while a third prisoner was leading his captors to a cache of arms.

The method of transporting prisoners was as nasty as it was efficient and as painful as it was simple. With bound-together ankles, each captive sat with knees up and arms wrapped around them, wrists tied together. A long pole was thrust through the space directly behind his knees.

As our section set off, two pairs of legionnaires each raised a pole on to their shoulder as the two prisoners inverted to dangle upside down and helpless!

It was awful for the victims, especially if the terrain were rough and the porters clumsy so that unprotected heads and faces got knocked about en-route.

It was a method of carrying prisoners brought back from Indo-China where bamboo poles were readily available. It not only served as a secure and handy mobile prison, but it could be conveniently suspended between two trees or makeshift posts without slowing down a march.

As we marched home I began to realise the purpose of the dug out prison I'd seen on my arrival and the two upright posts next to it, but not yet the whole ghastly purpose.

Later we marched and sang ceremoniously back up our hill like stylised hunters returning with game.

On reaching the summit, one captive's pole was unsheathed from behind his knees, pouring the man, still tied, into the dug out cage. While the other wretch, still dangling on his carrying pole, was placed across the two forks of those established upright posts to be dealt with later at leisure, or to be tortured immediately and left hanging in full view of the surrounding countryside. I thought it was an example to frighten their comrades, but it was bait to encourage a desperate rescue attempt.

The other poor man locked in his cage had little option but to hear and see what was happening.

Some of my so-called colleagues liked not only to watch but also to make suggestions. Or, like *Delouche* and *Carlos,* to join in.

The two fixed posts suspend a prisoner for torture with electricity and water. In the background two paras bring another prisoner similarly suspended.

The following morning as though everything was normal, we stood to attention for instructions. I was aware that some men were gathered around the still dangling and now naked prisoner torturing him, by one man winding a field generator as another poked electrodes into vulnerable parts of the victim's mouth and genitals, causing his body to convulse horribly.

As we set about our chores, still in the vicinity, I saw a bucket of water thrown over the man's still juddering body.

On asking a guy if the purpose was to make the victim's body cold, I got an enthusiastic reply. "Yes, and it conducts the electricity much better."

Another time in camp on a similar pole, I reluctantly watched a man holding a small square of blanket over an inverted victim's nose and mouth while another kept pouring water on it, to cause perpetual drowning.

Following their ordeal I think most prisoners were killed, others were held in the cage until extracted information could be substantiated, by leading us to a particular location for example. Then, of no further use they were probably shot by *Carlos*.

Later that day, an officer from the *Deuxième Bureau* was heliported in, to take possession of our two prisoners.

We accompanied him on a leisurely trek, which in the first instance, turned out to be a wild goose chase, but once that became obvious the first prisoner was shot.

The second prisoner then led us to a substantial cache of arms, so I suppose in the officer's terms, it justified the execution of the first man, but later I heard another shot!

The whole thing really troubled me, and I wondered what other men thought. Some like *Carlos* and *Delouche* clearly enjoyed it, and were ever eager to add their expertise.

But although quite a few men watched, including me, who knows what their thoughts really were. I want to think that most men felt quite differently and I believe *Sergent Angelos* and *Legionnaire Verma* were such men. I certainly know Johnny hated it.

Outwardly men seemed to take it in their stride as it must have appeared that I did. It was imperative for survival to fit in, crucial not to show emotions that might imply weakness or sympathy towards the enemy.

At *Zeralda*, I'd become well practiced at not showing emotions from those times spent glassy-eyed, trembling and nearly shitting myself at the foot of my bed.

One day out in the hills, I had a very brief encounter with an older looking English legionnaire from another section whose name was *Arcin*.

When I commented on how awful I thought it all was, he just replied, in a slow, soft, West Country drawl, "Agh, I dunno, it's not that bad."

I seriously wondered if we were taking part in the same life.

I'd known about the Geneva Convention ensuring some sort of fair play from my teens, but from this perspective in the wilds of North Africa that was just an 'armchair traveller's' fantasy.

....

CHAPTER FIFTEEN
'I'm made of Jelly?'

Visible in the distance from our own was another hill fort, which a company of *les Chasseurs Alpines* had recently occupied. It could have been that they were ill-informed or unfamiliar with the local situation, or maybe they were too casual or plain unlucky, who knows? But they woke up one morning to discover all their sentries had slit throats.

Little was said in our camp other than to be extra alert on watch. That night my stint was from three to four, and those slit-throat images had been playing havoc with my imagination all day.

The recently arrived *bleus,* who was the man I replaced, was clearly very jittery at having to stand so far from camp alone among the rocks and scrub, and who could blame him, but his sudden departure the moment I arrived, left an uneasy exaggerated vacuum. It was a space for thoughts to keep returning to those *Chasseurs* who were well armed and well trained, yet not one guard had raised the alarm and none had managed to save themselves from having their throats cut.

Long grasses moving took on scary forms as rocks changed shape and there were noises that hadn't been there before. Cloud came over, the rocks became black and suddenly visibility was gone. My heart was beating loud enough to lead a knife direct to my throat and in anticipation I made my neck longer so the slitting could be over quickly.

As light improved slightly I backed up against a rock and feeling a little more protected forcefully gained something like self-control, but not for long. Unmistakably now, there was a dirt scuffing noise and rustling of grasses that was definitely real, and another sound. I knew the *Fell* were closing in! Breathing stopped, but loud chest pounding wouldn't.

Caught between *Fell* and the camp and unable to see, I knew that to fire off a burst would expose where I was, and the whole camp would pour out lobbing grenades and firing with me in the middle. I forgot all training, gun, grenades, everything. I could have thrown a bluff grenade, and ran while they flattened, but a follow up grenade would have flattened our men as they rushed out to counter attack, yet if I hadn't thrown it, the same men would have come out firing on me.

I was mesmerised, not even a finger on the trigger of my *MAT 49*, staring and listening vacantly while the noises first got closer, then gradually further until they were silent, and I could gradually settle into an uneasy watch. Later the prospect of being replaced brought on a new rush of imagery that lasted an age until my replacement turned up, which was legionnaire *Carlos*.

With casual bravado I told him about sounds in the bushes, he just looked around, nodded, and took up a stance seeming unconcerned. I stayed for a while looking around, sort of punctuating my comment and being supportive, until I realised that *Carlos* had no need or desire for either support or company.

As I uneasily returned to bed I was having mixed feelings for all the things I'd seen *Carlos* do, and at the same time appreciating him for what he was, because with him on guard I felt safe enough to bury my head and get some sleep. However, sleep was short-lived, as before dawn an alert was sounded which had us rushing down familiar tracks hunting for the two prisoners that had escaped during the night.

Now I knew that what I'd heard in the bushes hadn't been my imagination, but was the two prisoners from our hillside cage feeling their way through the scrub. I was going through a lot of discomfort and confusion about my reactions, yet was glad I hadn't fired at them as they'd suffered enough, but I really wondered how they'd both got past the man guarding them.

Those thoughts soon receded as we raced about scouring the area for any indicators of their flight, until a couple of hours into the search news came that two fresh, headless bodies had been found by a section of *les reguliaires*. A small *équipe* was duly dispatched to photograph and verify that they were the bodies of our escaped prisoners, which they were.

By becoming captured, they had both become a liability to their comrades and been slaughtered accordingly. I was so glad not to have been on that *équipe*.

Of course *Carlos* and one or two others were eagerly waiting to handle the pictures.

We returned, to find a section from another company had been brought into our camp, and there was a palpable understanding that whatever was about to take place, was something special. These guys were different.

For a start, they were all good looking, seemed at ease together and were openly tactile as they nonchalantly relaxed in the sun applying Nivea to each other waiting for orders to carry out that something, that I suspected, would be quite lethal. I remember observing them with a curious fascination, not really understanding what it was that I was seeing.

They took far more interest in their appearance than we did, they were dressed in the same camouflage combat outfits, but had taken trouble to re-tailor theirs. They wore, what for us, were forbidden non-issue items such as silk ker-chiefs or cravats, and every one of them had, strapped to his thigh, one of those plaited leather sheath knives that among us were only worn by the battle hardened '*Anciens*'. In a macho outfit such as ours, a man would need to be very sure of his abilities to have himself stand out in that way.

As a group they were, to a man, not only tangibly sure of themselves and clearly tough as nails, but with the feline quality of Panthers. I felt something very important must have called for these men, as even though we too were about to be involved in the same operation, there was an element of secrecy surrounding them.

Yanoff, a fellow legionnaire that I'd begun chatting with, and who was permanently attached to our hill-camp, later told me that those men were related to the Sicilian mountain fighters of '*Juliano Salvatore's*' band. Descendants of tough, almost legendary men that had supported many of the poor villagers of Sicily, successfully eluding and keeping at bay both the Italian army and the *Carabinieri* for over twenty years. Finally, that Robin Hood of a man was betrayed by a cousin and gunned down by about forty soldiers in the courtyard of that same cousin's house.

Following those events of the 50's, the greater part of *Juliano's* original band dispersed mainly to the U.S. and South America, presumably with the help of the Mafia. Some of the more recent and younger descendant members of that continuing legend had found their way into the legion, where, according to *Yanoff*, because of their great expertise in mountain fighting, they had sought and been granted permission to operate together as an independent unit within the *2ème R.E.P.*

I thought no wonder they didn't seem like us, they were men of a different calibre, with an altogether different agenda. Like us, they were in the legion but there was one great difference. We were 'in' and 'of' the legion, where as they on the other hand, were in the legion, but very much 'of' themselves.

Thankfully, I missed out on the events which required those Sicilian men and other men of greater experience such as, sergeant *Batine, Carlos, Verma, Oblimov* and *Yanoff*, along with other *anciens* from across our company.

Johnny thought we were both going until, along with several men from our section plus a couple of new arrivals, we were ordered, "Report to *Sergent Angelos* to be assigned other duties."

That special event very successfully amassed a lot of arms and ammunition, killed numerous *Fell* and resulted in several prisoners. Three men were killed from the Sicilian group, several killed or wounded from our company and two men were killed from our section, one of whom was a *legionnaire Aziz* who, I only learned later from *Yanoff*, was actually *Carlos* who was Moroccan and not Spanish after all.

I was glad *Sergent Angelos* was in our company, even though he rarely operated with our section. I really liked him, as most men did.

He was a highly decorated veteran of *'L'Indochine'* who I believe had been tortured by the *Viet Minh*, yet there was no outward signs of hardness about him. His face was unlined, the whites of his steady grey eyes were uncharacteristically clear, and he had the quiet manner of a family doctor, rather than that of a hard-nosed 2nd R.E.P. sergeant. Unlike many of the thugs that trained us, whose control had been based on brutalising, he had always been fair and well able to assert himself both quietly and effectively. We had rarely encountered him at *Zeralda*, and here he only joined a few of our sorties.

I had a strange feeling *Sergent Angelos* protected me, and I've no idea why, maybe I reminded him of a brother or someone he cared about. For instance, when he swapped places with me on the truck, and when *Batine* held a gun to my head, and now during this latest operation, he had kept me out of it, ironing!

I had gradually become uneasily friendly with *Yanoff*, he was an *ancient combatant* of over four years when I arrived at the company and had some nasty mangled scarring on his shoulder to prove it. Because he was permanently attached to the hill-fort, he had the luxury of time on his hands. The more we became friends, the more he insisted on telling me about his nocturnal excursions.

A few hundred yards down from our camp there was a typical peasant's dwelling, which was just a few minutes sprint for a fit legionnaire. *Yanoff* said he had a good thing going with the couple that lived there, gradually confiding to me that he tied the elderly man up so that he could enjoy the man's younger wife.

He told me she enjoyed his visits as he brought her presents of food, which she and her husband both shared. At every opportunity in great detail, *Yanoff* would incessantly describe the women's white thighs, long black hair and other attributes, with the aim of getting me to join him in his fun.

Like many men of extreme vitality whose normal feelings had successfully been perverted, when he wasn't under extreme pressure, he was sexually desperate. It seemed to me that from *Yanoff's* 'warped' viewpoint, he had simply looked for and found a practical outlet for his needs and considered it honourable that he, as a decent guy, should be more than willing to share his good fortune with me, his friend. However often I told him I wasn't interested he just wouldn't accept it, nor would he believe that within our lifestyle, conscience could have any place.

Yanoff, like other men I'd worked with around the world, be it on ships, circuses, fairgrounds or construction sites, held sex high in their topics of conversation. But I was always struck that most of the legionnaires I came into contact with didn't. Whether they were being serious or joking, most of their conversations were about drinking, fighting, killing and, in many cases, torture.

On the lighter side they might mention the *bordel*, but mainly they'd talk about daily events, food and '*la quille*'. The latter referred to an ancient game of bowls that utilised old cannon balls and musket shot that would be played at legion camps in France by legionnaires when they retired.

So *la quille* was synonymous to a legionnaire's eagerly awaited dream of retirement, when he could peacefully idle away the hours playing *la quille* with his colleagues.

....

CHAPTER SIXTEEN
'Tea for Two'

Shortly before time came for visiting base-camp to re-equip for operations in another hopefully warmer sector, I received, totally out of the blue, about twenty pounds, possibly part of the originally promised enlistment money, or part of our pay. Including this pay out, to date I had received a total equivalent of about thirty-three pounds.

Johnny was going to field camp ahead with a supply detail so I gave him half my stash with great expectations of him bringing back some long desired goodies. Time passed, but Johnny didn't return along with his companions, nor did the eagerly awaited supplies.

Three weeks later we all went down, I eventually found Johnny who having got himself into some sort of trouble was condemned to shovelling dirt. He insisted that he didn't understand why, or worse still, how he'd come to lose all our money and got absolutely nothing to show for it.

Embarrassing as it feels now, I was really abusive to him, when in all probability he'd been set-up by some con men. I've since felt bad about it because it really wasn't his fault, and knowing his sense of loyalty Johnny would have given himself a hard time over it without my help. If you ever read this Johnny, "I'm truly sorry mate."

My frustration was also heightened as just before locating Johnny and discovering that loss, I had met the extremely tormented *Yanoff* so beside himself with lust, that I'd given him my remaining money to go and rent himself a prostitute in the camp *bordel*.

So *Yanoff* got his oats, but we didn't get our cocoa. Not comparable, admittedly, but in the environment of our hill-fort away from relentlessly pounding *la djebel*, it was a pleasure that oiled the wheels that kept us sane. Whenever we found moments, we planned our next cocoa binge, swapping cigarettes and brandy from our ration packs until we had amassed all the condensed milk, sugar and black chocolate necessary to satisfy our rich cocoa addiction in one of those rare breaks, when we could really enjoy it.

While *Yanoff* was getting his oats, there was a big upset outside *le bordel* due to a girl reporting a legionnaire for having come filthy to her for sex. I think it was unlikely given our discipline around cleanliness. But the result was very nasty, as some of us were ordered by the unfortunate man's sergeant to watch him being accused of dishonourable behaviour.

We were then ordered on behalf of the glorious heroes that had died for *La Legion*, to immediately redress this despicable outrage. In effect, the man was thrown to us, the pack, which immediately fell upon him. It was truly awful.

I had been involved in meting out similar brutality, in response to a similar order at *Zeralda*. On that occasion the 'so called' culprits were suspected of a homosexual act, based I am sure, on contrived information. I really hope that on both those occasions, I was not the only one to put up an effective show of ineffectual brutality. Unfortunately for such victims not everyone felt, thought and acted as I did.

Later that day, I got word of a South American legionnaire looking for me. As he was the first person I had ever had looking for me since England, I was both curious, and concerned, so went looking for him before he could find me.

He turned out to be a really friendly, chubby Argentinean guy called *André*, who having lost a leg to a grenade incident, had been given a stores job and was permanently attached to 'tent valley'. His reason for wanting to find me was that I was English.

He had been waiting months for an English man to appear. Why? Because he had, God knows how, come across a complete tea service and managed over time to access all the ingredients, including milk. Now he had an Englishman to share a pot of tea with!

So there we sat, two men from opposite ends of the world, in a most unlikely place, at a table complete with tablecloth and full tea service. We enjoyed afternoon tea in typical English style, chatting away in broken English, about English life, bowler hats, thatched roofs and cricket, things I never normally talked about, but nonetheless topics that made it for us both, a very special occasion. However eccentric that might sound, in that harsh crazy environment, it was for each of us, an hour of pure sanity.

....

CHAPTER SEVENTEEN
'It is Fear, Oh Little Hunter...'

The following day, our company set off for another mountain sector where the pattern of work was changing, and involved less of the devastating marches, it was soon apparent that we were part of something bigger. Helicopters and planes were more in evidence. We got whisked around a lot, and although I was never personally involved in any fighting, it felt more like a war.

Our numbers were deceptively diminishing as we lost a man here and a couple there without realising, mainly because we were strung out across, or along, such a vast terrain, operating with a whole lot of men from different sources. A few fire exchanges would take place here and there and it was only later that we might hear of casualties. Much more regular now were the running skirmishes that went on for hours, or days, with helicopters bringing other men, and taking away prisoners, bodies and any injured.

As the operation stretched over an even larger area more equipment was utilised, including various types of helicopter and planes, some of the latter were delivering napalm.

I'd no experience of napalm, and it was so eerie when I was positioned under a clump of trees at the top of a valley to have planes screaming overhead, launching their deadly missiles that seemed to pass through the branches above my head. Though probably what passed was just the violent rush of air through the leaves before their mindless fire splattered down the valley as a raging flood of flaming jelly.

There was a period of waiting, then sergeant *Batine* confirmed beyond all reasonable doubt that he was absolutely no friend of mine, by ordering me to take cover behind a clump of weed. He might just as well have told me to hide in an open football pitch because it provided absolutely no cover. I had to cling to the ground like a leach, utterly vulnerable, waiting for desperate armed men to come rushing out of what had minutes before been a blazing inferno.

In the midst of my discomfort I still appreciated the comical exchanges that passed between legionnaire *Delouche* and sergeant *Batine*, who was struggling to deal with that 'walking mouth' which used every opportunity to express itself about absolutely anything. And although '*la bouche*' was really getting up *Batine's* nose, he really didn't know how to handle the arrogant Frenchman, and after a couple of foiled attempts ended up frantically flapping his arms all over the place and screeching at an even higher pitch than usual.

"**Putin de merde Delouche! Shut your gob! (*Fermez ta gueule.*)** You've got more bloody gob than a runaway *AA 52*. And if you don't clamp your gob right now, you won't know whose bullets to duck!"

It was a real threat and 'the mouth' clamped, but not before sticking up a defiant finger. I thought from the expression on *Batine's* face that he'd plug the Frenchman there and then, but sudden activity in the valley brought us all back to task, and we started uneasily down the hillside.

What always added humour to these situations was the bizarre use of the Legio-Franco-German slang, coming about from so many nationalities using an alien language at all times.

It was a nerve-racking job descending into the valley, checking for possible desperate survivors who might still be gun at the ready, holed up in caves or tunnels. And there was the gruesome job that I hated, but *Delouche* relished, which was checking out the incinerated or part incinerated corpses.

The name of the exercise as far as I could make out from a passing sergeant who mimed it for me, was something like Operation Telescope. Its purpose was to man an ever-shrinking circle with all the forces that could be mustered, backed by air support. It had already been steadily closing in over an extended period, napalming of these inner valleys was to either flush out, or chase *Fell* into the net.

Various military units beginning with the conscripts had been withdrawn, and others would soon be pulled out including the various legion companies. It was now for we para's and the French red berets to shrink the circle further. Later, it would be down to us, the expendable foreigners, to actually close the noose.

I've no idea how small the circle eventually got, but when night came, I was aware that our section had been placed on a precarious ledge half way down a precipice, in mini Grand Canyon country.

Expectation was incredibly tense that night as we guessed at how small the noose actually was, and no one had any real idea how many birds might be in that noose. Wild rumours spoke of thousands. Common sense dictated there would be a lot of desperate armed fighters making a break for it during the night.

Men were dispatched to collect firewood for small fires to burn within sight of each other throughout darkness, so we could spot anyone or anything crossing the ledge.

Sleep was a requirement, so sentries were posted while others were allocated fire-tending duty. The rest of us, between guard-duties could lie on top of our sleeping bags at appropriate locations. I was allocated the 'three-to-five' stint and, on time, replaced the previous watch without incident.

It was a clear night as I munched quietly at my stock of breadcrumbs and garlic to fight the cold.

No replacement came, so once I'd made sure of the time, I made way along the ledge to wake my colleague. As I pulled at his bag my blood froze, there was no one there, and when I moved on to find the next bag empty, I wasn't sure whether to vomit or scream. I imagined myself alone on that ledge, my colleagues all dead, and at any moment cold fingers, or steel would find my throat and toss me into the void. The madness only lasted moments, but moments can be awfully long.

Relieved, I saw dim silhouettes around a dying fire as limited fuel was barely keeping the flames burning. Dawn would soon break so men were simply accompanying each other for added security, as this was the most likely time for the *Fellagha* to break out.

In spite of great expectations nothing happened that night, so the following day we remained covering the ledge as others moved in for the kill. Yet unbelievably not a single enemy was seen and none were caught in the trap.

It was apparent to all of us that a huge number of *Fell* had given the combined might of a huge chunk of the French military machine, ourselves included, a big run around, followed by the slip. They knew their territory and had melted through the maze of rocky tunnels and caves that was the ancient gift of their land, and it had protected them.

....

CHAPTER EIGHTEEN
'Sacrifices to a Sacred Order'

Following that embarrassing farce, our section was whisked south to an arid area of mountains that overlooked desert, we found no indication of the *Fell* in spite of some wide sweeping views with no obvious cover and I never even glimpsed a camel, or a half decent sand dune.

It was the nearest in the legion that I ever got to my fantasy of the desert, and as for *Le Compagnie Saharienne*, or *Fort Flatters*, although I was always asking, no one seemed to know anything about them. Our guys were more interested in the forthcoming '*Camarone*' celebrations with a lot of their focus on drink.

As my job was building a protective wall with *Yanoff*, I asked him to tell me what *Camarone* was all about and over that week we found moments for conversation, and in bits he told me much of the following.

April 30th, the legion celebrates its most glorious defeat, which happened at a place called *Camarone* in Mexico, in 1863.

3 Legion Company, having many men laid low with sickness, was protecting the *Vera Cruz* to *Puebla* supply lines, and were requested to send a detachment to meet a convoy on its way to *Puebla* with bullion for French troops. Sixty-five legionnaires volunteered under a *Capitaine Danjou* who, having lost a hand in battle wore a wooden one.

Following a series of mishaps, they eventually found themselves holding off two thousand Mexican foot soldiers and cavalry from within the meagre protection of a crumbling farmhouse. Eventually, in desperate conditions, against overwhelming odds, long deprived of food, water and ammunition, sixty men, including *Danjou* were dead. There remained 2nd *Lieutenant Maudet* and five legionnaires, who resolutely fixed their bayonets and moved forward into the mass of Mexicans.

Soon, only three men stood, *Caporal Maine*, and legionnaires *Wenzel* and *Constantin*, who prepared yet again to move forward and face certain death. A Mexican *Colonel Combas* intervened, ordering his men to avert their weapons and escort the three men to his Commanding Officer, *Colonel Milan*.

When *Milan* saw they were only three, he said, "Truly these are not men, but devils!" So impressed was he with the sheer bravery of the legionnaires, that he commanded his men to honour them and provide safe passage. It was a battle that later enabled a French victory at *Puebla*, and it was also a glorious legion defeat which has provided a powerful mythology ever since.

And the rescued wooden hand of *Capitaine Danjou*, now rests in the Legion's Hall of Honour to be traditionally kissed and honoured by all recruits passing through the museum on their way into *La Legion*.

"*Yanoff*, I never kissed any wooden hand, or saw any museum." I said, thinking I'd missed out on some essential ritual.

"Me neither." He said shrugging, "No matter where the legion finds itself on the 30th of April, it's a major, glorious celebration of drinking, eating, fighting and anarchy, with legionnaires' weapons withdrawn for the occasion, and with the French army brought into encircle and protect the legion from both itself or possible attack. It's a real day of craziness, starting with orchestrated parades and addresses and an officer reading out the *Camarone* story. We sing a couple of songs, then present arms etc."

I grinned, and asked, "Is that it?"

"Oh no!" he replied, shaking his head, "once that's over the day is devoted to us!" "How?" I asked.

"Well, they all suddenly start behaving like parents preparing our food, serving us at our tables, and even clearing them."

"Why *Yanoff*? It doesn't make sense."

"Oh it does! This caring is an important ritual. We are family, and they are our parents. These bizarre practices are the 'glue' that holds this family together. They're for remembering, drawing inspiration and honouring family members who have died victoriously in magnificent battles, and especially defeats like *Dien Bien Phu* and *Camarone*. Its underlying message is, we choose to serve, suffer and die honourably for the glory of this family."

"For Christ's sake!" I said, remembering that *Yanoff* had once told me of his pre-legion interest in psychology. "How the hell does it work?"

He went on to explain, "Well, psychologically its a special day for the angry kid inside each of their beloved sons to vent frustrations through drinking, fighting and even harming, all within safe confines, and with the loving approval of their 'parents'- our officers!"

So its hardly surprising I thought, if a man believed he'd chosen freely, that alongside his valiantly struggling colleagues he might 'give his all' in a misguided attempt to make things right. If not with the family, country, and religion he had deserted, then at least with this surrogate family that had whole-heartedly adopted him.

"Bit of a one parent family though isn't it *Yanoff*?"

"No, they make up for that through the Virgin Mary theme during the crib making competitions."

I was lost in that reasoning, because although legion Christmas is like legion *Camarone*, in our hill-fort it had been particularly low-key. We were each simply presented with a gift from the people of *Paris*. Then as we sat to enjoy a special meal, a false alarm saw us rushing along a familiar track.

During short periods on and off, I was able to ask *Yanoff* about certain things that no one seemed to question, like "Who is this enemy to me?" "What allegiance do I have to France?" and "What right do I have to be pushing around people, that I don't know, in their own land?"

"Yeah," said *Yanoff*, "the Legion is our country '*Legio Patria Nostra*', it's our religion I guess. Why did I choose it?" He'd obviously thought about it too.

"But did you really choose it?" I asked, watching his response.

"I chose it." He said, "And there were damn good reasons!"

He was irritated, and remembering legion code I changed the subject, at the same time realising that the code existed because the legion couldn't afford too much of this kind of probing.

"Besides," *Yanoff* went on, "there's a lot of call for our kind of skills on the outside, with a good life and good money to be earned."

Then I remembered that *Yanoff* had less than a year to go.

I got the feeling that there was both an official and an unofficial version of most legion facts such as: Men volunteered freely; Men were free to leave after five years; Men received regular pay; Men received an enlistment bonus; Men received a Parachutist's bonus.

And I wondered once again about creative accountancy regarding the numbers of men lost, given that we were given false identities, names, ages, nationalities, parents and countries of birth, etc.

I overheard stories between veterans, about numerous raw, untrained volunteers who came to fight alongside their comrades, being parachuted into the thick of *Dien Bien Phu* and told to pick up weapons when they landed, but not told of the six inch bamboo spikes sticking up all over the landing area.

"It was there," said *Yanoff*, "that a lot of young guys got to practice their first and final landing roll."

It was all pretty horrifying and my thoughts returned to how easy it would have been to juggle the numbers if all those men had, like us, been given false identities.

CHAPTER NINETEEN
'Paris, Almost!'

It seems inconceivable now looking back that by April of 1961, Europe would be on the brink of a piece of world shattering history. A time when millions would hold their breath as *Général Charles De Gaulle* addressed his Nation in preparation for an imminent invasion on *Paris* by crack paratroopers. I've often wondered how many people realised what a close call it had actually been.

But what appears to be less known, is that within the growing unrest there were seeds of similar plans the year before, because sometime in the early summer of 1960, several of us from *2ème R.E.P.* were unexpectedly heliported from the coastal hills west of *Philippeville,* to a place where other men of our company were already waiting. I'm sure that for several of us, it just felt like an isolated relief from incessant marching.

Swift allocations were made from the assembled men as to who would remain. Then the rest of us, without explanation, were kitted out with parachutes and other equipment. We were then, still none the wiser, transported to a small airport that was right next to the sea, where for a couple of hours, with parachutes on and our equipment beside us, we were kept on 'stand by' next to two planes with their engines both running.

First we were 'at attention', later 'at ease', and finally we were instructed to sit on our kit bags. It was all very exciting with everyone talking and joking about taking *Paris*! There were no orders, no explanation and no indication of what we would be doing once we got there. Presumably we were to be informed once airborne?

Some of the more informed men were pre-empting various possibilities believing there was a coup. They reckoned the million or so French military based in *Algeria* were desperate at the thought of losing out to politicians when for them, the war was all but won. Certainly, thirty thousand legionnaires weren't about to give up their spiritual home. Far too many friends had died on *African* soil for that*!*

Me and Johnny were dead excited and from our totally unreal perspective, it felt tantalisingly close to England. For some curious reason, we had no fear of what was to come, not even the usual pre-jump anxiety. We simply passed the time laughing and joking like the kids we still were, chatting and coming out with silly ideas, all around the subject of how we could steer our parachutes across the English Channel. The other men were all in good humour, encouraging and joining in with our absurdities. Then while still in this jovial mood, we were mysteriously taken off alert, the plane engines fell silent, and we were again ordered into trucks.
    By late evening we were back in the hills, marching.

We had no real understanding what it had been about, but later as I chatted with Johnny, we had both noticed that the two French guys, '*la bouche*' and an obviously French legionnaire from another section, had not been on the airport adventure with us. We joked a lot about the opinions that we thought '*la bouche*' would have mouthed off had he been there, and how frustrating it must have been for him to have missed out on an event that he could have really sounded authoritative about.
    We all reckoned they wouldn't have included *Delouche* on the *Paris* invasion anyway, because with his big mouth, *De Gaulle* and the whole of *Paris* would have heard us coming!

Yanoff, who was no longer at the hill-fort but now marching with us, told me there had been a plan but the expected support hadn't materialised, so the pilots backed out. He went on a bit about how French *Algeria* had become 'one whore of mess'. "Nobody trusts anyone. It's true within the Legion and it's true throughout all the diverse French units including the Colonials and even the French conscripts. The Algerian French are breaking into factions and so are the Arabs. None of them trust each other. It is one big fucking mess!"

Johnny found out that the French guys weren't included in the plan as the legion wouldn't send men into situations where they might have to fight in their homeland.

I couldn't imagine how the legion could possibly know who was French given that so many of our nationalities had been changed, or how they could enforce such a decision within moments, without risking a man's cover.

There had been an earlier occasion when we were taken to an airport, similarly prepared with our combat gear, but on that occasion there had been no visible planes standing by. We were just inspected or reviewed by some American high-brass Generals. That incident occurred just after we completed our training at *Zeralda* in late 1959 and were still part of the *1er REP*. Nothing more was ever said about it, but a rumour circulated that we were being considered for use in *Cuba*.

A few days after the mysterious non-*Paris* drop, we found ourselves operating in yet another mountainous terrain, where for the first and only time I was actually shot at, and it was just the sort of place where I had been most afraid it might happen.

We had been proceeding along a high mountain track with plenty of cover in the form of thick scrub both above and below. Unbeknown to me, the cover was also disguising the precarious nature of our position, which wasn't apparent until we came to where a section of the rock face had sheared away from some hundred feet above, right down to the chasm below.

The men in front of me seemed to show no fear in traversing the precariously narrow broken ledge, and I hoped to hell I wouldn't. Swallowing hard, gritting teeth and desperately wishing to be somewhere else, I steadily side-stepped, eyeballing the rock and allowing my vision no further down than my chin.

Past the point of no return, about two-thirds across, right when I was thinking I had a chance of looking professional, something jumped where my hand had just been. 'Snake' I thought, bounding the last yard like fear of heights was suddenly on holiday. I had no hesitation at diving into a bush as I heard, "**Rutand - Look out!**" *(Fais gaffe!)* Only then from the safety of cover did I hear the second shot, I don't think I even heard the one that nearly got my hand.

I was pleased and exhilarated that I had cleared in a split second what before I had been really scared of, and hadn't let myself down in the eyes of my colleagues. It was the second event where fear hadn't paralysed me, and I thought maybe, just maybe, I was gradually overcoming it!

Our section went on to find a large cache of arms, several *Fell* were killed and three prisoners taken. We had three men injured and heliported down to base camp. One of them was *Yanoff* who got shot in the leg.

....

CHAPTER TWENTY
'Time To Leave'

By late May things had been quiet for some time, and we were held up in some low hills not far from the coast awaiting orders. I was enjoying a munch at my supply of garlic and stale bread crumbs on a particularly nice day and observing a large eagle or other bird of prey that was perched on a rock nearby.

Framed between two hills was the deep blue Mediterranean Sea and my eyes were drawn from the bird, towards a white liner passing along the distant horizon as I became lost in thought for the minute or so that it took to pass.

A well of sadness came up, as I imagined it heading for England and pictured my family and friends back home. I had stopped writing letters after being accused by a corporal of placing my section at risk by making notes, and had only ever received two letters and one food parcel from home, so it was clear to me that letters weren't getting through.

As the ship disappeared behind the hill, I looked for the bird which had now left the rock and was soaring high and free overhead, and I remembered that a year had passed since telling Johnny in *Marseille*, that I would give it a year, then leave. It was now time for me to fly high and free.

Our annual parachute jumps were due and we would soon be in *Philippeville*. I figured that in spite of the high security, there had to be some way of getting on to a ship, preferably a British one as I had been led to understand that no foreign authorities could touch a British subject once they were on 'British' property.

I would definitely go on my own, as escape had proved impossible for the several men I'd heard of that had tried it in pairs, and all without exception had come to a bad end.

In one case a French naval ship had picked up two Italian lads making a dash for home in a stolen boat. Two others were spotted, reported, then picked up by Gendarmes and passed via the French military police, back to the Legion. All were caught while still in French territory. What had happened to some others was less clear and more ominous.

Getting caught wasn't a nice thought. I'd seen enough of brutal legion punishments including *la pelote* and they were all bad enough, but there was also the dreaded prison of *the 2ème REP's Compagnie de disipline.*

That was an isolated, man-made nightmare based near *'Collomb-Béchar'* where men worked extremely long hot days under the Sahara sun, often subjected to unthinkable brutality. Several legionnaires had spoken of prisoners being driven insane or killed. I was surprised that anyone survived it, and from what I gathered some men were never seen again.

Lastly, there was the threat of being caught by *La Fell,* where torture would likely be both vicious and terminal.

Yanoff had told me of a deserter from his original section who had somehow survived *Collomb-Béchar* and been returned to the regiment.

"Five of us," he said "had been out on our own, cold and soaking for several days and our *équipe* seemed to be getting a lot of thankless shit. Our *caporal chef* was a real pig called *Rodriguez,* an angry *Dien Bien Phu* survivor, who'd been getting meaner by the day. It was during a lull as we waited for radio orders that *Rodriguez,* who really had it in for this legionnaire called *Otto,* started goading him again.

Otto was really jumpy when *Rodriguez* announced to us. 'This man is a deserter, and what happens to deserters is the legion punishes them, but I think that's far too good for them. Here at *2ème REP* we consider they are sick animals and should be treated as such.'

Otto sensed what was coming and made a run for it, but *Rodriguez* was ready and caught *Otto's* thigh with the side of his boot, crumpling him and causing him to drop his gun. Then *Otto* made the mistake of reaching for it. We all knew he wasn't going to use it, but for *Rodriguez* it was just what he'd wanted. **'Threaten me you scum, would you?'** He shouted, raising his *mitraillette*. *Otto* ran.

Rodriguez shot him stone dead in 'self-defence', then coldly ordered us two new guys to get rid of the corpse and to get our hair cut. He detailed the other man to give us both a *'boule à zero'* and when it became obvious the guy didn't have his clippers, Rodriguez yelled, '**Demerdez vous, just sign for the bloody haircuts and pay me later.**'

It was just after that incident that we ran into the *Fell* where I caught these lovely scars on my shoulder."

I had seen the minced-up looking flesh on *Yanoff's* shoulder shortly after meeting him and when I asked him about it he'd told me, "A tiger did it."

"What do you mean?" I'd asked naively.

Leaning forward, baring his teeth in a mock grimace that was also a smile, he hissed, "An *A.A.52* tiger did it!"

To conclude *Yanoff's* story, *Otto* had escaped from *Algeria*, made it to *Paris*, where looking out of place he'd run from two Gendarmes, smack into an army patrol that delivered him straight to the Legion. They sent him back to *2ème REP* in Algeria, who immediately subjected him to a big dose of *la pelote*, before dispatching him to *Collomb-Béchar*.

Then having survived their brutal regime and surely paid for his actions, he had been uncharacteristically sent back to his original company, which was what had really got up *Rodriguez's* nose. For a hardened combatant like him, having a deserter back in service was not only dishonouring the *2ème REP*, but it was an unpalatable insult to all of his comrades that had died at *Dien Bien Phu*.

I was on duty at our hill-fort for the final time when trucks arrived for the trip via 'tent valley' to our Base Camp *Philippeville*.

Verma, who was now a Corporal, informed me that I was to go with them.

"What for corporal?" (*Pour quoi Caporal?*) I asked, realising I'd been singled out. "Maybe punishment." He replied, shrugging.

"For what, Corporal?" I questioned.

"You'll know soon enough."

That was his final comment and there would be no further dialogue.

Our annual training jumps weren't due quite yet, so being sent ahead didn't bode well. There was no reason I could think of for being punished, unless they were digging up some old issue, but the *boule à zéro* I received on arrival at *Camp Pehau* did worry me a bit.

The purpose of a bald head was so that those of any rank who didn't know a legionnaire personally could keep him active and on the run at all times, and of course he wasn't allowed to cover his head.

I'd only been twice to the camp. Once on the way to join my company after training at *Zeralda,* and the other was when a truckload of us for no apparent reason came and left three days later. Now I was bald headed, running everywhere simply doing *corvée,* preparing vegetables, peeling potatoes, scrubbing, cleaning, etc.

In practise it wasn't that bad and I was far too fit to be put out by the running, and the minders were noticeably slack anyway.

The first evening after *corvée,* I was shown a sandy track to the beach, and subsequently I managed in the mornings and evenings to go for a cooling swim, which within that lifestyle really was a major luxury.

There was no further mention of punishment, and it was just possible that the real reason for my early descent to *Philippeville* was something else. One or two of the corporals and a sergeant had on occasion, jokingly confided that I was going to be promoted.

I'd always assumed that they were kidding but thinking about it since, in spite of my fears, I hadn't actually failed at anything. I had a good record and was an excellent marksman under pressure, and perhaps most important was the fact that I'd always kept myself to myself. Useful qualities for the right job I guess. One corporal had joked that I would probably be sent to Tahiti.

As the time got closer for my company to arrive, I grew progressively uneasy at the prospect of doing a series of training jumps. Rumour was that we would be doing night jumps over water. So, I began to let my escaping desire draw energy from my rising fear and began actively addressing the way out.

'Time To Leave'

On the third day, I bumped into *Yanoff*, who was still his horny self. He'd been at *Pehau* since getting shot in the leg and it seemed to be doing fine.

We were both pleased to meet up and actually managed to organise a swim together that evening. A curious bond and mutual trust had developed between us and, while still on the beach, I confided in *Yanoff* that I intended to leave. I was pleased that he was readily supportive, and immediately addressed my intention with some of the obvious problems I might confront.

I told him I would sneak my dress uniform down to the beach, change into it after washing in the sea, bury my work clothes, then stroll nonchalantly along the beach to *Philippeville* like a man on leave, find a way onto the docks, and get on to a boat, a British ship if possible.

Yanoff reminded me that as there was a war, there would be a curfew, he also pointed out to me that getting onto a ship might not be that easy, plus finding a British ship might be very unlikely.

I told him it was my time to leave and once he realised I was certain, he began pointing out how he could help.

He said as few people in camp knew either of us personally, and we both had shaven heads, if he did *corvée* in my place, no one would be any the wiser. He reckoned it would provide me with the time needed for the casual stroll into *Philippeville* and a bit more, before the legion and every other mob would start looking for me.

....

CHAPTER TWENTY-ONE
'A Smokey Freedom'

The following morning when circumstances were right, I cautiously headed for the beach, hoping no one would see me, bald headed on the track carrying the large wrapped parcel that was required in order not to squash the pristine contents, which included my ironed light khaki summer dress uniform, waist sash, shoes, stiff white kepi and big red hairy *épaulettes*.

At the beach I snatched a quick wash in the ocean, then spent an awkward and wary time trying to keep my balance while avoiding yellow staining sand from marking the immaculate dress uniform. There was also the added complexity of correctly attaching the long blue centuron, red lanyard and *épaulettes* without being seen.

Once the dirty old clothes had been buried deep in sand, I carefully placed my white *képi* and began strolling west.

Fortunately, that part of the beach had remained clear of people, so far so good, so far un-spotted.

The road from *Camp Pehau* to the town runs more or less parallel with and close to the shoreline. It was, as I remember, a raised sea wall along most, if not all, of its length.

On that particular day the road was busy with a flurry of two-way military traffic and there were already a fair number of people on the beach. I knew full well that any military person of rank, be it Army, Navy, Air force, Gendarme or Policeman, had the urge and the duty to check a legionnaire over at any time, at any place, for good conduct and correct dress.

This included making sure that uniform and behaviour were immaculate at all times, right down to ensuring that buttons were securely sewn on. In fact, Legion dress code was so extreme, that a legionnaire on just a day pass was not only continually checked out, but was also expected to report to a police station at regular intervals. Immaculate really meant immaculate.

Before leaving camp, not only was there a fanatic inspection which included checking that the thirteen creases on his summer shirt were precisely ironed, but a legionnaire was also expected to produce for inspection, his regulation needle, cotton and buttons, along with a clean, neatly ironed and precisely folded handkerchief.

I'd only ever managed one pass *'quartier libre'* throughout all my time with the Legion, and that was when we unexpectedly dropped into the camp. During that twelve hour permission, I had to report three times to the *Gendarmerie* during the evening and the overnight option was to register in a sleeping centre provided, or with a girl at the military brothel. I naturally chose the latter, but not having *Yanoff's* sexual characteristics, I was somewhat turned off by my pre-paid 'potential promise of bliss' vomiting at regular intervals. Clearly, I hadn't yet become a hardened *ancient* in terms of sex.

With hindsight, I realise that she probably specialised in pulling off that scam on every naive *bleus* that she encountered. I was pretty disappointed particularly as she had got practically all of the money from my traded goods, but in the early hours before returning to camp I came to terms with it over a black coffee and croissant.

So long as my progress along the beach appeared unhurried and I remained smart and soldierly, I would draw little attention. So, however keen I might have been to get to the docks it was a matter of being disciplined and ambling my way towards freedom. On reaching the end of the beach, I was confronted with a peninsular of rocks, which together with a breakwater, extended out to sea, and beyond that was my first objective, the harbour.

I had already been absent for quite a while, so didn't want to risk the road, that I now discovered passed through a narrow rock tunnel, and would expose me in close-up to all vehicles passing through it. There seemed little choice but to swim for it, so once more, this time feeling even more exposed I hurriedly undressed, furtively burying all but my briefs in the sand.

Either the tide was against me, or there was a steady current because it took far longer than I'd expected to swim out level with the end of the break water, only there to be challenged by a gun wielding French soldier, standing on the wall. After a few antics and attempts at appealing to his better nature, by exposing as much of myself as possible, trying to show that I was a European and a tired one at that, it became painfully obvious, that he would have none of it, as he aimed his gun directly at me in no uncertain manner, indicating very clearly that I should swim back. So I did, while waving to make my intentions obvious in the hope that he wouldn't find it necessary to raise the alarm.

Ironically, the currents still seemed to be against me because although I was a powerful swimmer, it took a hell of a long time for me to get back to the beach, only too aware that by then I would certainly have been listed as missing and that whatever happened now, I would be considered a deserter.

Back at the beach the water had crept in and out over the sand beneath which my uniform was buried. Getting dressed was crazy, it meant finding and digging up my light summer-wear khaki shirt and trousers and the snow white *képi*, all of which had definitely not benefited from their burial in the now wet, yellow-staining sand.

By the time I was dressed, incredibly one of my huge red hairy *épaulettes* was nowhere to be found. No mirror was required to see that I looked an absolute and complete wreck and would stand out like a sore thumb anywhere, never mind here in a garrison town. What now?

Exploiting a lull in the traffic, I clambered up the rocky slope to look down the tunnel. There definitely wouldn't be time to make it through there between vehicles and it was absolutely certain now, that I would instantly be picked up or reported by practically anyone. Well there was nothing for it, I would just 'trust' by stopping a taxi and throwing myself at the driver's mercy. I did just that.

As soon as the kindly looking middle-aged Arab driver had stopped, I told him straight away that I was English, I hadn't meant to come to his country, I didn't like what I was doing in his country and that I wanted to go home. He nervously hastened me into his cab, while agreeing to help me.

Seeing my bald head as I removed my *képi,* he said first he must get me a hat, and meanwhile that I should do everything I possibly could to make my clothes look non-military. He told me to get all the insignia off, roll up my sleeves like a workman and hide the *képi*.

While he was saying all this he was driving into the city and down a back street where he parked the car behind some unidentifiable buildings. He told me to keep down and out of sight as he disappeared into the rear entrance of what he said was a store to buy me a hat!

After only a few minutes, I spotted some hundred yards down the hill the dark *képi* and distinctive epaulettes of a Legion Sergeant walking slowly in my direction. He was still some distance away. Oh shit, I thought, suppose the taxi driver has, or is reporting me to the authorities right now? What if he's calling his friends? Or worse still, what if he's calling the *Fell*?

Scary stories continued to gang up on me of how taxi drivers, or any other Arabs, got paid handsomely for handing legionnaires over to the French, or were given protection for handing them to the *Fellagha*. However I waited, keeping low as instructed in the back seat of the car.

Then every bit as good as his word, the somewhat portly and deliberately unsmiling taxi driver came strolling back, allowing a smile to break out on his kindly face as he murmured, while passing me a brown paper bag, "Take care, we have a soldier nearby." (*Prenez la garde, on a un soldat par là.*)

Inside the bag was a white Panama hat. Keeping low as we drove past the Legion Sergeant, I put the *képi* inside the bag to hide it, then took the canvas hat and began re-shaping it.

My Arab saviour then drove me down towards the docks, along a road that ran parallel to the railway track, pointing out various relevant features. He showed me a place where there was a flaw in the boundary fence through which I could pass to get into the stationary train that was temporarily parked. He said I would have the advantage of the train's cover and length to safely spy out the docks and hopefully find a way in.

I thanked him warmly and profusely, insisting he take the pitifully small amount of change that I had in my pocket towards the price of the hat. He reluctantly accepted, only on the basis that I would have no further use for it. It wasn't safe for either of us to hang around any longer, so I took my paper bag and he wished me luck and Allah's blessing before driving off. With gratitude I hurriedly disappeared through the fence in order not to draw attention, only wishing that there had been more time to thank that generous spirited human being.

Once through the fence getting onto the train was amazingly simple, which considering it was a country at war was surprising. With care, it was possible to walk up and down the corridor at will.

As luck would have it, I immediately saw between a couple of buildings, the fluttering Red Ensign of a British cargo boat, and would later find out that she was the first British ship to have docked at *Philippeville* in over seven months.

Without too much trouble and being extremely fit, I lost no time in erratically negotiating the prison-style wire perimeter fence, whilst expecting a shout and even anticipating a possible shot at the top of the fence as I was in full view of the town's streets. Once on the ground it was urgent to blend quickly, so still carrying the crumpled bag, I strode workman-like between buildings and crossed the concrete area as if having every right to be there.

By taking a deceptive right and feigning a short walk along the quayside, I could suddenly turn left up the gangway of '*The Estonia*' and duck through the first available door. When I pulled that door open, it threw me face to face with a startled, young crew-member.

"**Quick,**" I said "I'm an ex-British seaman escaping from the Foreign Legion, **where can I hide?**"

The door was already pressing against me, as he blurted back, "**Don't involve me mate, go and find your own bloody place to hide.**"

What a let down! Somehow having been a seaman there was a sort of expectation that he would want to help me.

Ever mindful there was a possibility of being observed, I swung round the first corner and continued up some steps to discover the oval ship's funnel. A metal panel on the side of its otherwise smooth surface immediately caught my eye. By pulling a lever which opened a hatch, I was able to step inside, discovering unexpectedly, that the inside of the ship's funnel was actually a metal room with a meccano-like structure creating two levels inside the outer shell. The narrow exhaust pipe from the ship's engines simply passed up through the closed roof of what was in effect an imitation funnel.

Climbing instinctively to the upper level, which was not a floor so much as a ledge, I was provided with a perch where, like a chicken, I could squat and peer through downward-slanting ventilation slats, similar to those in louver doors. I could clearly see an area of the ship, a portion of the quayside and the gangway that I had just come up. To my astonishment, a legionnaire was guarding it. Had I seen him before coming aboard, the outcome might have been very different, he must have picked that moment to nip round some corner for a piss.

As I settled on my perch carefully watching both legionnaire and gangway, various people came and went. Some were crew-members, some didn't fit any role that I recognised until, as anticipated, a Legion search party arrived on the quayside, they were smartly brought to attention and their sergeant came aboard. Minutes later he was back instructing his men, who were quickly aboard and searching the ship and I knew just what they were looking for.

It wasn't long before several of them appeared within in feet of me, yet no one seemed to register the hatch-plate on the funnel. They must have been 'land lubbers' who saw a funnel as a large smoke stack, in which case they would probably assume the hatch-plate was for access to clean the chimney.

Remaining very still, becoming progressively more uncomfortable and knowing how much sound would echo in that iron box, I was carefully controlling the sound of my breath, as I watched them through the vents.

I realised that a legionnaire was looking directly into my face, we were literally looking straight at each other's eyes and it went on for what seemed like a hell of a long time. Then, as a corporal called the men to search a different area, that legionnaire showing no sign of recognition, and turned away with the others as they left the funnel area. I am convinced he saw me, although having been Legion trained his expression was impassive. Why else would a man look long and hard at a blank expanse of metal. I believe he did what I would have done had our roles been reversed, he had inwardly wished me luck and let well alone.

The patrol kept hunting for me for well over an hour, eventually filing down the gangway and disappearing from view between the dock buildings. Evening came. There were different activities taking place but the only life I could see was a replacement legionnaire guarding the gangway.

Then I became aware of engine vibrations and warmth radiating from somewhere deep below.

To avoid disappointment, I quelled any hopes that the boat might be getting ready to leave, but the gangway went up and the ship began almost drifting along the quay. I saw buildings move slowly past, and the gap begin to widen between dock wall and the visible ship's railings. We were leaving!

I began to perk up as we moved further from the stone wall, but it seemed to be taking one hell of a long time, yet we were now actually clear of the quay and therefore clear of the land, and I was on British territory beginning to feel a certain amount safer.

As I perched patiently waiting for sight of the harbour exit, I became aware that we were slowing down and were very close to the quay again. It took me a while to realise that we were once more alongside. It only became real for me when the gangway was lowered and made fast. I didn't see anyone leave the ship or come aboard, but while all these manoeuvres had been carried out, darkness had crept in.

I kept staring through the vents, but no one moved either on the quay or near the well-lit gangway. I must have dozed on and off, occasionally wavering on my perch as the night passed with no apparent activity. Yet, when daylight came, I saw that another legionnaire had been posted at the gangway.

What had happened? What was wrong? Why were we back at the quay?

I wondered if the guy I'd made eye contact with had been motivated by second thoughts, or maybe the soldier on the breakwater had reported my swim.

Suddenly there was the same patrol on the quayside, it was the same ritual as yesterday, but they came more deliberately up the gangway obviously aiming straight for me. I waited for them, shuffling about like a parrot with my head bobbing about at the various ventilation slats, peering this way and that, tilting my head for better vantage points. I could see the patrol checking all the possible hiding places with the crew assisting. They were even opening up the tarpaulin covers that protected the lifeboats. This was a serious in-depth search.

I thought they must surely find me this time, especially with the help of the crew, but I must have been wrong about the legionnaire reporting me because they clearly didn't know where I was hiding.

Once again after an immeasurable period, they filed down the gangway to begin searching the surrounding area. Then a string of other uniformed people came aboard; customs, police and other agencies, searching for guns, stowaways and general contraband. Yet not one of them so much as glanced at the funnel, I could hardly believe my luck, they eventually all left, empty-handed!

Soon once more came those familiar engine sounds from below, which reassured me that we were again preparing to move. The gangway was taken up, and quite quickly this time. The space between quay and ship widened and kept getting bigger as the ship smoothly moved, gradually gaining speed and much more clearly going somewhere. The end of the breakwater sped past, complete with a gun-wielding soldier, like the one who had foiled my earlier attempt to enter the harbour.

Yes! We really were heading out to sea, this time I'd made it! Elation! It made sense to remain in place until we were definitely well out to sea, by which time it was getting uncomfortably hot in the steadily pulsating funnel.

When I actually came out of that black, fumy container that had served me so well and for so long, it felt wonderful. The fresh sea air entered my lungs, the cool wind blew and aired my hot sooty skin as the ship motored on, with its long wake curving back towards the receding coast of North Africa, which was now well and truly in the distance.

Quickly, I threw my *képi* overboard with the shirt that had all the dark tell-tale silhouettes where patches and various military insignia had been, along with anything else that might have identified me with the Foreign Legion.

I did keep one very important item though. It was my canvas webbing belt that not only kept my trousers up, but also had stitched carefully to the underside of it, a small square piece of folded satin, my protection and amulet. It was a fragment of my little brother's satin sheet, that as a child he had always used whilst sucking his thumb and passing the satin between his fingers.

It had come in the first letter (in my legion name) I received from my family and he had enclosed it especially for me, a six-inch piece of his well-loved, well-used, pink satin comforter. Besides having kept it for sentimental reasons, I'd been looked after and protected so well by it over and over again during the past months, I wasn't about to get rid of it now.

....

CHAPTER TWENTY-TWO
'Sod's Law'

I'd been sitting happily on the iron deck with my back against the warm funnel enjoying the ship's smell, the sea air, and that beautiful view of the Algerian coast receding into the distance, while experiencing with the seagulls the sweet taste of freedom, when a young red faced, uniformed cadet came up from below, presumably to attend to the flags. One shocked look was apparently enough for him, and he disappeared.

Not altogether surprising considering that he had just seen a stripped to the waist, lean, bald, bare-footed man, shiny black from soot grease and sweat, with a two day stubble on both head and chin, that was also black from the long hours spent languishing around in the filth of what was after all, the ship's exhaust system. What probably helped to scare him further was the contrasting clear blue and whiteness of a white man's eyes looking at him from that black greasy face.

Within moments the same ruddy-faced boy returned, more confident now that he could linger behind the secure presence of a uniformed First Officer, known on board ship as the 'Mate'.

From a safe distance, and keeping one prepared foot back on the last but one rung of the steel ladder, the tall officer beckoned me with his fore-finger to come closer. Then, in that peculiarly patronising way that we English seem to always manage, he asked me very slowly, "Do--you--speak---English?"

"Yes I am English!" I told him, with a grin. "I'm a merchant seaman and I've just escaped from the Foreign Legion."

"Ah ha. Now you had better be a good fellow and come with us." He said.

Then turning to the red faced cadet, told him, "Now you had better stay with me and not breathe a word to anybody about this, until we have seen the 'Old Man'."

I think the Mate as a human would have liked to be supportive, but wearing the hat of First Officer, once we were on the bridge he became totally compliant with the Captain's reactions, which were very much not supportive.

That bad-tempered old Captain was definitely not a happy man, barking in his gruff northern accent, "**I don't want 'is type foulin' up my bloody ship an' contaminatin' my bloomin' crew! Lock 'im in t' fan room an' put bloody good guard on 'im. I'll get on radio right sharp an' 'ave bloody authorities pick bugger up in t' next port!**"

Then towards me he mouthed, "**Tha deserves wha'ever tha bloody well get. If tha 'adn't meant ta do time, tha shouldn't 'av joined bloody Foreign Legion in t' first place, an' I'm not 'avin likes of thee on ma bloody ship!**"

Well so much for that universally believed myth, that once aboard a British ship a British person would be safe!

The Mate showing no expression along with the now scarlet-looking cadet, took me as ordered to an unused utility room, a sort of square, smaller, cleaner metal locker-like version of what the funnel had been, all iron, including the floor and the downward slanting ventilation slats that I could see through. The heavily welded lock on the iron door was made secure by a key turned shut from the outside, and I was left to await my fate.

But very soon the *Old Man*, now very inflated with his 'jailer' role, arrived followed by two more of his shocked-looking cadets.

"**I'm porstin' these two young men 'ere ta make bloody sure tha don't bloomin' well try ought.**" He said. "**I've given 'em orders an' a couple a stout iron bars. One bloody wrong move, or ought funny business on tha' part an' they're to 'it ya bloody aard!**"

Those two boys now looked even more horrified than the original red-face one. As for me, I just settled on to the iron floor fairly untroubled, as there was no imminent threat, and fell asleep.

I later learned that the *'Estonia'* was a troubled ship, with a troubled Captain and crew. It was one of those set-ups where the crew had been flown out to join her in a foreign port where ship owners could, and often did, by-pass U.K. labour and safety laws. She was one of those freighters known as a 'tramp ship', picking up and dropping cargo anywhere, then awaiting the next assignment in whatever port she found herself. So with no predictable schedule, the crew had no way of knowing just how long they would be away from home.

Consequently, there was a lot of animosity between officers and crew. Later I found out that the crew, through their shop steward and his pal, had come together and managed to exert pressure on the Captain to honour human rights and treat me in a civilised manner. So it came as a nice surprise when I was suddenly awoken and taken from my iron cell, to be provided with a lovely hot shower and food, plus clean soft bedding, and courtesy of some crew members, a tee-shirt, jeans, footwear and even a denim hat.

For the first time in a long while, I slept with full belly and clean between fresh sheets on a soft mattress with pillows. Even if I was locked in an iron cell with guards, it was total luxury.

Some hours later the clatter of metal on metal woke me up, as someone had thoughtfully posted a knife through one of the ventilation slats while the cadets were changing watch. I looked at it for a while and made an ineffectual attempt at sharpening it on some of the iron fittings, then placing it under my pillow I was again quickly asleep.

Through those same ventilation slats moving shafts of morning sunlight reflecting off the sea woke me. The ship was turning about, preparing to enter the harbour port of *Mostaganem*, which is situated towards the Western end of the Algerian coast. Sure enough, looking down through the slats, just over there on the quayside a mere few hundred yards away, was the Legion patrol that had obviously come to make its collection, courtesy of the ship's English Captain.

Now I was concerned, and began anxiously peering from various angles. It was quickly evident that the two cadets had gone, probably called away to fulfil their docking duties and there was, for the moment, no one in sight.

Looking about for a means of escape, the knife came to mind as a tool for loosening the lock, but the welded fittings were totally impervious to my feeble attempts and being a hefty mechanism that could only be activated from the outside, the knife never even managed to make an impression.

Then I noticed a twelve-inch length of block steel that was held to the bulkhead by two screws, which the knife could and did unscrew. Using the length of steel as a hammer, I gave the lock an almighty blow, only to stop alarmed at the colossal noise in that all-metal environment. Someone must surely have heard and would come quickly. There was a minutes wait holding breath while anxiously seeking a way to muffle the next blow, but the door moved and it became apparent that the hard single blow had actually sprung the lock's mechanism.

No one came, so without further hesitation I walked out of the cell, stepping through the nearest available door.

Under normal circumstances this would probably have been the worst possible choice, as one foot was now inside the fully manned ship's bridge, with the Captain, Officers, Cadets and Seamen all standing in a wide row and looking out through the panoramic window, as they carried out whatever tasks their role demanded.

I instinctively knew that any hesitation or backing out was more likely to draw attention. So simply choosing to believe that I was part of the scene, and behaving like any crew member, I strode across the full length of the bridge and out of the far door, totally unnoticed. It occurred to me then, that I might just have been gradually mastering the knack of invisibility, just like a wise old dog I would one day get to know called 'Gyp'.

I was driving a lorry in the south of England years after these events and found myself near Aldershot, so went to see if I could find my Elvis look-alike friend, Greg. I found him playing with his youngsters, a couple of their friends and his two Alsatian dogs in their council house garden. I had turned up on an emotionally-charged day for this smashing family man that Greg had become, as his elderly mother was moving into a home, having to leave her house and six dogs. Accompanying Greg for the sad event, I noticed amongst the yelping pack, one quiet, very shaggy, male dog that stood out from the others. It may have been that because we shared similar looks and characteristics he also noticed me. He was Gyp, apparently the runt of the litter.

When time came to leave that sad house, as I walked to the lorry Gyp was beside me clearly asking to be taken along. I explained to him that I lived in a busy part of London with no garden. It didn't seem to matter much to Gyp, because as soon as the cab door was open Gyp was in, taking up an observation position on the passenger seat that he maintained all the way back to London. The following day, we both sat for a while at the very busy intersection in the centre of Notting hill Gate so I could tell Gyp all about traffic. He learned well, because, with no previous experience of life outside of that old lady's house, Gyp went on to live an independent life in the busy heart of Notting Hill Gate and the Portobello Road area, quickly becoming a well known regular visitor of all the quick serve food outlets in the vicinity. He even bought home half a chicken for me one day when I was sitting on a mattress in a bare room, and broke.

One day I watched this wise old dog in the presence of a ferocious looking large Alsatian. From mooching along the pavement contentedly, Gyp's whole body posture changed, for twenty yards or so he became invisible to that Alsatian. So much in fact, that the hyper-alert pedigree never even noticed him. Once Gyp had reached the far corner of the street, he peeked back. Then feeling safe once again, he reverted to the bumbly carefree Gyp that I knew.

Having stepped from the far door of the ship's bridge and mounted the first steps available, I knew my invisibility had worked, but why there was this tendency to go up I don't know, as the bridge on most ships is already pretty up and this ship was no exception and I was at risk of running out of up-ness. The ascent was all happening in full view of the Legion patrol and faces were watching my every move as the ship tied up.

The last option was in the lower rigging, a sort of flat maintenance platform that when I reached it via some metal rungs, was about the size of a single bed. Once on the platform, I pulled off another 'Gyp' trick by looking up at the sun, removing my tee-shirt and blatantly waving to the watching patrol, while making a macho fuss of my body as I disappeared from their view to sunbathe.

I was trusting that rigid military thinking, combined with the ordinariness of the scene, would erase any concept of it as a hiding place from the minds of those hunting me, and it worked. There I remained, in various positions of flatness for the whole day, thankful for a light breeze, and covered myself as best I could so not to get burnt under that North African sun.

From spying through convenient rivet holes it was quickly obvious that the thwarted 'Bligh'-like Captain had given total freedom and encouragement to search every corner of the ship. They worked long and they worked thoroughly, intent on covering every detail, including some seemingly impossible places. These white *képi* Legion infantry clearly didn't want to return empty-handed as the Legion patrol at *Philippeville* had.

By the time I watched them searching large concrete pipes and other construction materials on the quay, the sun was low in the sky and I was very uncomfortable. Yet, only when it was dark did I feel safe enough to risk finding my way down the companion ways to the deck-hands' living quarters and introduce myself to the crew. I felt certain that they, unlike the officers, would be supportive and to a man they were, quickly organising a meeting to decide how they would help me.

Before long there was unanimous agreement that the workspace, 'up front' near 'the sharp end', was the safest place for me to hide. This actual space was to the front of the several cargo holds, just before the bow. It was reckoned that officers would have little reason to go there and that it should be safe enough so long as I kept clear of the panoramic view from the officers' accommodation and bridge. At night I could move about the ship freely for exercise, toilet facilities, etc.

My new home, that turned out to be the size of a decent living room, had metal lockers and work surfaces running around three sides, with a large work bench standing in the centre. Most important in that overheated space, was that just to the right of the entrance was an opening back into the two cool dark steel compartments which, between them alternately housed the massive resting iron links of the ship's anchor chain. It was a dark place where I could quickly disappear whenever necessary.

As it turned out, I spent most of my time quite happily sitting in that darkness on top of the smooth, pleasurably cool iron links. Of course at that time I hadn't heard the story of a woman who stowed away in a similar place, to then die of heart failure from fear, noise and vibration as massive links rumbled through their iron sleeves when the anchor was unexpectedly dropped.

Nights were spent wandering freely, exploring the dimly-lit communal mess room and ship's galley, a curiously eerie experience hearing the sounds that pulsed away in another world as barefooted and silent, I haunted the big sleeping machine. Everything on board was so efficiently stowed, there would have been nothing to do or even see, except that thoughtful well wishing crew members had left sandwiches or other items of food and drink in hidden places for me to discover.

I had amusing visions of a loyal cadet presenting proudly to the captain a sandwich that he had discovered hidden behind a lifeboat stanchion, I always cleared away any traces to ensure nothing gave the game away.

Night freedom meant actually using the toilet, which was luxury compared to living all day in the close proximity of a 'turd' wrapped in oily rag, until under cover of darkness it could be enthusiastically hurled to leeward. Furthermore, I could shower, wash my few clothes and then dry them on hot pipes before morning.

The 'Newport', a British ship from Liverpool, pulled in around the third day docking diagonally opposite, a good ten minutes walk along two sides of the smooth concrete and fairly barren quay. Our crew quickly found out that she'd be heading directly for England in about three days, which would be a much better bet for me than staying with the *'Estonia'*, which was unpredictable and showing no signs of leaving for a while anyway. So, on my behalf, the crew from both ships met up to work something out, resulting in the following scenario being contrived.

I would be referred to as the brother of Stan, one of the 'Newport's' crew, on the basis that we rarely had the opportunity of being together, due to opposing sea schedules. Permission would be sought for me to spend time with Stan, helping him paint the ship so as not to disturb routine. With that plan I'd be freer, and it would relieve my hosts while putting me in a position to hide when the 'Newport' came to sail. I would be back in England in just a few days.

The plot was hatched.

Under cover of darkness, in spite of curfew, a shallow painting punt was silently paddled across the inky black harbour to collect me. I felt uncomfortably observed by the expectant crew as I made a pigs-ear of scrambling awkwardly down the side of the ship to the guys standing by, in the punt.

I'm sure my new colleagues who were all leaning out and watching, expected a real Legion para-style descent. They didn't know about my fear of heights!

Thankful for the absence of moonlight, the men glided the punt silently back across the black water.

For the next two days I dangled over the ship's side on a maintenance cradle helping my 'brother' paint the ship's hull.

Outside of working hours there was freedom to enjoy walking about the ship and socialising, especially as by now, part-bearded, in denim cap, tee-shirt and jeans, I was just one of the crew. Just before the 'Newport' was due to sail, the Legion patrol came aboard to carry out what was little more than a basic search. Luckily I was over the side with my 'brother' and another man painting, and therefore taken to be crew. Once the patrol had left, the cradle was raised for deckhands to take up their various tasks in preparation for the 'Newport' to sail. A guy showed me a cabin in which to remain out of sight.

As I lay on the bunk waiting for the ship to move, I picked up the only book on the shelf, which ironically happened to be about a man who'd escaped from the Foreign Legion.

I was just beginning to believe I might soon be back in Southampton, when the door opened and an officer poked his head in, probably checking that there weren't any crew members avoiding work.

"Who the devil are you?" He asked pompously.

"I'm an Englishman escaping from the Foreign Legion and trying to get back to England." I replied, already certain from this man's face that it was not about to happen now.

"Well you certainly can't remain here old chap. Better get 'orf' now before the old man finds out. Now be a good fellow and follow me."

Just as the gangway was fully up, it was lowered on my behalf so that 'poncy' officer could see me 'orf'. Once again I was back on Algerian soil, well Algerian concrete to be precise, and feeling decidedly vulnerable.

CHAPTER TWENTY-THREE
'Algérie Encore'

Getting back to the *'Estonia'* in broad daylight would have been risky enough, as even a brisk walk round the naked concrete harbour would have involved long uncomfortable minutes of total exposure. Once there, the ship's layout would have necessitated a walk up the forward gangway and over the long open deck, all in full view of the panoramic windows, but now there was an added problem.

The Legion patrol had been standing at ease all this time on the quay, watching the 'Newport's' departure and would have seen the gangway raised, then mysteriously lowered to deposit me onto the quay. These weren't legionnaires from *Philippeville* who could personally recognise me nor, I hoped, did they have a photograph, but the fact they were there at all meant they were keeping an eye out, and by then would certainly have a description of me.

Admittedly, in denims and with stubble I now looked very different, but in view of the circumstances I was incredibly noticeable and any half-bright sergeant would wonder at my not having sailed out on the departing ship, and whatever story I might have chosen to tell him he would only have needed take me to the *'Estonia'* for verification, where I'm sure 'Bligh' would have been only too happy to seal my fate. Well I had to do something and do it quick! If I hadn't learned much in the Legion, I'd learned to *demerde-vous*! It was time to be invisible and become who I was not.

So calling and waving goodbye to imaginary people on the departing 'Newport', I took on the stance of one of those pissed British holiday makers abroad who cover their inadequacies with obnoxious behaviour, passing a couple of feet in front of the row of waiting legionnaires, swaggering, raising my thumb to ear level and grinning like an idiot.

"*Bonjour eh*! *Ça va bien*, yeah! *Bon*, good eh, Legion *bon*, yeah?"

More thumbs up, more grinning. Their eyes watched from expressionless faces, I was beginning to enjoy it.

"**Boom Boom**, gun *bon*, yeah!" I said pointing to the sergeant's gun and grinning. "Sten gun, English, yeah! *Très bon*, yeah!"

At that point one or two of them looked expectantly towards their corporal, so a switch back to waving enthusiastically at imaginary friends on the departing 'Newport', even though it was by then too distant to see anybody.

I never faltered in my progress towards the '*Estonia*', acutely careful not to make any movement that hinted of order, discipline, regularity or even normality, knowing full well the role must be played out to the end, or until well out of sight. The final stretch up the gangway and along the exposed deck of the '*Estonia*' also required acting a part that cadets or officers wouldn't notice, and it worked!

Entering the lower deck of the seamen's accommodation and coming to the open sided section, several of the crew were drinking and raising bottles in the direction of the 'Newport's' departure.

Legs, the tall ex-guardsman was calling out, "**Here's to our stodge-away being back in Blighty soon!**"

"**Yeah, to our stodge-away!**" echoed another man.

"**To our stodge!**" chorused the others.

Then I burst their bubble with, "Sorry guys, I'm still here!"

They all registered some obvious dismay, both disappointment for me and concern for themselves as what for the crew had started out as a supportive adventure, a chance to band together and help a fellow seaman in trouble, was now becoming a liability and a couple of them, Vince and Reggie, were obviously a bit pissed off.

Merchant seaman were employed by the Merchant Navy, or in some cases contracted to a shipping company. In either event, a career could be severely damaged by a dishonourable discharge at the end of a trip and assisting a stow-away could lead to just that. On a ship with as much bad feeling between crew and officers as the *Estonia*, there would be no 'blind eye' from the Captain.

A serious meeting was hurriedly got together, with various suggestions put forward, which included how to hide me more thoroughly. In spite of their concerns, every man was still behind me. An idea soon came up, for what everyone agreed would be an excellent hiding place.

We went straight to a metal hatch on the main deck, which was unscrewed and lifted. Inside, was a fixed metal ladder, down which I partly descended. Once satisfied that I was in agreement, someone hurriedly closed the hatch, noisily screwing the catches down which in effect sealed me into a dark damp tomb! I remained with my limbs sort of hooked onto the iron rungs. There was absolutely no light, only the sound of water splashing around and echoing in the metallic depths below, which made it feel enormous and set me wondering how far the ladder reached down, how big the space really was, and how the hell was I going to get comfortable.

I was busy entertaining myself with the lights that eyes conjure up in pitch-blackness when I heard above me the sound of catches being unscrewed. The hatch opened and I'm sure anxious faces must have peered down at me, though in the sudden light I couldn't see them at the time. They were calling and reaching down to help me out. Ernie, who was the same crew member that had posted the knife to me as I slept in the iron room, had discovered that I was likely to be drowned.

Concerned about the safety of the hiding place, he had done some quick calculations and concluded that the current cargo, being light weight cork, would require ballast to stabilise the ship, and to that end all ballast tanks, including the one they had put me in, would have to be flooded. Not a nice thought for me, and one that really disturbed the crew.

Further discussion led to general agreement that the anchor locker room was still the safest place. So several more somewhat boring days were spent in that familiar environment with nightly excursions for exercise, cleaning up and discovering food.

Its interesting how the crew of this and presumably other tramp ships never seemed to know or even care when or where the ship was going next, so it was only through concern for my circumstance that a couple of them were motivated into trying to find out.

It was Ernie again who said, "We'll be leaving for Gibraltar soon, you'll be safe there, they'll send you home I expect."

Before the *'Estonia'* eventually did sail, there was to be yet another series of searches from customs, police and a Legion patrol. These infantry guys were markedly different to the guys that I had left. Even as I had watched them from my observation platform as they first searched the ship, they hadn't seemed as crisp, or come across nearly as well-disciplined as had the *2ème R.E.P.* guys. Nor did they have that same aura of pent up vigour. Some even wore beards, which as I had passed close to them on the quay sparked a quick memory of the endless sharpening of worn out razor blades on the insides of bottles at *Zeralda*.

When it came close to leaving time, I was no longer willing to hide in the anchor locker having heard of that unfortunate woman's fate. Ernie foiled their search attempts by having me lie hidden on the work bench, right out in the middle of the workroom, cleverly covering me with two or three good sprinklings of the old oily, shredded cotton waste that is used for mopping up oil spillages and the like. Then he completed his camouflage work by throwing some other things on top.

Not one of the various searching agents, including the legionnaires, ever came near me as I lay quietly in the middle of that room for over an hour, practising again the art of invisibility.

Then came a lengthy period of trying to get some idea of what was happening. As I heard no one for some time, it was likely that searchers had left the ship. Unlike inside the funnel, where engine vibration and warmth were apparent, a light trembling, muffled by layers of cotton waste, was all I could feel from inside my cocoon.

Try as I might, I could find no indication as to whether or not we were still in the harbour, or if we had left *Algeria* for the second time.

CHAPTER TWENTY-FOUR
'North Africa Receding'

By the time it felt safe enough to lift off the stifling layers of oily covering and stiffly ease myself off the wooden bench, it was a surprise to find it so dark with only a grey silhouette where fresh air streamed in from the doorway.

Stepping cautiously outside it proved safe enough to sit in darkness breathing deeply and enjoying the fact that we were now well away from the coast and making good headway on a gently breathing, black satin sea. It was a relief to know that I had all night for the long operation of removing stains and stink from the foul smelling oil, that had impregnated the layers which had hidden me so well.

At early light, I made myself scarce and remained in hiding as we headed for Gibraltar. The intention had been that in order to minimise implicating the ship or her crew, I should slip off the boat that night then hide until she had sailed, before handing myself over to the British authorities. We all 'knew' that as I was a British citizen they would quickly repatriate me.

Well so much for intentions, new instructions meant the ship could only remain in dock to shift cargo for a couple of hours and then sail. Immediate new plans were called for, and quickly drawn up.

It was decided that I should take a calculated sprint across the ship's deck, on cue from the crew, and then jump from the handrail across to a flat roof on a nearby dock building. Not a big jump for an ex-legionnaire they assured me. So while unloading from the hold, with an additional officer overseeing work to speed it up, I was to wait in the doorway of my cell for the 'thumbs up' to be passed around all the crew whenever they saw the officers were otherwise occupied.

Then at a final signal from Ernie, I was to go for it. Following a couple of false starts the moment of action was on and there was no turning back. I shot off without hesitation, blissfully unaware of the long drop to the concrete below. An enthusiastic leap from the handrail took me safely on to the roof of the adjacent building, and I was now on British territory.

The quay the ship was tied to was at the end of an open-sided causeway or pier, the other end was blocked by a big wrought iron gate that was manned by a very tame looking English-style bobby.

After killing time round the limited space for several hours, it became evident that the *Estonia* was not sailing out that night after all. So new action was needed.

Escape from Gibraltar would be unrealistic other than by boat, as Spain and *Morocco*, *France* and *Algeria* all had reciprocal arrangements for the handing over to each other of military deserters. Anyway, there seemed no reason to consider it, as being British I would soon be sent home. My concern was not to cause more problems for my shipmate friends aboard the *Estonia*.

While I had passed time trying not to look conspicuous, I'd noticed a laid-up British naval vessel with an officer in whites, entertaining a couple of attractive, apparently English ladies on it's deck. I approached, excusing myself and asking what he thought might be my best line of action, given that I wanted to cause no further problem for the *Estonia's* crew. The officer was spontaneously charming and supportive in the presence of his female admirers, who in turn were sociably *very nice*.

He spoke to me smiling, mostly at his admirers, "Ehh –yes-s, mm- just hang about over there for a bit old boy, I'll just finish this drink orf with these two charming ladies ehh, then we'll get you sorted soon enough, ehh what!"

It was a relief.

"Thanks." I said, more than happy to wait.

Twenty minutes or so later, I was being driven in this officer's very fine car, towards those big iron gates with the bobby, and hopefully freedom, or so I thought.

Cutting the shabby part of this story to size, once in the presence of the policeman, amidst smarmy smiles, this spoilt young officer was sucking-in congratulations as he proudly upped his kudos by arranging, over the police telephone, to have me handed over to the authorities as his 'successful discovery'. He did this in the full knowledge that I would be handed back to the Captain of the '*Estonia*', who would in turn do his best to hand me back to French authorities somewhere, anywhere.

So much for being safe on British soil!

When I was led by an official, with the young officer proudly in tow, on to the '*Estonia's*' bridge in order to present their 'catch', the Captain was more than just a little put out.

"Thought I'd got rid of this bloomin' problem three hundred miles back!" Ignoring me, he shook his head in disgust. "S'pose I'll have to keep 'old of 'im till I can get 'im to some damn Frog port. 'Ere lock bugger up!"

He ordered the same troubled looking cadets, who promptly led me to my familiar iron cell, apologetically shutting the door and turning the key.

Late afternoon a young official in a suit came to see if I needed anything, I wasn't altogether surprised to learn that his visit was triggered by one of the crew, Ernie. The friendly official told me he would see what he could do to get me released and as he left said, "Hopefully I'll be back soon with some good news."

CHAPTER TWENTY-FIVE
'A Future Beckons'

Anticipating that young official's return, while patiently watching evening light fade through the metal ventilation slats, two curious experiences happened.

In the first, grey moving images floated spontaneously across my vision as if on a screen. There was a scene of many hands reaching upwards from grey bubbling mud, through slow swirling mist, as if clearly beckoning for help. It lasted only minutes, yet long enough to leave a profound realisation that the future would someday require repayment for the good fortune and protection that had accompanied me.

The second experience was, the evening light that I had earlier watched diminish, quickly brightened after that vision faded, and morning activities began. It was undeniably dawn, and in what seemed to be only an hour or so, a whole night had passed away!

As the morning developed, I scrutinised the various personnel that came and went, still expecting someone to collect me. But the familiar vibrations of engines, coupled with the crews' preparations to leave, indicated that we would soon be underway. And as the gangway went up it was clear that no official was coming, and another myth about being safe on British territory was blown.

The direction the ship was facing as we slipped away made it hard to get a sense of which way she was going, so it was some time before I could allow the belief that we weren't heading back into the Mediterranean. Half an hour later I was certain that we were heading more or less west and could feel a sense of relief, even though I knew there were several possible French ports we could head for.

Once we were seriously underway, the red-faced cadet came to sheepishly take me to the bridge. As we climbed the companionway the land was an irregular line along the horizon, and we were definitely travelling straight out from it.

West!

Bligh dismissed the cadet, then looking somewhat resigned said, "Seems I'm bloody stuck wi' ye fer a bit longer, but never ye mind. Sooner or later we'll pull into some damn frog port, or better still, we'll find a frog bloody ship so I can 'and yer over. Till then yer' t' stay up 'ere on't bridge so yer canna contaminate me bloomin' crew. If yer thought bloody foreign legion were rough, don't yer go thinking life's going to be any bloody easier 'ere. Now, see, take bloody bucket an' carbolic soap aft an scrub ya self clean. Coz when your done wi' that, you're gonna scrub this bit of damn deck spotless, then when ya finished ya'll damn well scrub some more!"

Walking aft with the bucket to a section of deck directly behind the bridge to be out of sight, I was grinning at the absurdity of this man's idea of being hard. Little did he know as I plunged my hands into the luxurious, steaming hot water, just how good I felt. And I knew we weren't going anywhere French just yet, and I was getting closer to Australia day by day.

For a couple of days the old man kept up his 'Captain Bligh' fantasy, commanding me to repeatedly scrub an eight foot section of bridge, then stand waiting for him until he was ready to repeat his pompous inspections over and over. Meanwhile, he allocated me the adjacent self-contained pilot's cabin, where he could keep an eye on me and forbade me any communication with the crew. Of course this also meant I could keep an eye on him!

That, and the fact I was so obviously content, must have undermined his fantasy and got to him in the end, because abruptly and without comment, his silly game stopped and I was left free to enjoy the luxury of my accommodation. There was ample space and I was entertained by endlessly watching the ocean, sky, activities of the crew, and of course Bligh!

For a while I had good reason to feel content, but it was slightly marred by the realisation that our apparent course could just be taking us to French Guiana, which was not the best outcome I could have wished for.

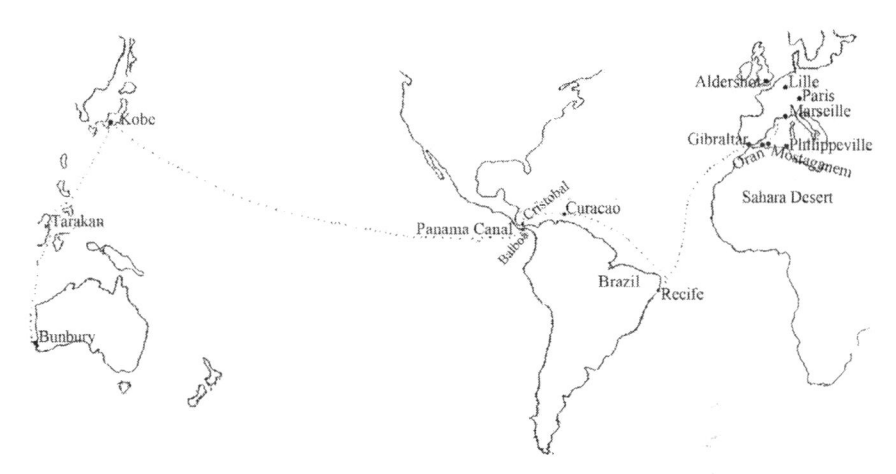

Part of the incidental escape route on 'The Estonia'.

Little by little, short encounters developed with some of the crew, through which some really good news came that I could hardly believe! We were heading for the port of *Recife* in Brazil, which felt to me like a homecoming. *Recife* had been the favourite port of call when I was a boy rating on the old 'Alberta', that same ship on which I'd had that childish knife fight. I felt high as a kite.

Recife. I just loved the place for all kinds of reasons. Not least, because it symbolised the true beginnings of my sexual education.

That once majestic 'Alberta', by then due for the scrap heap but still much loved, was one of those big beautiful old passenger ships, carrying a crew of several hundred men.

Before I joined her, some older man had 'knowingly' winked and told me, "You'll see boy. It's not for nothing that she's known throughout the Merchant Navy as the 'happiest ship afloat'!"

Certainly what my naive eyes saw for the first few days seemed to confirm his statement.

She was my first ship if I don't count the old 'Vindicatrix', that German training ship which in a dry dock at Sharpness served young boys as a Sea school.

I had left my one-road village on the Isle of Wight, turning up at the Southampton recruitment office known as the 'Pool', as a five-foot, slight, blond, freckled, nicely spoken boy. One glance seemed to decide it. A man said, "Join the 'Alberta', noon, Wednesday, and don't be late." In retrospect the assumption seemed obvious, if I wasn't already queer, then I probably soon would be.

That huge ship felt overwhelming and desolate when I first boarded her on that grey morning. They had directed me to join much too soon as there were only shore maintenance workers aboard who could tell me nothing.

Consequently, I spent the first twelve hours sitting forlornly on my ridiculously over-loaded suitcase in a draughty corridor, until an elderly crew-member arrived who kindly lead me through many corridors on several decks to where he thought I might be staying, and then showed me where I could eat.

She turned out to be an exciting first ship and we were three days at sea before I discovered that the pretty girls I'd been ogling at in the crew's large recreation room and dance floor known as the 'Pig', were not girls at all! Having never seen men dressed, made up and behaving as tactile women, or heard 'camp' voices using words like 'darling', 'bitch' and 'queer', my initial impression was that the whole ship must have been the same.

On sailing West from Southampton, and once beyond that magical two-mile-line where most seamen believe national law is replaced by laws upheld at the Captain's discretion, the ship became one six week party until the moment she again crossed the line on her return voyage. During my three working trips aboard that ship in the mid fifties, I saw three hilarious weddings, conducted and participated in by crew-members. They included the 'bride', groom, and all their pretty 'bridesmaids' and guests! There was also a sprinkling of passengers from 1st and 2nd class, along with a few impoverished Spanish and Portuguese migrants who were travelling 3rd class, that sneaked up to watch. Those in the know, along with those presumably not in the know, cheered, little old ladies cried, and most took part in the amazing parties that followed, which were some of the most wonderful and memorable I've ever experienced.

That aspect of shipboard life naturally became my fascination until, that is, we had crossed the Atlantic and arrived at Recife. Then my real interests emerged to be re-ignited at each of the seven ports we twice called at along that South American coast, all awash with beautiful girls eagerly awaiting our arrival. Wherever we went, the fun went with us, as like many sailors, we frequented the sleazy bars, brothels and cafes of those vibrant ports. Given the gender preference of some of the 'Alberta's' crew, once the girls had finished their long nights of attempted seduction to no avail, but nonetheless, done a wonderful job of encouraging liquor to flow, there would nearly always be a girl, or one of the older Madams, who in the absence of paying clients enjoyed the idea of taking a young boy home with her, to either teach or play with. So it was, that much of my early education began.

It wasn't only the women that excited me about South America and Brazil in particular, it was also the sheer vibrancy of the Brazilian night people, combined with music, food and the exotic balminess of those tropical nights.

Now unexpectedly, while still escaping from North Africa, and as far as I was concerned on my way to Australia, I was actually returning awhile to *Recife*!

The remainder of the Atlantic crossing was long, drawn-out and uneventful, with whatever contact I had with Bligh a sort of civilised indifference.

It was tempting, having travelled that way before, not to compare, unfairly of course, our new tub's long-winded journey, to the short time taken by both the aging 'Alberta' and the brand new 'Southern Cross' on which I'd also made a crossing.

In the early hours of morning, as we prepared to enter the port of *Recife*, Bligh had me summoned and said, **"I'm orderin' tha to remain 'ere on't bridge where I can see tha."**

I was really chuffed.

There I was high up on the ship, with a privileged view of *Recife*, watching the whole process of negotiating our way into the harbour, docking and tying up. Once the ship was alongside and the gangway securely down, Brazilian officials came aboard to carry out usual formalities.

After a bit, Bligh called me over saying, **"Just go ashore with these gentlemen, an' they'll take good care of tha."**

We were all smiling as I followed them off the boat and stepped ashore in *Recife* thinking that maybe I was being taken to the British Consulate.

CHAPTER TWENTY-SIX
'A Cell with a Stone Pillow'

The stone cell they locked me into was about eight feet wide, fifteen deep, twenty feet high and with a small barred window about fifteen feet up the back wall that let in daylight. It wasn't dark in that cage as its front had wall-to-wall bars right up to the ceiling of the ground floor on which it was situated, just like a cowboy jail. Other than those bars everything was stone which included the built-in bed, which somebody had thoughtfully designed with a raised pillow, also of stone!

It was possibly the only cell in use at the Port Authority's Police station, a building that had other floors, but I never had cause or reason to go upstairs and see them.

Framed within the building's large wooden rear service doors was a little door that I would later find led out into a fifteen-foot stone alcove facing onto a busy part of the harbour. It was in fact the landing stage where boats could pick up and deliver goods, and presumably where the Police launch could bring in villains and contraband, not that I saw any evidence of that activity.

Two small offices that the police guards inhabited, directly overlooked my cell and were manned at various times during a twenty-four hour day by one, two, or three officials, although when only one man was on duty I figured his mate was probably grabbing a quiet kip somewhere.

I was held there for nearly six weeks, while labour disputes, combined with seasonal rain, held up both the unloading of cork from *Algeria* and the loading of raw sugar for *Japan*. Although the Legion had involved a lot of space, it had in fact been very restrictive, so that I hadn't found the ship's funnel and later limited spaces a problem. This cell was no different and as things worked out I wasn't confined there very much anyway, and when I was it was generally very pleasurable.

Recife had, among seamen, the reputation of having the highest number of night ladies in the world, and on the very first night of my imprisonment I was amazed when the lanky screw that I would later christen 'Slim', opened my cell door for a couple of policemen to shepherd in to my new home, five raucous Brazilian slinky ladies.

It seems that these girls were so numerous in *Recife*, that there was a rule limiting each girl to a section of pavement. Transgression meant a night in nick, 'my nick'!

I assumed there had been a mistake or that for one night we just had to double up, but no, it happened every night of my six-week stay. Nor did it end there, as over the course of each night other groups of girls were brought in, and mostly under hilarious circumstances.

The capacity of those girls for outrageous fun was incredible and it often took a full twenty minutes of coercing by the two policemen and my guard to get each girl in through the door.

Night watch seemed to be down to only one screw on duty, or at least awake, and once the girls were locked in and the screw was back in his office trying to at least doze, the fun would begin with the chorus,

"*Senior, Senior, Maria* **needs a pee,** *Maria* **needs a pee!**"

The chorus quickly became a chant until the screw just had to come over and open up for *Maria*, without losing the other girls, then escort her to the toilet, wait for her awkwardly, and bring her back. All this was while mercilessly being teased and taunted by both *Maria* for the benefit of her audience, and by the girls screaming out obscenities, jokes and accusations throughout.

Getting *Maria* back into the cell with out letting the others out was another fiasco. Then no sooner did he get back to his office and prepared to nod off, than the next chorus would start up, "*Senior, Senior. Yvette* **needs a pee,** *Yvette* needs a pee."

And so on for the rest of the night.

'Slim', took it particularly well and the excitement would peak as every so often more arrested girls were raked in, which all added to making absolutely sure that he would get no rest until all these unrelenting ladies would be released before dawn. I loved the whole show but was disappointed that none of those gorgeous women had showed any signs of even noticing me.

Daylight triggered a big wash-down which was carried out by a boy that I guess was about twelve. He gave the whole stone floor and walls a real hose down that was very effective for both cleaning and cooling in preparation for the long hot day to come. Soon that same lanky night guard, now wearing a police type uniform and a nose that was at least three sizes too big, came in chattering away in Portuguese and plonking a tin slop bucket with a lid beside me, while pointing at his own chest and indicating that his name was *Pablo*.

"Slim." I said, grinning.

He nodded his head with a smile as an unfriendly, fat sweat smelling man, came in and clanged a plate of fish heads and sloppy rice onto the stone bed, I quickly dismissed it for much later, or never. Obviously I'd been too long and too well fed on board the *'Estonia'*.

Later crew friends came to see me and gave me a pack of cigarettes, concealed in an oil-cloth. By the time they had each made rude gestures or twisted faces at the staring fish eyes and left, they had promised me bedding from the ship, and decent food to be delivered from a local café. I quickly hid the pack in a bucket keeping one un-opened packet of 20 in my pocket.

Later when *Slim* passed by I offered him one, which he put behind his ear smiling while sticking out the long, nicotine-stained fingers of the other hand for another one. I passed him a third and asked to use the toilet and washing facilities, he grinned, nodded and left, leaving the cell door ajar. I strolled carrying the bucket and dumped the fish heads and rice. Then while washing myself, I also thoroughly scrubbed the bucket but deliberately made the rim area on one side look messy, before returning to recline on my cool stone bed and dream nostalgically of past times in *Recife*.

Slim was replaced by my day guard *'Marcel'*, a short plump, sweaty man with sleek black shiny hair, who in that tropical rainy season, loved to wear his black suit and carry a black umbrella while moping his brow frequently with a neat

'A Cell with a Stone Pillow'

white folded handkerchief. When he looked in on me I offered him a cigarette. Realising that I was English, he got very excited and thanked me in very careful English.

After spending a lot of time struggling with language and telling me how much he respected England and English people, he seemed to say something along the lines of, "Could there be a very small chance, that perhaps, one day, you might find it in your heart, to send to me from England a black bowler hat?"

He knew, he said, that I was a really trustworthy person, and to emphasise this point he would give me the key to my cell, on the single condition, that I honour our agreement like an Englishman, by staying in my cell from four in the afternoon until six in the morning! Four in the afternoon, he emphasised was particularly important, because that was when his superior came to inspect things.

I tried to explain my situation to him and how I was on the way to Australia and may or may not get there. Therefore, I might not manage to get a bowler hat, but the communication wasn't working. He just smiled and held out a very clammy hand, insisting that we shake on the deal, and the next day sure enough he passed me a key.

Meanwhile I enjoyed daydreaming about the previous nights antics and particularly *Yvette*, who I thought looked pretty good.

Much later my café meal came, brought by the same boy I had seen that morning hosing the place down. He hung about awkwardly, then I realised he was waiting for a tip. I tried to indicate that I was a prisoner and had nothing, but he just stood waiting. There was a badge on the denim cap I had inherited from a deck hand, I gave him that, and he went off happy. The food wasn't much, but it was delicious, coming in the form of sweet black Brazilian coffee in a glass tumbler, along with what could be called a flat egg, a sort of basic omelette complete with buttered crusty bread.

Over a long day, time was slow in my situation but naturally the café staff didn't share a prisoner's sense of time. So that each day the eagerly anticipated treat might arrive any time from eight in the morning to mid-afternoon, by which time I was pacing the floor. But wow, was it good when it came, and thankfully I never once had to resort to fish heads and sloppy rice.

Ever since that experience, I've been addicted to sweet black coffee, flat egg and buttered crusty bread, but the coffee has to be in a glass tumbler to fulfil the nostalgia.

It was halfway through the second night before any of the girls even acknowledged my presence. So far, none of the girls had sat down, seeming to prefer involvement in the teasing and taunting of *Slim*, and the continuous interaction that they so clearly enjoyed with each other.

It was *Yvette* who first spoke to me, in that familiar, teasing type of interaction that 'working girls' the world over normally adopt for easing themselves into a safe upper-hand position. I had discreetly offered her a cigarette, which she put straight between her breasts asking for another one for her friend. The whole packet was emptied as she invented more and more absent friends.

Once she realised that I was discreetly favouring just her, she became decidedly physical and I was suddenly her friend. I didn't push it and by morning she was making comments about seeing me the following night.

I was pleased to notice the girls had all avoided my bucket where a little poured coffee had successfully created a spillage stain on the stone floor, supported by the deliberate mess that I'd made earlier on the bucket's rim, it was the perfect hiding place! It had been a fun night, and well worth it.

I was now ready to play a game with *Yvette* of wheeling and dealing that we could both enjoy.

Meanwhile I had a key and the daytime run of a large area, including the cool outside loading bay with its harbour view of incredible activity. There was a little old man on the water each day who looked for all the world as though he had been 'put out for the day to get some air'. He just sat about fifty feet away in his bobbing wooden boat like a toddler in his pram, just looking at me with a big smile, while I looked at him with an even bigger one. Aah what bliss. Maybe we were both enjoying our own little secret.

With my new freedom I could stockpile cigarettes and allow only a limited amount into my cell. Following a few nights of consistent generosity, which included donations to *Slim*, I had sorted out the regulars, and with *Yvette's* help soon had a group of generous, sexy friends, with *Yvette* making sure that all favours to and fro, sexual or financial, were passed via her.

Soon my incarceration had become an enjoyable period of looking forward to days recovering, and smiling in that cool stone alcove from hectic nights that were spent making up for almost two years of abstinence.

I never had reason to feel hostile towards my jailers who were always friendly towards me, and whether or not I passed cigarettes around they remained that way all through my stay. I only saw one bad thing that happened towards the end of my time, which rudely reminded me of where I was.

A young 'mulatto' boy was roughly hauled in one evening, presumably for some 'no good' reason. *Marcel* and *Slim* between them, violently interrogated the frightened kid right in front of my bars. Locked in my cell there was no choice but to watch. It was upsetting but also a sort of relief to realise that I could still be affected by outright cruelty and violence.

I trembled as I watched *Marcel* question the boy, while *Slim* systematically and repeatedly, kicked the boy's ankles sideways from under him, each kick sending the lad heavily onto the stone floor with progressive loss of control. The punishment lasted about ten minutes before they sent the boy trembling, limping and in tears, back to the streets.

I could only hope the boy had learned whatever lesson had been intended, and would now keep out of further trouble, although I doubted whether his life circumstances would allow that. It was surprisingly the only really unpleasant incident throughout my six weeks in jail.

Very early on the last morning, when our intimate indulgences were requiring considerable focus to ignore the presence of *Yvette's* many mates, we were both uncomfortably surprised to be physically separated, by two grinning officials that *Slim* had let in. They had intended whisking me away to avoid waking, then having to deal with the reactions of my woken fellow in-mates.

However, *Yvette* immediately launched into screaming as I was dragged out and away from her by a background chorus of mocking screams and shouts like, " How could you, they haven't finished yet!" and raucous laughter.

With no time at all for goodbyes, I was escorted straight to the '*Estonia*', up her gangway and into the view of an irritated Bligh who began shouting at me to **"Bloomin' well get up 'ere, an' be seen 'ere standing on my bridge."**

I think I was now classified as something like 'bonded cargo' so authorities ashore had to actually 'witness' my departure.

So beneath the sky an approaching dawn, I once again enjoyed a mysterious view of *Recife* harbour as we chugged out and soon began following the Brazilian coast North.

....

CHAPTER TWENTY-SEVEN
'Negative Headway'

Someone once told me that a bucket of water scooped from the sea a hundred miles out from the mouth of the Amazon River would bring up fresh water so powerful was its flow.

Fascinated that we would be passing it on our way to the Caribbean, I thought maybe I'd raise a bucket and see! The mouth of the Amazon is over two hundred miles wide and we must have spent ages passing it, but I had imagined it would be a brief period so dropped the intention as impractical.

Meanwhile, for some of that time I was in the ship's galley learning to cook.

Two hours out of *Recife*, with waves crashing over our starboard bow, Bligh summoned me to the bridge in order to proposition me. Standing with his back towards me, he spoke at the panoramic window with exaggerated gruffness.

"Fact is, Secon' Cook 'as gone missin'. So, I'm offerin' thee chance t' take over 'is bloomin' job. Tha never know, if tha keep tha damn nose clean an' do tha work well, tha might just get half decent discharge ent o' trip. Maybe, even tha bloomin' job back as a bloody seaman." Only his head tilted in my direction briefly, "S'up to thee, tha can take it or leave it!"

Then it tilted back indicating indifference.

There was a long pause, which gave me time to think. I knew we were taking sugar to *Japan* so would have to pass through the *Panama Canal*, and I was concerned that *French Guiana* was along that route. What the Captain was suggesting would surely make me a replacement crew-member and therefore less simple to hand over to the French. After all, it would have to go on the ship's records. I agreed.

Bligh nodded ordering me, **"Report t' cook straight away."** I quite liked the idea of learning to cook and that same day under the great teaching of *Alphonso*, the ship's extremely hairy, five foot, Maltese cook, I made bread for forty men and it was damn good bread at that!

I was really beginning to enjoy myself, particularly when confirmation came that we only intended stopping off at the Dutch island of *Curacao* to take on fuel. As I felt I would have little to worry about for quite sometime, I settled into my new situation intending to enjoy the voyage, while learning to cook from *Alphonso*.

Later that day Ernie came by to tell me that after *Curacao*, he thought we would sail via *Cristobal*, through the *Panama Canal*, then *Balboa*, stopping at only one of those places to pick up provisions, and after that, he figured, it would be non-stop across the Pacific to *Kobe*.

Having twice before passed through the forty or so mile canal and lake in mostly daylight, night progress through the illuminated lock systems was a totally different experience and particularly enjoyable, especially when viewed from the balmy comfort of a ship's deck.

It was a visual feast of vibrant industry, as men beneath bright floodlights sat at impossible angles on vehicles called Mules, repeatedly straining the cogs of their tracks to keep pace with our ship at each ascending lock, where they would tow us safely in. From the salty waters of the *Caribbean* we were raised over eighty feet to the fresh waters of the jungle-lined *Lake Gatún* above the Isthmus.

A near silent cruise through darkness and morning mist brought us into steamy daylight some eight hours later, when more men on mules eased us down the eastern locks, where it was fascinating to look back up at a ship that followed us down the steps, periodically poised in a massive trough, with only a seven foot thick gate holding back its massive tonnage, along with unbelievable tonnes of water.

As we exited the last lock, along with our many gallons of accompanying fresh water, numerous struggling fish, having survived the journey from their lake, were now for all their efforts destined to a miserable death by salt, in an otherwise wonderful ocean, but totally alien to their kind.

I took in most of this between making the crew their breakfast, and when clearing up was finished and lunch preparations begun, we were out in the *Gulf of Panama* on a calm sea setting out on what would turn out to be an extremely long drawn-out, uncomfortable trip across the Pacific to the port of *Kobe* in *Japan*.

In one region of ocean the weather became so bad that, according to the crew, for three days we were making negative headway, yes, travelling backwards! It was by far the roughest sea I'd ever seen, but endlessly mesmerising just to look over the aft rail from the galley and watch an enormous mass of challenging sea froth up behind the ship like an angry mountain, to fall right away down into a boiling valley below and see the ship's propeller spinning desperately in mid air, shaking the whole structure of the ship which itself was protruding from a solid wall of water.

The lines put out for hands to scramble about the ship's deck were absolutely necessary, though seldom used, in fact no one ventured on deck during the worst of it. The *'Estonia'* was less than a year old and apparently suffered minimal damage, but the sea remained very rough for the rest of our trip.

On the slippery rolling steel galley deck *Alphonso,* with legs set firmly apart, assumed a purposeful stance and let the floor slide him from side to side along the width of his working space, while instructing me.

"For checking if spud is cooked, you take 'im like so."

Shooting his finger and thumb into the boiling water as he skated past his big cooking pot, without even a glance he whisked out a potato tossing it over his shoulder in one move. Then sliding past on the return journey with an acquired sieve in his hand, he noted the consistency of the small dollop of pulp on the galley floor.

"*Eez-a cooked*!" He said approvingly, simultaneously picking up a huge bowl, in preparation for his next journey past the sink.

It was too much for me, I was just happy to keep my balance and not feel woozy. Once the weather eased, *Alphonso* made me woozy again as he taught me how to make a baked bean dish for forty men by using several tins of haricot beans and a large tin of golden syrup, all buried and cooking slowly beneath a whole belly of pork.

Having worked as Second Cook seven days a week, for the six weeks since leaving *Recife,* it was generally accepted that I was now part of the crew and, therefore, on the Merchant Navy pay roll. So with several of the guys, I was looking forward to some nightlife fun ashore in *Kobe*.

The '*Estonia*' anchored off in the large watery space where all the other ships were either off-loading from or loading onto waiting barges. All travelling between ship and shore was done on one of the frequent Liberty boats provided for that purpose.

It was interesting to notice that it only took four days to unload the sugar using the barges at *Kobe,* whereas it had taken five weeks to load it in *Brazil* directly from the quay.

The Japanese workers competed with each other the whole time. Once a barge was loaded there were celebratory noises, as a flag went up to indicate the winning team, and when they took a break, each worker had his neat and orderly food arrangement, which included a bamboo fabric lunch box with chopsticks, and a mat to sit on. Following this brief picnic-style meal, the man was back in action with no time wasted, and in complete contrast to any of the dockworkers I'd seen in any of the countries I'd visited so far.

Most of '*Estonia's*' crew-members, including myself, queued up for a sub ready to go ashore. I had no great expectation of being paid, but the crew were convinced, saying the old man couldn't have me work full-time and then refuse to pay-up, as it would be flying in the face of both union rules and Mercantile law, and even he wouldn't risk that!

However, when it came to it, Bligh with a look of exaggerated contempt, intervened in his gruff manner saying, "**Don't tha go giv'n this blighter nothing.**" Then with a half glance in my direction said, "**Tha' adn't got some fool idea I was goin' t' damn well pay thee, ad' tha?**"

I just shrugged it off, I hadn't really expected it anyway.

Then he rubbed it in by confining me to the ship while threatening, "**Bloody '*nippon*' police 'ell have 'thee locked up in't no time, an' they'll be a bloomin' sight tougher on tha' than those damn lazy buggers in *Brazil* were.**"

The crew on the other hand were disgusted, and when out of Bligh's earshot muttered things like, "We're not having our stodge-away miss out on the fleshpots of *Kobe*, are we?"

That evening, discreetly hidden between several of the crew, I was slipped quietly on to one of the shore-bound Liberty boats. Once ashore, having no money beyond what Ernie had pressed into my hand for a few drinks, and not keen to be a hanger-on, I downed a surprisingly tasteless token *sake* with the boys before wandering off to sample the night life of *Kobe*.

CHAPTER TWENTY-EIGHT
'When Girls ain't Girls!'

Simply enjoying the freedom and strangeness of an exotic city as a non-drinker, with little idea just how strong the almost tasteless *sake* had been, there was no sense of being pissed. Yet, as a very communicative open foreigner I soon attracted a lot of seductive Japanese night girls, both curious and fascinated with the few months growth of beard, and seemingly not put off by my lack of money.

Once again with the help of a few cigarettes being passed around, I would soon be making up for time spent in all male company, or so I thought. *Sake* hit my lips as it was repeatedly passed around and these smooth skinned Oriental beauties became deliciously more amorous by the minute.

I'm not sure how far things had gone, or how long before I noticed some very 'firm' evidence, that at least some of those beauties were not quite the 'girls' they purported to be. Although by that time, *sake* had created clouds of silken amnesia as the night faded into an oblivion where, even had I had wanted to, I could have been of little service to any one of them, whatever their credentials.

The next memory is of being prodded into wakefulness by four policemen on the tiled floor of a scrupulously clean powder blue public toilet where they had found me. Unscathed as far as I could make out, not even a headache, and perhaps even a little wiser for the experience.

Those Japanese policemen showed a lot of concern for my welfare, carefully seeking out the right Liberty boat to take me back to my ship whilst making sure that I would be there in time. Oddly, it appeared that no one saw my return and nothing was ever said about my absence.

Probably Bligh couldn't be bothered to follow up the inevitable, and he was so wrong about how the Japanese police would treat me.

Following the shoddy non-payment episode, the crew couldn't allow me to work anymore due to union principles. It was disappointing because it had been enjoyable especially working and learning with *Alphonso*, who in turn, had appreciated my help. His response was simple, *"Aah, eez-a life-a, life eez-a bitch-a!"*

Without work, life aboard '*Estonia*' was beginning to drag. It was, after all, several months since escaping from the Legion.

Next stop was *Tarakan*, somewhere near the northern tip of Borneo, where for some reason Bligh had me confined to a cabin for what turned out to be an overnight stop. I was reading a book about The *Panama Canal* when we pulled into what from my porthole in the semi-darkness, looked like a jungle clearing, where even if there had been a chance to go ashore I probably wouldn't have bothered as it didn't look remotely inviting.

Next morning, as breakfast was brought into me by Paul, who was the union shop steward, he told me that a crew member had been sent to the hospital with a health concern, "He's on his way back and we won't be sailing till he's back on board."

He placed the precarious tray of food on to my dresser saying with a nod, "Looks like *Alphonso's* made sure you've got plenty to eat."

It was Paul and his friend George that had argued for me to be treated humanely when Bligh first locked me up without bedding, food, or even a means of washing.

It was strange that I hadn't really talked with either of them since and come to think of it I'd hardly even seen them. It wasn't at all unusual on a cargo ship of the '*Estonia's*' size, for the forty or so crew to keep pretty much to their own small groups, or even to themselves as in Ernie's case. The result was that there were quite a few men on board that I hadn't even seen.

Half an hour later, through the porthole, I saw that it was Ernie coming aboard with the gangway drawn up behind him, and within a few moments we'd set sail. Once out at sea, the familiar red-faced cadet came to give Bligh's clearance for me to come out of my latest lock up. There was no explanation, and I could think of no reason why I'd been locked up in such an uninteresting place.

A friendship had been growing between myself and Ernie and it was he, who having completed first watch, came down from the bridge with great news for me.

"Hey, guess what! Our next port of call in about five days will be Bunbury in Western Australia, not far from where your mate lives and I've looked at the map and can't see anywhere French between us and Australia."

Once he'd convinced me, I began to get really excited. It suddenly felt like after a year and a half, I might soon be turning up at Ken's door!

Then Legs joined us very excited about a letter from his brother Vince who having travelled for a year overland to Australia, had landed himself an unbelievable job manning a barge around some idyllic tropical islands in the Indian Ocean. Legs read on.

"It's ninety miles out from the remote northwest coast of Australia, in the exotic sounding Buccaneer Archipelago at Yampy Sound. The island is called Cockatoo Island. He says he's earning unbelievable money and to top it all, the food's fantastic and free, and the cabin accommodation which is cleaned out once a week, is free as well!"

The letter even described where the island was, and included the address in a small town called Derby where he had applied for work on the Island. From Derby it was 90 miles to the island, but workers were sent there by plane, free.

There and then I decided to go and man a barge in that wonderful sounding Buccaneer Archipelago. It soon became our main topic of conversation especially when Fred, another one of the crew, came up with a large scale map of Western Australia, which we all eagerly poured over, looking at the thick red line that ran right up the left side of the page, marked 'Great North West Highway'.

Sure enough, there among a lot of dots, way up off the top left corner of the page, were those wonderful sounding words, Buccaneer Archipelago, Cockatoo

Island, Yampy Sound and Derby. It was real, it was exciting, it was where I was going, and visiting Ken disappeared from my mind.

Also, the fact that I was still incarcerated aboard the *'Estonia'* didn't seem to figure in my thinking.

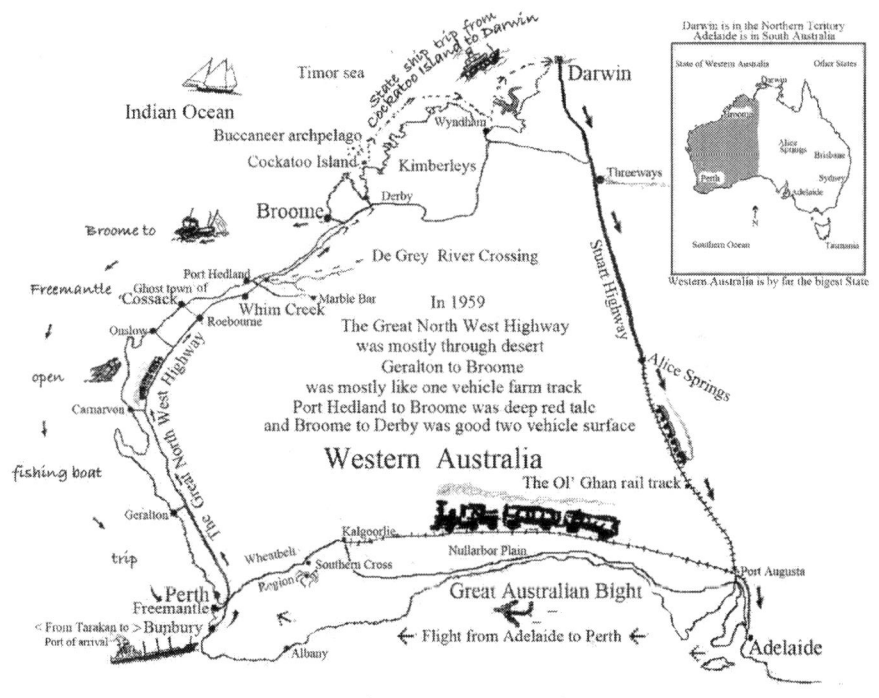

Map of Western Australia.

We all concluded, that as it was the only road north and was probably dual carriageway for most of its length, and that in order to manage the immense distance of nearly two thousand miles, it would be best to break the journey into two stretches. Roughly halfway the clearly marked town of 'Whim Creek' looked a reasonable choice, we thought it should be possible to pick up a bit of casual work, rest a while, maybe take in a film, and then when refreshed, continue the second leg of the journey on to Derby.

Once there, it would only be a simple matter of finding the office and getting a job on Cockatoo Island!

At crack of dawn, the *'Estonia'* anchored off Bunbury. I was eagerly watching the land, when I was once more summoned to the bridge.

Bligh was pacing the deck, and as usual speaking without looking at me.

"I'm nay botherin' to bloomin' lock tha up, coz' if tha's daft enough to damn well get off 'ere, I don't think tha'd make it 'alf way afore sharks'd 'av' thee, an' tha'd be out of ma 'air fer good. An' damn good riddance too, s'far as I'm concerned."

He stopped for a bit and was silent while I waited expectantly.

Then still not facing me, he waived a dismissive hand.

"S'all I got t' say t' thee. So now get off ma bloody bridge!"

I left wondering at the strangeness of human nature, but pleased with the new situation.

Later, tied up at the docks and still free to roam the ship, I chatted with the dockworkers, knowing that all over the world those guys tend to spread information, and by repeatedly asking questions about the road east to Sydney planted a rumour about my intended direction which of course, was the opposite.

Friends that knew I was leaving came to see me off. Legs passed me a message to give to his brother on Cockatoo Island. Paul and George gave me a dark blue suit and shirt, etc. while another deckhand, Joe, wished me well with an undersized pair of black leather shoes for my two thousand mile journey. *Alphonso* came looking really sad and handed me a huge wrapped stack of sandwiches.

Then Ernie arrived, surprising us all by confiding that he was abandoning his career by jumping ship and tagging along with me.

Half an hour later on the 30th of September 1960 having set off from Aldershot in the spring of 1959 and escaped from *Philippeville* around the 4th of June 1960, I was now heading with Ernie, a stack of sandwiches, tight shoes and a smart suit, for a place that looked to be nearly 2,000 miles up in the remote tropics of the far north of Australia, beginning our journey towards a paradise island.

....

CHAPTER TWENTY-NINE
'Headin' For Paradise'

I wondered how safe being in Australia would be, given that the British ship and Gibraltar had definitely not been.

I figured if the Australian authorities got me they would lock me up pending deportation by the '*Estonia*', or another ship of her line, and if it was the '*Estonia*' I would once again be at risk from any of the French ships or ports dotted around the globe.

But for now, I was here, very optimistic and intending to make the most of it.

A quick series of short lifts saw us well on our way, during which we discovered that the most common car in Australia was the Holden, that a Pick-up was called a Ute, an Articulated lorry was a Semi-trailer or Semi and that everyone, no matter who, seemed to call each other mate.

We were soon passing Perth and there was temptation to turn up at Ken and his mum's house, particularly as Ernie kept saying we would have a much easier start if we had contacts in Australia. As much as I agreed with his logic and knew they would have really welcomed us, fed us, and put us both up, I wanted to be able to contribute something before allowing that to happen. Besides, I was now fired up and keen to see the wonderful sounding Buccaneer Archipelago before getting myself deported.

Ironically, after those thousands of miles travelled we may just have passed within a few hundred yards of Ken's home.

Between lifts as we progressed north out of the Perth area, standing at the side of the dusty road with no shade became uncomfortably hot, especially wearing a dark suit and no hat, plus the tight shoes were already painful. I saw a young bronzed guy, working on the roof of what we would call a bungalow, but just a house in Australian terms.

He was wearing shorts, singlet and a wide brimmed hat.

I went over to him and called, "**Here mate do you want to swap those clothes you're wearing for mine?**"

"**Ah good on ya mate, too bloody right I do. Hang on, we'll be straight down fellas.**"

Him and his mate were already half down the ladder with big grins. "You blokes are pommies right? Where yer both headin' then?"

We told him we were heading for Derby.

"**Strewth**, she'll be bloody hot up there mate, that's a dead cert. Yer sure gonna need water bags. Reckon we could sort a couple out for these poms, what do you reckon Dave?"

"Ah no sweat, and fix 'em up a couple of swags while we're at it."

After a lot of laughter around swapping clothes and jokingly showing them off, we were hitching again, but now I had an Aussie bush-hat, shirt, shorts, and boots that more or less fitted. On top of that, the guys had provided a full water bag between us and made us up a bedroll each.

It was a great boost to our journey and made us much less conspicuous as well as being a great introduction to the easygoing Australian way.

Along the way we had seen several cars with these water bags dangling off their big front fenders, and they're a pretty ingenious invention, a sort of 'hang-up-able' closed canvas pouch, with a nozzle and plug at one top corner. When they're new the water just runs through the fabric, but as the saturated fabric swells it only sweats, which in a breeze, results in making the water inside really cold. Conveniently for drivers a thick layer of dust on them quickly becomes mud, which works even better.

Shortly after the clothing exchange a big semi pulled up a long way ahead of us. We hesitated to follow, until we saw the passenger door fly open for us, at which point we both ran forward until we could look into the hot tin box in which sat the sweating driver.

"I'm headin' for Port Hedland guys, if that's any help. Sorry for makin' ya's run like that, but I couldn't 'ave stopped any quicker with this bloody load of rail track up, strewth not even if I'd wanted to! Jump in fellas, an' make ya-selves good, ay!"

We thanked him enthusiastically, both scrambling into the hot fumes and noise of the rumbling diesel engine, which inside that rattling cab sounded like the demolition of a corrugated iron shed.

The oil blackened grinning red-haired driver was lean, sinuous and greasy, wearing a black singlet and the skimpiest pair of shorts I'd ever seen which were also black, and in his driving position failed to cover the very parts they were meant to cover. As I introduced us as Ernie and Steve, I noticed he was driving with bare filthy feet.

"They call me Bluey, same as every other bloody Australian with red hair!" He called out to us, as if that were explanation enough!

Having no idea how far Port Headland was, I asked how far north he was going.

"Ah, she'd be a bit over a thousand miles I reckon!" Is what I thought I heard him say, as he crunched into the first of a series of gear changes with the engine becoming progressively louder at each shift.

Once under way, we could see how quickly oil fumes spread about the place and Bluey's dirty appearance began to make sense and we knew we'd both soon look the same.

Cutting the revs between a gear change, Bluey part-leaned across the engine that was situated between us so he could shout loudly with a grin,

"Hope you blokes don't mind helping off-load this stuff at the other end, she's a fair 'ol lift?"

"Yeah!" We both shouted while nodding enthusiastically.

There was no point in talking, but a fair 'ol lift it would turn out to be, and not far off a thousand miles up the original old dirt forerunner of today's modern bitumen highway. It would be to a cattle station, just south of Port Hedland, where we would work up a sweat helping Bluey unload the heavy, hot, railway lines to provide corral fencing for the property.

We would come to feel pleased to have worked our passage, as not only was it a long lift, but it would also turn out to include bed and board! Bed, mostly the hard sand beneath a massive dome of stars that at that time of year in the northwest felt almost touchable. Board, would be the 'billy' – an old dried milk tin with holes pierced for a wire handle and blackened from regular dangling over a campfire.

We would all stand anticipating as water was boiled over a raging spinifex grass fire, until the liquid became smoky. Once fiercely boiling, a handful of tea-leaves would be thrown in so it could boil again and rise fast, then following one more lift off and rapid boil, the billy would be lifted off the fire real quick and tapped vigorously to create surface vibrations that would make tea-leaves sink to the bottom.

With an overdose of white sugar, the smoky brew would taste wonderful, especially if accompanied by steak and damper, a flour, salt and water bread, fire-baked in the hot ashes beneath the Australian sky. Finally, sand was thrown over the hot ashes where the remaining damper would retain its heat overnight to be ready for breakfast.

Because the engine was between us and Bluey the racket only allowed for shouted words which not only felt awkward, but also necessitated the engine's revs being cut which slowed our heavy truck's progress.

Little was said until, some hours later when we had been driving along an endless farm track, I picked up Ernie's look of concern and shouted, "**Bluey, where are we going now?**"

The answer came back straight enough. "**North mate.**"

Half an hour later, still concerned, I tried again. "**Bluey, why have we turned off the highway?**"

He dropped the revs right down, "**Whad'ya mean mate?**"

He looked genuinely puzzled and I hesitated, not wanting to show mistrust. "**Why are we going along this track instead of the highway?**"

He looked across with a huge grin, nodding vigorously and dropping the revs while shouting, "**Hang on a bit fellas, I'm stopping.** Ah that's it guys, she's right."

We had come to a halt.

"This 'is' the highway, what were you poms expectin'?"

Surprised, I looked about at the endless farm track.

"Well," ventured Ernie, "I thought it would be like a normal road, you know?"

"Ah, fellas, this is the good part, wait till we get along a bit, she'll get a whole lot rougher than this, **my oath she will!**"

Gears crunched, revs picked up again drowning any further talk and the truck lurched forward, two or three more sets of crunching and soon it was as though the track moved endlessly towards us.

We sat mesmerised for what felt like endless miles as the odd incident of a vehicle passing became progressively less, but I noticed how cars now had the same big heavy duty fenders that I would later know as 'roo bars' on their fronts, from which hung the familiar canvas water bags.

When Bluey pulled over for a piss, a stretch and drink, we got to sample water from his mud-covered water bag and were amazed at just how cold the water was.

"Shouldn't we try and get some of this mud off Bluey?" I asked.

"Ah jesus no mate, y'd ruin it, she's just comin' real good."

Following that first stop it wasn't long before we saw the reason for roo bars, as we began hitting kangaroos with sickening regularity. The poor creatures, many the size of a calf or large dog, had an unfortunate tendency to run along as a group ahead and parallel to us, only to then suddenly veer across our path, and thump! Bluey didn't even lessen the revs.

The fact is, that in that heavily laden truck, there was no way of avoiding them. The roo bars didn't help them, but it did the intended job of protecting radiators and windscreens.

Night was even worse, when their eyes shone out of the blackness as they stood transfixed in the middle of the road waiting to be hit, and we hit them at the rate of eight or ten a night.

As we constantly shuddered over seemingly endless mile upon mile of rock-hard corrugated sand, there was an essential driving technique for dealing with it, which was to maintain a constant fifteen, thirty or forty-five miles an hour (depending on the vehicle's ability), or it would literally rattle itself to bits. Any abrupt stopping, particularly in a heavily laden articulated vehicle was out of the question as, even if it were unladen, it would surely jack-knife.

A great deal of tenacity, skill and vigilance were required to negotiate regular hazards, such as numerous hard concrete-like, rimmed pot-holes and the larger skid hazard bulldust pans, virtual mini lakes of fine dusty sand having the same abrupt concrete hard edge at their far side that could, and sometimes did, break a truck's back.

Heavy rain falling many miles away on ground so dry that water flowed over its impermeable surface sometimes unpredictably crossed the highway, and formed temporary ditches by boring its way through a soft sand crack in the concrete-like sand. These were called run-throughs. If a driver were lucky he might cross it while the edges were soft, even crumbling it for the next vehicle, but if a hard-edged version was encountered there could be serious consequences.

As Bluey had said, the further north, the rougher it gets!

In that relentless heat on long hauls sleeping drivers were not an uncommon problem, and where the terrain permitted, drivers could be coaxed out of their slumber by driving parallel while sounding the horn progressively and moving closer until the message got through to the sleeper's consciousness. When it worked, the awakened driver gave an acknowledging wave, re-oriented his vehicle, and drove on.

On one occasion much further north, I saw a driver running parallel to the road through a region that was dotted with trees. It was a nerve-racking process waking the driver, but he eventually did wake and miss all the trees, he was a very lucky man.

Overtaking was another dangerous and nail-biting business, especially when it involved blindly over-taking one of the massive lumbering road-trains, with its renegade trailers swaying wildly in alternate directions. Because a road train driver could see in his mirror no further back than the bank of dust that followed close behind his cab, he had no option but to leave an overtaking driver to gamble his or her life and lives of passengers in a desperate manoeuvre to overtake. As the road was not wide enough for two vehicles, the overtaking vehicle's offside wheels would have to drop along the water table gradient that sloped outwards from the road.

Anyone that risked overtaking one of these on the Great Northwest Highway in 1959 placed themselves in the lap of the gods!

Just negotiating the opaque trailing dust cloud, often many times longer than the already lengthy road train, was hard enough but then the over-taking driver had to hope the truckie would be awake enough to maintain a steady course, and that the two, three or four trailers would remain relatively steady.

Finally, unable to see ahead, the over-taker had to trust that fate wouldn't send a vehicle, coming the opposite way! It was a case of trust, foot down, drive blind, cling to the water table, hold breath and pump the horn over a prolonged period, maybe praying.

Often, the first indication that an alert road-train driver was likely to know about being overtaken, was actually seeing the vehicle emerging from the dust far too late for evasive action in the event of an oncoming vehicle.

On a seemingly unending drive seeing one vehicle in five or six hours, it was not unusual, having sat behind a road-train for over an hour in a vehicle that should be speeding across the corrugations rather than rattling to pieces, to risk a blind pass. Many took the chance and most succeeded.

But a few didn't, and on meeting an oncoming vehicle were wiped out, or violently nudged off the road by a swaying trailer to somersault off the gradient without the truck driver so much as noticing. Bluey told us a couple of times that the big road-trains up the Territory, often pulled four or more trailers.

"Yeah but, they got the bitumen up there, and a thousand miles of beaut' straight road but!"

The land we were passing through was truly a land of vast panorama. Not a cloud in the sky, apparently for months at a time, and dancing dust spirals or willy-willies and bigger roaring cock-eye-bobs playing endlessly across the whole gigantic vista. Often the heat limited visibility, creating mirage like impressions mostly of small or large expanses of water that mostly disappeared into a haze. I was convinced they were water as we trundled relentlessly towards them, only to watch them move further ahead, then eventually disappear.

Bluey liked emphasising that the further north we went, the bigger things got. Flies and their swarms, mozzies, ants and snakes all got bigger, and even the relatively harmless willy-willies and cock-eye-bobs sometimes turned into huge devastating Cyclones.

"Like I told youse, even the bloody road-trains get bigger up north. Strewth, ya don't overtake one of those bastards without holdin' yer breath mate, I can tell ya!"

As we travelled further up the Great North West Highway, we saw fewer and fewer vehicles of any sort or anything else other than wild life. Three trucks and one car was all we saw on the long drawn out day before reaching our destination which was a cattle station near Port Hedland. We parked up for the night so as to arrive at the homestead early enough to unload the iron rails before they would become too hot to handle. If we hadn't stopped to open a gate I'd never have known we were leaving the highway as we drove another twenty or so miles up what turned out to be the front drive of the homestead.

An old man waved us to the unloading area half a mile on and we passed a distant group of, what Bluey told us, were aboriginal families that lived and worked on the station, but they were too far away for us to see properly.

After a few hours of unloading the hot lengths of track, Bluey called us for some tucker. It was the biggest plate of meat I'd ever seen, just meat, oh, and beer! But between the hungry three of us we did a bloody good job of demolishing the food and Bluey was happy to knock back enough beer for three blokes, and that was breakfast!

We spent most of the day sitting about in the shade while Bluey did some maintenance work on his truck, then he decided to take us the remaining miles into Port Hedland. On arrival, he insisted we accept at least enough money to get some eats, even offering to find us somewhere to bed down for the night. We thanked him, only accepting enough money for fish-n-chips and a couple bottles of soft drink, telling him we wouldn't sleep there as we really wanted to keep heading north.

"Oh yeah, you blokes might be interested to know that the station owner heard something on the radio a few days ago about road blocks on the Nullarbor for two absconding seamen from a ship in Bunbury. They were supposed to have been heading east for Sydney. Stewth, fancy that, ay? Good luck to 'em both I reckon, 'an good luck to you blokes too. Best keep on the road but, ay."

We were both grinning and a bit unsure, but then seeing Bluey's obvious enjoyment, we were soon having a good laugh as we realised that my ruse with the dockers had truly paid off, they had obviously spread the word perfectly.

(The Nullarbor is that vast tree-less plain on the long highway east.)

Following goodbyes, thanks and good lucks from us two, Bluey, in his now un-laden truck, gave a big wave then roared into sudden action as we scattered to avoid the whirling dust cloud.

Then we headed enthusiastically for the 'Eats' place where we not only satisfied our hunger, but we also got a free shower thrown in. By the time we were through it was dark and pointless to risk hanging around. So, we walked blindly out along the bitumen causeway to wait for our next lift.

CHAPTER THIRTY
'The Great North West'

Port Hedland, having around three thousand people, was the biggest town in the whole four hundred and twenty four thousand square mile North West, an area roughly three times the size of the UK. It definitely felt like a town where we could have picked up a few hours work, rested and maybe watched a film, unlike the original choice of Whim Creek that aboard the '*Estonia*', we had all thought would be a town somewhere along a dual carriage way.

The fact was, we had already past Whim Creek, noticing it only as a rickety, corrugated iron, shanty type building that stood isolated in a vast landscape. There was nothing else visible other than a few tin windmills, scattered among acres of short, dry spinifex grass that reached to the horizon in every direction.

Curiously, that single storey 'hotel' had a heap of empty beer bottles half its own height standing right next to it. Given that only three vehicles had passed us during that whole day it was a bit of a mystery as to where the people came from who drank all that beer. I didn't like to ask Bluey about it, as it would have necessitated a gear change and slowed us up, just when the uncomfortable hot, dirty journey was nearing its end. Both Bluey and the lift had been fantastic, but we were all relieved and looking forward to it ending.

Out on our misty dark causeway, the fish-n-chips and warm shower had really

The isolated Whim Creek Hotel with its famous mountain of beer bottles, with willy-willies dancing on the distant horizon.

set us up well, but now we were out there in such a blanket of darkness, we became uneasy that our narrow strip of road was surrounded, judging from the frog and reptile sounds, by either Mangrove swamps or mud flats. As everything was getting bigger up North, we had no idea what might walk, crawl, swim or fly in that darkness around us as we stood waiting uneasily, glancing dramatically towards every sudden noise. But it was what flew that really got us - millions of biting, illusive sand flies that seemed to get at every bit of skin, covered or not. It made any chance of normal stillness impossible. We covered skin as best we could and sat tight, back to back in the middle of the road as far from the mud as possible, it was all we could do.

Later in what felt like, but probably wasn't, the middle of the night, we were suddenly brought to our feet by the roar of a big approaching engine. Eagerly grabbing our scattered bits, we stood up waving our arms and other items hoping to be seen. Moments later, blinding head-lights bore down on us with a truck's horn blasting, we thought it was to show that the driver had seen us, but when the lumbering semi finally come to rest, in what turned out to be an urgent stop, we had to run a hell of a long way to catch it.

By which time the engine was off, the passenger door thrown open and a loud voice was hollering.

"**Stone the bloody crows fellas, you'll never know how bloody lucky you were! Sta-ruth I could have killed ya both. Bloody oath that's given me a nasty turn, I thought ya were a couple of bloody boomers and I wasn't gonna stop.**"

We couldn't see the driver, but he sounded good.

"Well if ya wanna lift to Marble Bar, yer can both jump right in, an she'll be right."

We didn't need to think twice, Marble Bar was way off our route, but anything was good that could get us away from those nasty little biting buggers, along with whatever else might have been lurking around that causeway.

"How far is Marble Bar?" Called Ernie.

"Oh we should be there come daylight, she's not a bad road. Feel free t' spread yer swag n' make some space, there's plenty of it in here. Yea, n' grab some shut-eye if you want, coz once I crank this ol' girl up it'll be too noisy to talk. Name's Dave by the way. **Strewth, that gave me a …**"

Before he had finished the sentence the engine was roaring, and in less than five minutes the noise had lulled me to sleep.

We were thrown into sudden wakefulness by the rock-n-roll of the swerving semi as the big bearded driver, now clearly silhouetted, was swinging his wheel, revving and crunching through numerous gears, while climbing, dropping and steering erratically among small steep hills.

Occasionally he thundered across a dried-out riverbed, precariously negotiating the twin concrete tracks that were provided for that purpose.

"**Not too bloody far now fellas.**" He shouted, during the break between a less frantic gear change.

A few miles of gentler driving followed, before steaming, creaking and lurching like some prehistoric beast our truck came to a shuddering halt in the middle of nowhere and Dave cut the engine.

"Here we are chaps." He said, sweating and grinning in a mock English accent "That is how you pommies say it, don't you?"

It was light enough to see now that as well as being big, Dave was muscular and his beard was black. He was wearing the same type of black singlet and shorts that Bluey had worn, only his shorts did a better job of covering the parts they were meant to hide, and unlike Bluey, Dave wore boots.

As we all clambered from the cab he was already down and knocking his bush hat into shape while taking a long leak against a front wheel. It was then that I realised an advantage to those minute shorts.

"It'd be a bloody sight better for me if you guys walk in the last bit, it'll only take about fifteen minutes." He said, with his back still partially towards us. "Only see I'm not meant to carry anyone with this kind of load up."

"What are you carrying?" Asked Ernie looking at the various boxes.

"Oh mainly mining stuff, but its the explosives are the main reason! Hey strewth, we wouldn't 'ave looked too good if that lot had gone up ay?!"

I caught Ernie's eye and didn't need to say anything, I knew that like me, he too was remembering those scary dry river crossings.

"What kind of explosives are they Dave?" Ernie called out, but the engine had already started and Dave was on his way, we stepped back to let the dust settle as he waved and trundled out of sight.

In spite of the dust and noise, I managed to hear Ernie shout, **"I don't think I want to know."**

We were still talking and laughing about the journey, when some thirty minutes later, we were looking at a scene that prompted us to turn about and hitch back the way we had come.

Marble Bar, reputed to be one of the hottest towns on Earth, it may even be the hottest, sits inside a big doughnut ring of ironstone hills, black, hard rock that rings like a blacksmiths anvil when struck and retains the heat.

"You can fry bloody eggs on 'em mate, yer really can!" was what we heard repeated many times.

The ironstone hills not only retain heat, they build it up, making the days in Marble Bar like a furnace and the nights really suffocating. The town's temperature rarely drops much, and I read somewhere that it has been known to remain at over a hundred degrees Fahrenheit for two hundred and seventy consecutive days and nights!

What really put us off was the sight in that early shimmering heat of the few dark rusted corrugated iron buildings. Even the iron roof of the pub/hotel was dark. It was as if the residents knew that painting it a light colour would cool it down, but couldn't be bothered in the heat, especially with the lure of cold beer so compellingly close and available.

We expected a long wait but incredibly in less than twenty minutes, a beat up old short wheel based Land Rover came along and stopped for us. Inside, were four men wearing bush hats and, as I got closer, I could see that the two guys in the back were black men and the first Aboriginal people I had seen other than the distant group of Aboriginal families on the property where we had helped Bluey unload.

All four men were really smiling and had a sort of picnic air about them. Once we'd said our bit to the driver, who turned out to be another 'Bluey', he said they would all be happy to take us, but that they would be travelling bush and only as far as the Great North Highway at De Grey crossing which was, he said, "A pretty much dried up river crossing about seventy miles north of Port Hedland."

I looked at Ernie, it didn't mean much to either of us but we both nodded gratefully, it would get us back on our journey North, so our nod was an emphatic yes.

"Sling your swag in the back guys and squeeze in alongside Tracka fella."
"Hey move up Cook fella an' make some room for these guys."
"Yeah, bloody oath I will."
"She'll be right fellas."
Everyone, good naturedly adjusted to us, and our gear, smiling broadly.
Later as Bluey fended off an invading marsh fly with his hat, I caught sight of the ginger hair I'd been anticipating.
As we crushed our swag into suitable spaces, Drew, the front passenger called out, "Be plenty of bloody shade and water at De Grey guys."
"She'll be right there mates." Said Cook Fella.
And another voice, "Bloody good water tank so ya's won't go thirsty I reckon."
"Crocs won't go hungry but." Threw in Tracka fella.
"Bloody oath they wont, not with a couple of nice tasty poms straight from the old country, ay!" Called out Drew.

It all felt really good-natured and somehow it was how I imagined Australia would be. While the guys had been pitching in their comments and laughter, we had squeezed our gear and ourselves into the available space and were already 'out bush'. It was then that I realised 'bush' was a term that meant away from the road and nothing to do with bushes.

All four men were stockmen, the Australian version of cowboys, wearing the traditional hat, shirt, jeans and high-heeled pointed boots of their trade. They were on their way back to a cattle station somewhere west of that long highway that we were getting to know so well.

Driving cross-country was a whole lot better than driving on the so called main road, as most of the land was flat, rock hard sand between sparsely growing spinifex and with none of the familiar corrugations, pot holes or bull dust pans to negotiate, and no cattle trains to sit behind, but it certainly wasn't always possible to follow a straight line. A land rover or similar vehicle was essential though, as its characteristics were often called on to negotiate dry creeks or pockets of soft sand. It was near the end of the dry season and as Bluey pointed out, the track was now at her best, but the coming 'wet' would change it real fast.

Although wild life had been plentiful all up the highway, here it was prolific with rabbits, kangaroos, goannas, snakes, lizards, emus, camels, and a multitude of colourful birds. Their trails were everywhere in the red sand, and we saw a massive goanna, which to everyone's amusement, I thought was a crocodile.

It was exciting, and worrying, when Tracka fella announced. "We're in croc country now."

"Real bloody man-eaters." added Cook fella. "Dinkum sea-going buggers."

"Yeh, Salties." Said Drew. "The massive estuarine buggers that can grow up to forty feet!"

"There's no trees to climb here." I said, looking around and trying to sound casual. "Wouldn't do you much good mate." Said Tracka fella, the guy whose voice I could now put a face to. "My oath it wouldn't, a forty foot salty could reach up thirty feet an' grab ya in his paw just like that!"

"Yeah, an' the buggers can run fast." Said Drew. "Well over twenty miles an hour for a short distance."

It didn't take much to capture our imaginations, especially as we pointed out that we were about to sleep in our bedrolls next to the De Grey River.

"Bloody dangerous near rivers." Said Cook Fella grinning, as all four of them relished in our obvious concern.

"Bloody oath guys." said Drew. "All this talk about pom-eating crocs has made me real hungry, must be about time for some tucker I reckon."

"My oath." said Bluey.

"Bloody oath!" came the general chorus of agreement from everyone, including us poms.

Bluey parked us near a spiky tree and we all helped rig a tarpaulin to the Land Rover from a couple of sharp branches. Although we had stopped to boil the 'billy' and cook tucker in the shade, I think it was just as much so those guys could sit down with their rare captive audience, and embroider the facts. For no sooner had we shared a pan of steak and hash knocked up by Cook fella, than they all launched off in earnest about man-eating crocodiles, massive man crushing pythons, deadly venomous snakes, sharks, lethal box jellyfish, cyclones, floods and raging bush fires. All with Cook fella and Tracka fella constantly and willingly drawn in to lend native authenticity to the popular Australian hobby of yarn spinning, such as…

Drew: "Do you remember that python that got a hold on Larry's foot?"

Cook fella: "Yeah, 'im bloody big snake, my oath 'im big."

Tracka fella: "Bloody thing start swallowing 'im leg not let go."

Bluey: "I'll say, he was halfway up Larry's leg when we had to cut the bugger off him with an axe, ain't that right Drew?"

Drew: "Bloody oath we did mate, that was some snake, my oath if it bloody wasn't. We couldn't get it all off but."

Bluey: "Yeah poor Larry was really crook, he was left with the rest of it hanging off his foot."

Tracka fella: "Bloody right,' im couldn't get the bugger off no matter what."

Drew : "We talked about burning the bugger off, but Larry wouldn't 'ave it."

Cook fella: "No, Larry not 'avin' none of it, can't blame the poor bugger but."

All four men were seriously muttering and nodding. Ernie looked at me, dead serious.

"So what happened then?" He asked, looking at all of them hopefully.

Tracka fella: "D'ya remember Bluey? D'ya remember what happened?"

Bluey: "No mate, dammed if I can bloody remember. What about you Drew, you saw 'im the other day. What happened to Larry an' the snake?"

Drew: "Well far as I could make out, poor ol' bugger's still got it mate and he's wearing the bloody thing as a boot now."

Tracka fella leaned forward frowning earnestly and said quietly, "Jesus I reckon that would be a bloody tight boot!"

Chorus.. "Bloody tight boot," "My oath she'd be bloody tight!"

I laughed, nervously. Ernie didn't. We'd been well and truly taken in by all four stockmen and now they were happy.

With a very straight face, Ernie changed the subject asking Drew something about the tree we were under.

"That's just a shrub mate, wait till ya see the Boab trees we got further up North, they look like bloody fat arsed milk bottles, with branches coming right out of their bloody necks."

"Them upside down trees." Said Tracka fella seriously. "Them show off too much, now them been punished!"

Bluey took over, telling us how somewhere back in the 'Dream Time' those trees grew the other way up, but they were too proud and showed off by growing too big which upset the other trees. So, the wise Ancients ripped them out of the ground and planted them upside down as a lesson for having been too proud.

I was fascinated to know more, but the conversation didn't stay informative for long, as all too soon, in spite of our efforts to avoid it, the talk returned to hungry crocs casing a man for days and watching his every move, then at the right moment grabbing and dragging him into the water to roll and drown him, then take him to his underwater larder! What was true and what was fiction we didn't know, especially when Drew told us of an incident that year where all that was ever found of a man that disappeared, was his pile of neatly folded clothes beside croc tracks to the water!

Time was being passed pleasurably at the expense of pommy naivity, but Ernie's dry humour did redress the balance a little, when he managed to lead Drew and Cook fella into earnestly correcting their story, by assuring us that the croc hadn't actually folded the pile of clothes on the river bank.

Yep, we poms were certainly being exposed to the North West, and were quickly discovering that up there even yarns get bigger!

CHAPTER THIRTY-ONE
'Roo Tail and Damper'

De Grey crossing, when we got there, comprised of two long concrete tracks beneath a few inches of slow moving water. It linked the tree lined banks of what was mostly dried-up riverbed, and was where we would have crossed had we not gone to Marble Bar. Now it was where we would turn right on our journey towards Derby.

The large trees that grew all the way along the top of both steep banks provided plentiful shade and other than the sandy Highway, there was just a typical mechano-style windmill accompanied by its round corrugated iron, five-foot high water tank. Besides those, and the unbroken tree line running both East and West, there was only the ocean of spinifex stretching in each direction towards a horizon that had long disappeared into mirage or heat haze.

Having pressurised Drew into showing us crocodiles, he now volunteered, saying. "Alright mates, s'pose I'd better dig out the old croc gun an' show youse poms the only kind of good croc there is. A dead one!"

After he'd pulled out the gun I grabbed a chunky log before running to catch up with him and Ernie, then the three of us strolled along the nearside edge of the almost waterless riverbank. Both banks were high, steep muddy hills right up to the trees. Half a mile on, I was becoming progressively disturbed that Drew was looking up towards the top of the hill at gaps between the tall trees, as if expecting to see the brutes up there and not down towards the river bed, where I thought they should be. The Aboriginal guys had only that day been colourfully explaining to us, how never to get between a croc and its water.

"Them big fellas mate. Run straight past you an' bring their big bugger tail round an' sweep you in water. Then that big fella gonna roll you mate."

Drew was disturbingly non-committal when I questioned him, which reminded me of an experience a few years earlier where I had responded pitifully to a charging wild boar in New Zealand.

At that time I was an impressionable 16 year old boy-rating, working a 'round the world trip' aboard the 'Southern Cross'. I had foolishly, thinking it was a manly thing to do, shown off by jumping ship in Wellington. Following various naive incidents, such being unprepared at an interview for a store job in Auckland, where I had fled when the lady interviewer went for help, concerned that I had told her I didn't live anywhere. And another occasion, having been dropped off in pitch darkness by my 'lift', it seemed only natural to put on my required 'boy rating kit' pyjamas to sleep in a remote field and to carefully arrange newspaper over myself, as I'd heard 'that's what tramps did'. In spite of such inexperience, somehow I got a job on a sheep farm where, after heavy rains, my job was to help waterlogged sheep stand up as their thick growth of wet wool made them too heavy to get up by themselves.

Graham, the very fit farm owner that employed me, talked a lot about pig hunting which sounded really exciting. One day when he was telling me about his 'Maori' farm hand losing a calf muscle to a charging pig, and the numerous wounds and loss of ears of his pig dogs, I reminded him of his promise to take me pig hunting. "You're right." He said, spontaneously grabbing some cartridges from the mantle piece. "We only seem to have three here, I suppose they'll have to do." Then, accompanied by three battle-scarred 'pig dogs' we set off into the bush and it wasn't long before we heard that his dogs were on the scent.

I got very excited grabbing a heavy stick as we both ran towards the commotion, which we couldn't see through the scrubby trees, but which indicated that the dogs had bailed up a pig. Closer, the scene was hectic. The boar was massive and ferocious. Suddenly my stick didn't count!

Meanwhile Graham had calmly dropped to one knee, aiming his rifle while commanding the dogs to stand aside, at which the angry beast charged.

"Stand behind me." He muttered, as the first shot went off.

We were among tall, flimsy tea trees too thin to hide behind, too dense to run through unless you happened to be a dog or pig, and certainly they were far too weak to be climbed. Seeing the third shot fired at an enraged monster that was close and still charging, I dropped the stick to frantically scramble up the nearest tree, which only curved over and put me back on the piggy-drome with the beast still coming!

In blind panic I just kept jumping, frantically willing that rubbery tree to stand up. Thankfully, unbeknown to me, the gun had more than just the three bullets that I knew of, and the fourth shot that I didn't even hear dropped the boar in its tracks.

Graham just fell about laughing at my antics while patting his dogs who were now already well behaved and happy. I was still shaking like a leaf and feeling stupid as between us we only managed to carry half the pig home.

Now here we were casually strolling along a riverbank looking up in the hope of seeing crocodiles! And me with just a log of wood, clearly a slow learner!

We did see plenty of tracks, but no crocs, in fact sadly all we managed to find was a poor cow up to its shoulders in mud which Drew shot, saying, "It's gotta be better than one of those bastards getting her, makes me crook just thinking about it. Strewth, what a bloody way to go!"

When we got back to the others, a road grader with a small white caravan and trailer attached was parked not far from the water tank. The trailer was laden with oil drums, pump, and other gear for servicing the grader and its driver, who Bluey was now talking to.

"Come and 'ave a drink." Shouted Bluey calling us over. "**Come an' meet this old bugger. This 'ere is Bill McCloud. Upset him, an' my bloody oath, you'll be good as dead!**"

Ernie was slightly ahead and by the time I got there, his hand was no longer his own but in the vice-like grip of the big overweight, sweating, saggy-bellied Bill McCloud. The black curly hair on his overhanging gut made up for the lack on his sweating bald head, and it blended well with his oil splattered, historically, but no longer white singlet.

As the singlet did a fine job of emphasising his bare, fat, hairy shoulders, so his grimy shorts, tied up with packaging string did an equal job of showing off his bare calves and feet that were stained by a mixture of red desert sand and diesel oil.

'Roo Tail and Damper'

Bill McCloud, I later found out, had once been a rodeo rider.

Now dropping Ernie's hand as he spotted me, he downed more beer before chucking the bottle to his other hand and snatching mine as though it was something overdue that he had every right to.

"I'm Bill bloody McCloud." He roared, his eyes narrowing. "Who the bloody hell are you? Another pommy bastard, I s'pose?"

He was hauling me close, shoving his face into mine, his blackish brown eyes boring deep in some ritualised onslaught of Wild West masculinity.

"I'm Steve Martell." I said firmly. "Steve Martell." I repeated, suddenly uncomfortable that it wasn't my real name.

His eyes narrowed even more, as for another ten seconds I got an almost mythical image of an older man trying to make me, the younger man, believe he could read my mind.

"Yehhh." He hissed, while nodding. "Yehhh." He said nodding again. "That'll do, bloody good enough for me. S'pose you'll be wantin' some bloody tucker now? Don't s'pose you bastards 'ave got any!"

He spat the words out, hard-eyeing us up and down with exaggerated disapproval, then he spat for real and stared at the frothing smudge on the sand.

The hard-man act went into a lull, as the two Aboriginal guys came back from somewhere in the land rover. Wherever 'somewhere' was, they'd got some turkeys and were keen to leave for the homestead before it got dark.

Once the several 'good luck' and 'good-on yer's ' were over, the land rover soon disappeared behind its cloud of dust as it trundled west along the tree line.

Bill bloody McCloud wasn't giving off an air of welcome, so we kept our distance. That was until we heard a shot. Curious to find out what he had hit, we ventured over in the general direction of the bang. Bill was holding up something and there was blood on his hands.

He shouted, **"You pommy bastards 'ad better like roo tail."**

We both decided there and then to bloody like roo tail!

"See here," he said later, wielding a big sharp knife, "you can both bloody watch me. You might just learn something. First, you cut the bastard tail off here, leave a bit of skin from the bastard's back like this, then you got yourself a flap, now you sink the knife in deep to carve around the bloody tail bones like this, until you can pull the bastards out, see!"

We could both see the bastards very well.

"In a few minutes I'm going to pack her up with vegetables, add a bit of flavouring, then I'll bring the flap over the top an' tuck her in. Then I'll wrap a bit of wire round her an' she'll be ready to go straight under the fire with a bit of damper. It'll be a bloody good meal, you'll see. **Now, do you bastards want a beer?**"

We both said we didn't drink, which wasn't the best thing we could have said. But neither of us drank, especially beer, nor did either of us like the taste. Besides which I always felt uneasy around the men who drank it, and I definitely would have felt uneasy about drinking with that angry man out in the middle of nowhere in the state he was in.

In those remote parts of the Australian Northwest it was practically a social problem 'not' to drink, and often taken as an insult by those who did, now we were encountering our first experience of that curiosity. In just refusing to drink his beer it was as though we were refusing to drink with him, so now any offers by us to help were disdainfully dismissed.

Meanwhile, he not only independently got on with the fire and the cooking but also laboured his point by indignantly moving his rig to a distant location. We were very hungry, but when the food was practically thrown at us, we were obviously grateful, but unable to really enjoy it knowing that Bill was angrily eating and drinking alone at some self-imposed location less than five hundred yards from us and many miles from any other living soul.

For a man whose work area spanned around three hundred miles of isolated road that he proceeded along day after day alone, grading the water tables at a rate of about three miles a day, it must have been a huge disappointment to meet new people, only to discover, that they didn't do what every civilised man in that vast territory did, i.e. drink beer. We both agreed there was little we could do but to try and improve matters with the sober man in the morning.

However, when we peered out of our sweltering bedrolls at sunrise, the blue sky, sun and flies were all there but no sign of the man. Bill 'bloody' McCloud, his grader, caravan and trailer were all gone.

Regrettably at that time, I'd yet to acquire the generosity that comes with maturity and experience. If the clock could be turned back, I would definitely share a beer or two with Bill McCloud.

....

CHAPTER THIRTY-TWO
'Magnetising Ants'

The numerous tin windmills dotted around the north west were for topping up water tanks that supplied animal drinking troughs, and definitely not for swimming. But hanging around for hours in that burning heat, a million miles from anywhere and on our own knowing full well that the tank beside us was full of cool clear water, eventually became too much, so to hell with the law! Singlets came off, shorts were dropped and in moments two hats floated on the surface above their wearer's who had sunk in five feet of luxurious cool artesian water. Soon of course it became sheer enjoyment.

So much so, that in the middle of wild splashing, ducking and laughter, we both failed to hear the sound of an approaching engine, nor did we see the truck until it was practically upon us.

Bizarrely, having waited hours for a lift, we reacted with a mixture of guilt and embarrassment, lowering ourselves into the water and hiding, relieved when the truck didn't stop. Then fingers and noses sticking over the rim we watched like a couple of cartoon 'chads' as the last of its dust disappeared into haze.

Both of us, totally oblivious to the fact that it would be the last sign of human life we would see for over five days!

For a time we chatted with enthusiasm about various possibilities such as swimming on Eighty Mile Beach, which was on our next leg of the journey. But by the end of that day Ernie was getting frustrated and kept climbing the same tree straining for a better view, as hour after hour he convinced himself that he could hear an engine coming.

For my part, I was happy enough most of the time trying to control the take off and landing behaviour of a marsh-fly having made an intriguing discovery. If I combed my hair to charge it, then inched the static-electric-laden comb towards an ant, the ant would first run, then struggle, then freeze, depending on the proximity of the comb. But whenever the comb was withdrawn, the ant seemed to carry on as usual, apparently untroubled by the event.

I knew that controlling the flight, landing and take off of one of those bee-sized, stinging, dry, marsh-flies wasn't going to be easy, but it kept me entertained for our whole period of waiting, and as with most discoveries, set off a chain of thoughts that have ramifications to this day.

For example, if a creature the size of an ant can't move in such a small, still, static electric field, what happens to the cells that make up our bodies when say a nylon or silk tie is worn over a cotton shirt and maintains a static field? Could that field inhibit cell function and contribute to conditions such as throat, breast or cervical cancer? After all they do seem to occur a lot in areas where nylon or silk is separated from the skin by cotton. I wondered if seeds would grow faster under moving static magnets or slower, or not at all, if the field were still?

Meanwhile, in the shade of that water tank during five days of waiting, both hunger and the long gone truck were discussed, many small creatures were magnetised, and the same tree was often climbed.

On the sixth day after arriving at the crossing, five cars roared past in quick succession with their occupants all waving at us, but without stopping! When the first car passed we were disappointed, but by the time four more had passed, frustration was really rising. So it was with uncertain relief that we walked towards the sixth car, as we could see that it too was full, and towing a trailer heaped high with iron beds.

A young sandy-haired driver, with some difficulty, extricated himself from the car and began kicking his tyres as in a German accent he called out.

"**Maybe stopping here was not good, it could be trouble to move now.**"

Then looking at us, he added, "But I could not just ignore you here. After all, it is sure the 'wet' will come, and I am the last car travelling from Port

Hedland before the 'wet'. Now is so dangerous for you here and it will be big floods, yes! I am *Schultz* by the way. Look you can see my car is so full, the only space will be on top of the beds, which I am taking for the Hospital in Broome. That is the only option I think, but maybe that is better than to drown!"

Seventy miles from Port Hedland, even more bush miles from Marble Bar and with some two hundred miles of sandy desert to cross before Broome, with a crocodile infested river about to flood, we all agreed that perhaps it was the only option. So, with *Schultz*'s help, we clambered gratefully on top of the iron beds. Then *Schultz* twisted himself into the car and started the engine.

Wheels spinning, swerving uncertainly, the car inched forward gradually accelerating to a driving speed that *Schultz* could maintain.
    Within a quarter mile I knew we were in an unbelievably precarious position, hanging on to iron beds that were unstable, likely to crush fingers or worse still be shaken adrift by the rumble of corrugations, as we erratically swerved and bounced around bull-dust pans.
    Then a mile further we ran into miles and miles of six-inch deep red sand that in the north west's dry season could only be described as talcum powder.

Isolated on our lurching world of dust and noise we could see nothing. As for *Schultz*, or his passengers, they could neither see nor hear us and there was no possibility of *Schultz* stopping the car to check us out and then get moving again.
    So, for several tense and sometimes panicky hours, we droned through choking dust unable to even communicate with each other for risk of choking, as we clung for all we were worth, to something that we hoped and prayed wouldn't break off. We both knew that to fall, or jump, would commit us to the mercy the Great Sandy Desert and Indian Ocean without drinking water or shade. Or, as the rains were imminent there might have been water, but with it the risks of snakes, crocodiles and/or drowning! Somehow the car didn't throw us off, we didn't fall, we didn't jump and we weren't suffocated.
    Schultz's sheer driving tenacity got us through the ordeal and safely on to the short bitumen road that led into Broome, and all without so much as a glimpse of that long anticipated Eighty Mile Beach.

The Compass of Naivety

On arrival at Broome hospital, as agreed, Ernie and I between much throat clearing and nose blowing, unloaded the beds and packed them into a small room. Meanwhile *Shultz* went to arrange for us to get cleaned up. By the time he returned he had not only organised wash facilities, food, bed and laundry for us, but also a lift into Derby the following day by a boyfriend of one of the nurses that had travelled in our car. Next morning, after washing away even more of the fine red sand, the same nurse surprised us both with breakfast.

Later, I took a short stroll around town which, at first glance, was a square dominated at one end by a sizable general store and hotel pub.
Down one side was an open-air cinema and small Chinese restaurant that formed part of a long row of corrugated iron houses that was China Town. Behind that, I realised, as a large passenger plane flew over extremely close, was the runway of Broome airport. A row of old rusting corrugated iron sheds ran down the opposite side backed by dark green mangroves and the rich coloured waters of Roebuck Bay.
The central area of the square, which was really a rectangle, appeared only sparsely filled with wood and corrugated iron houses.
I was immediately captivated by such a curious ramshackle place with its balmy tropical feel and pungent mangrove smell. It could have been anywhere remote and hot, except oddly enough Australia, and as I didn't see any white folk but did notice several obvious foreign-looking people, that impression was intensified.

Down by what I found to be the old pearling sheds, I met a white-haired, dark skinned, wiry old man who told me a lot about the town and its history. His name was Dev.
He told me, "I was sent here as a pearl-diver when I was twelve-years old from one of the Islands up north east Australia near Papua."
He went on to tell me how Broome, once a small insignificant backwater, had experienced a 'rush' for pearls, which suddenly swelled its little population to over five thousand people.
"They came from everywhere, all countries." He said, telling me how opportunists and adventurers had flocked with all that mixture of humanity that is magnetically drawn towards such events.
They included honest traders of goods and services, and perhaps less honest dealers in liquor, guns, drugs and the flesh, which created the need for boarding

rooms, hotels, drinking and gambling places, brothels and even opium dens.

Of those newcomers, around three thousand were divers, crewmen or workers for the four hundred pearling luggers, and most of them were Asian men, some with their families.

As Dev continued, the story came even more alive as he pointed at a pearling lugger actually out on the sea.

"Over four hundred luggers like that one used to sail in and out of that narrow channel through these mangrove swamps to this Jetty."

From a position up on a sort of veranda, Dev showed me the old hulks of two pearling luggers lying in the mud alongside the skeletal remains of a third.

Then turning about to overlook the unpainted rusty, yet curiously charming, miniature China Town, he drew my attention to the expanse of dried mud that served as the town's runway, and explained that two rusted engines still lay there from Japanese fighter planes that had crashed during the bombing of Broome in World War Two.

I knew that beyond that lay thousands of miles of the red heart of Australia.

I could have stayed longer listening to that white-haired old man, but I had my lift to catch.

"Which island are you from Dev?" I asked.

"Thursday Island." He replied, with a big smile lighting up his face.

"I look forward to seeing you again for more history lessons." I said, shaking his hand, and I meant it. I was hooked, and would definitely be back.

Walking back to meet our lift, I was wondering about what Dev had said and the hard work required in a pearling boom, thinking how the luggers that looked so serene and picturesque out on the blue waters were, in all probability, terrible sweat shops.

The fact that a cyclone, hitting the pearling fleet in 1887, resulted in a hundred and forty crew-members' bodies being washed up along Eighty Mile Beach, shows how sudden and dangerous weather in the cyclone belt can be. Devastating storms come up really fast. Immense local tide ranges create drastic currents both above and below the surface.

Yet it was in that environment that a diver day in, day out, hour after hour and many fathoms down, toiled away his years, totally dependent on the stability and reliability of the fragile ship above, along with its often ancient equipment. But perhaps even more, he depended on the sensitive alertness of his guide and communicator, that man or woman, who sat so patiently turning a handle to literally pump down 'life' through the long frail umbilical hose, all the time having to watch weather and sea, feeling for any hint of trouble.

Those divers were not only dependent but extremely vulnerable, being heavily restrained in stiff, ill-fitting, heavily-weighted diving suits. A man was condemned to moving awkwardly, almost blindly, across uncertain terrain of the ocean floor, toiling while hampered by tunnel vision as he peered out through the small, thick glass of his clumsy cell of a brass helmet.

He operated in a world of ongoing risk at depths where giant clam, shark and swordfish were just some of the threats. Large, friendly, but unwelcome, groper could playfully injure him or damage his precious air hose. A turtle might also mistakenly snap open any section of that life-line between unsuspecting diver and oblivious drifting lugger.

Yet, no matter how devastating the event, the diver knew the fatal consequences of a quick assent. Such a man could but live in trust to survive long enough to send sufficient money home, as for most divers it was a short, dangerous and painful life. Most aged prematurely and were often crippled and several did die horribly.

The pearling boom was greedy for lives, as nearly six hundred Japanese graves in the Broome cemetery testify.

Dev had also told me fantastic tales of intrigue and gambling as fabulous pearls changed hands for fortunes. He spoke of terrible things; murder, piracy and 'Blackbirding', which was a form of trading female slaves for diving without equipment. Often those women were abused at sea and still made to dive, even while pregnant.

I had felt strangely close to history, when Dev had told me of personally seeing aboriginal men brought into the town, chained together for marrying off to the valuable foreigners. Then later sent 'bush' just so the officials could satisfy their bosses down South, that only Australians lived in Broome!

Then the boom collapsed, the masses moved on to make new killings elsewhere, or perhaps to invest their new found, and in some cases ill-gotten, wealth into safe or lucrative options.

Broome continued at a much lower key, reaping the harvest of gold-lipped mother of pearl shells, used for buttons, combs and various trinkets, for the ladies of Europe and America. But fashions changed and more people from Broome moved on.

What remained, was a population unlike anywhere else in Australia, a town that was totally at odds with the rest of what was then, White Australia.

The Broome I encountered was apparently the only place in the whole country where whites were outnumbered and living harmoniously among Aboriginals, South Europeans, Chinese, Japanese, Koepangers from Timor, Thais, Malays and Torres Strait Islanders.

The individuals who had chosen to stay were there because that's where they wanted to be, in Broome, a ramshackle, mosquito and sand-fly infested town, practically surrounded by smelly mangrove swamps, but with an independent spirit and, although I didn't know all that at the time, I felt that spirit.

Much later I discovered that I had stumbled upon an unlikely 'bush Bohemia'.

Our house, backing on to Streeter's Jerry, as seen in 1962 from the open air cinema with China Town off to the right.

Back at the hospital, Ernie was waiting for our promised lift, which arrived ten minutes later in the form of a V.W. Beetle and its driver, who introduced himself as Paul.

He told us he would take us right to the Derby office where we intended to get our jobs in the Buccaneer Archipelago.

"It's a good road so it should be quick."

Five minutes later we were purring along the bitumen out of Broome and soon back on our old friend the Great Northwest Highway. But this section had been recently graded and was a smooth wide road, free of the awful pot-holes and bulldust, but alas not the corrugations.

Luckily Beetles were renowned for maintaining a safe sixty mph plus over uniform corrugations and for being dust proof!

I'd been looking forward to this last section of our journey taking us through boab country and sure enough we were soon passing through mile upon mile of Tracker fella's upside down trees. Their crazy waving arms looking, for all the world, like Alice in Wonderland figures dotted about the landscape, strange chess pieces rising out of a communal carpet of hard sand.

Boab trees like crazy wonderland chess pieces.

As only monotonous scrub followed the boab tree section, there was enthusiasm as we reached the intersection that marked for us the end of our long hitch north. Having reached its northernmost point within the state of Western Australia, the highway turns right skirting South of the Kimberley's and on towards the Northern territory. But we turned left and enjoyed the brief luxury of cruising into Derby on the smooth bitumen.

Paul dropped us right outside the wooden veranda house described in the letter that Legs had read to us on board the '*Estonia*'. It seemed an unlikely office for 'Australian Iron and Steel' and 'Broken Hill Propriety', but we lost no time in asking Kenny, the young guy in the office, for work on the islands.

"Ah, sorry guys there's no work at Yampi right now, but if you hang about there should be some in a few days."

I thanked him and explained our financial situation along with the fact we hadn't eaten since breakfast.

His response was immediate. "Ah, no sweat, guess youse both can do a bit of weeding round the place. Tell you what, I'll pay up front so youse can get some tucker for energy, ay!" He pushed forward a pen and chit. "Ah, sign this will youse?"

So we got to eat and do a few hours weeding before the day was over and had work for the next day, which meant we didn't have the problem of hanging about the small town and drawing attention to ourselves.

Several mornings later Kenny woke us on the veranda behind the office.

"No more gardening fellas, no more weeding work, but no worries, youse'll be flying out to Yampi this arvo."

Sure enough, that afternoon along with two truck drivers, who were returning to Koolan Island, we left Derby aboard the company's small plane.

....

The Compass of Naivety

CHAPTER THIRTY-THREE
'Islands in the Sky'

The company's Fokker Friendship flew northwest for a time up the King Sound, before veering north over colourful hill contours and white rimmed blue inlets of the Kimberleys, to then come out over exquisite blue waters before touching down to drop off the two truck drivers on Koolan Island. From there it was just a short hop above the Timor Sea to our eagerly anticipated destination.

Responding to our enthusiasm, the friendly pilot generously extended the hop to give us a glimpse over some of the islands that make up the wonderful sounding and beautiful looking Buccaneer Archipelago.

As far as I had been able to find out from Kenny in the office and the two truck drivers, Koolan and Cockatoo were the only islands being mined and the only ones having generally known names. At low water there were said to be over a thousand islands but no one seemed to really know how many, as forty-foot tides regularly covered many islands that later reappeared.

It seemed such a wasted opportunity that no one referred to this wonderful world as anything more exotic than Yampi.

Circling in, we saw the island was hour-glass shaped, but with one sphere larger

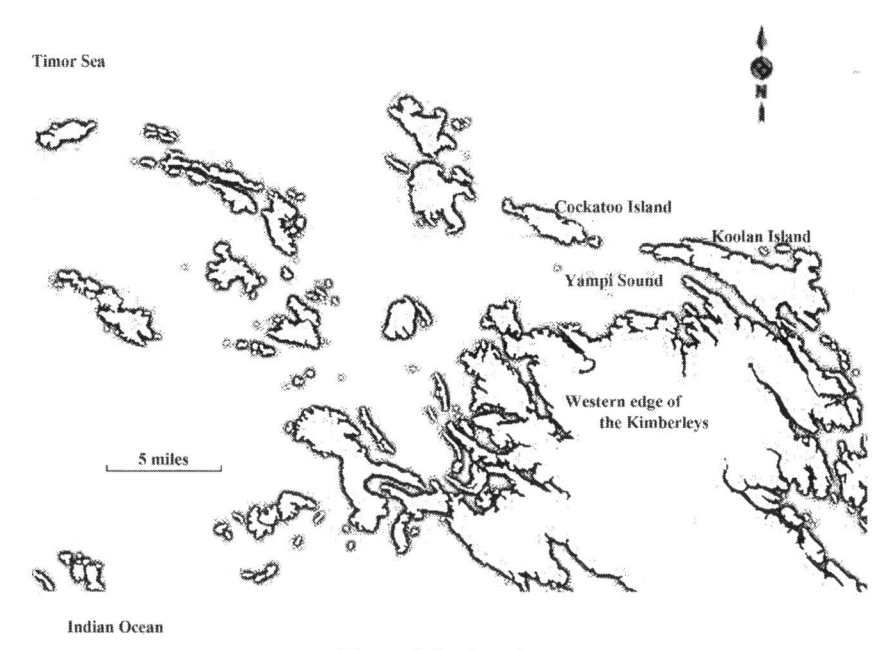

Map of Archipelago.
40 foot tides of the BUCCANEER ARCHIPELAGO
can expose over 1,000 islands at low tide.

than the other. As we flew past green vegetation and red cliffs of the larger segment, the open-cast iron quarries reflected blue in the sunlight as, like dinky toys, massive dumper trucks were being loaded by giant diggers, which inched about on huge steps that were the man made excavation levels. Everything was focused towards a long narrow extension that protruded seawards.

"That's the conveyor belt." Shouted the pilot. "And that long jetty across its end with the ship alongside they call 'The Dolphins'."

As we banked over the small sphere end of the island, a shallow bay the colour of jade with a perfect crescent of white sand flashed beneath us. Then a green hill over which stood a scattering of wooden houses sloping down towards the narrow waist of the island, which contained rows of huts and tents, an open-air cinema, a small tidal swimming pool and a concrete wharf.

A final look at the surrounding sea, islands and inlets confirmed that it was all as beautiful as we had imagined it would be. Wheels bumped along on Cockatoo's landing strip, and we'd made it, both grinning from ear to ear. Well, I was grinning, Ernie was sort of smiling.

Considering the significant part that Ernie had played in my life, and the time we spent together both before and after Cockatoo Island, it's surprising how little I got to know about him.

He was about five foot six, well-built, good looking with dark brooding eyes and black hair, mostly serious and didn't smile a lot, although he did have a dry sense of humour.

Ernie kept his cards so close to his chest, that when I asked him what his other name was, he replied, "Ernie."

I said. "No, I mean your other name."

"Ernie." He stated emphatically.

"What, Ernie Ernie?" I asked.

"That's right." He said, with no hint of a smile, so I left it at that.

On one occasion he told me that he came from South West London, had a mother and father and that the Merchant Navy had always been his career.

Beyond that, I saw on board the *'Estonia'* that he was a hard working Able Seaman and a loner who kept to himself.

Yet, he definitely reached out of that role when he chose to help me by taking several risks on my behalf, such as posting the knife to me when I was locked up and camouflaging me with oily cotton waste to prevent the authorities finding me. And certainly his calculations regarding the flooding of the tank I'd been locked in had probably saved me from a nasty death. Then much to my surprise, he blew his career by jumping ship to come with me and never really said why.

Perhaps in some way it represented a door, or an opportunity to change his life. Whatever it was, we never discussed it, but remained friends and re-connected several years after those events when he visited London with his wife.

Soon after arriving on the Island, as with all newcomers, we were accommodated at 'skid row', a line of tents each of which was a fully equipped room in itself, and a mere stone's throw from the sea. Later, as space became available, we were moved into single huts that were airy, clean, well lit and also faced the sea, but no longer quite as close.

I soon discovered that our floors were polished once a week when we received a generous supply of clean linen, including towels.

The communal shower blocks were immaculate and provided a twenty-four hour supply of hot water in abundance, which was amazing, considering that all water had to be brought to the island in the form of ballast on the otherwise empty iron-ore ships, that came thousands of miles from the eastern states of Australia to collect the iron ore.

There was a large airy dining room providing an endless variety of well-prepared food in large quantities, and not only was all of this provided free but we also had free use of the open-air cinema and tidal swimming pool.

On the hillside that we had seen from our plane, the wooden houses we spotted turned out to be for executive personnel and their families. There was also a shop for purchasing general goods, and what would later turn out to be some quarter of a mile scramble beyond the hilltop, there was that appealing crescent shaped white sandy beach. On the opposite slope from the houses, beyond the cinema screen and swimming pool, a steep single concrete lane led over the crest before turning into a red dirt road which crossed a mile of low trees and undergrowth towards the working area of open-cast mines.

Day one was spent receiving a really thorough medical, plus safety goggles, hard hats and steel capped boots in readiness for starting work on the following day. My actual job when it came to it was hard work and a far cry from manning a barge in a tropical paradise.

Wearing a harness, safety gear and nothing more than the same type of skimpy shorts that Bluey and Dave had worn in their trucks, I dangled precariously, in more ways than one, over the gaping throat of a broken crusher, alongside a young American traveller called Sam. We both wielded heavy sledge-hammers and energetically laid into each resisting rock until it yielded and fell crumbling and tumbling through our sleeping crusher and down into the wide awake pulsing jaws of crushers two, three and beyond.

Sam had just arrived on the island having achieved the feat of hitching overland from England in the days before the backpacker rush. He was a tall, well tanned 22 year old with shoulder length sun-bleached hair and a ready sense of fun.

We worked well together, enthusiastically hammering and sweating through our twelve-hour day or night shifts, both very fit and enjoying the sensation of using our bodies in that way. Once the latest rock had succumbed, we perched on the crusher's edge wiping away pints of sweat, chatting and joking, as the next thirty tonnes of ore was side-tipped by crane into our empty waiting crusher, from one of the giant chain driven 1937 Mack trucks, that waited in a long continuous queue.

They were unbelievably noisy work beasts that, with the help of a twenty-four hour maintenance program, had been kept running day and night for over twenty years, throughout extremes of wet muddy or dry dusty conditions, all of which they seemed to be at home in.

It seemed illogical that we two mere humans should be the key to that huge operation's speed, as the outcome of our hammering went tumbling through ever-smaller crushers. Eventually everything no larger than a fist was patiently fed on to a conveyer belt, by a man controlling a vibrator and wielding a sledge hammer whenever compacted ore clogged the outlet. He laboured alone through twelve-hour shifts in a compartment the size of a telephone kiosk deep underground, constantly peering through a cliff face window to witness the crushed ore rumbling steadily towards 'The Dolphins' for loading on to ships with names like 'Iron Yampi'.

It wasn't long before I noticed that many of the men on Cockatoo seemed to be there on self-imposed sentences to earn big money. They were clearly working their contracts unhappy and quite blind to the beauty around them, whereas Sam, like myself, was optimistic and with a grand sense of the ridiculous. We shared a similar appreciation and uncomplicated attitude.

Following each long dirty night shift, we were returned to our huts, riding on an open truck fast enough for a cool morning breeze to blow away some of the dust from our nights work. Because we knew hot showers, good food and comfortable beds awaited us, even a swim if we chose, we were able to fully appreciate the stunning view as we came up over the hill. A vista that would have defied photography and ridiculed any attempts at painting it. Suspended on an ever-changing backdrop of ocean and sky, partly due to the combination of light and extraordinary tidal conditions, was a scattering of variegated green and brown petal islands with red patches and white sandy beaches.

Like a fantasy image, they floated like 'Islands in the sky', and it was just as if we were actually floating in the midst of them.

Islands in the Sky.

Unfortunately, for those men who had seriously miscalculated and expected quicker rewards, time dragged. Money wasn't coming quickly enough and sadly, for most of them, it probably never would. Meanwhile they were closed to such experiences, their only pleasure coming from drinking.

In fact there was a bizarre behaviour pattern that was endemic among some of the workers, as every so often a couple of men would convince each other they'd had enough and get drunk with the lads to celebrate their determined decision to leave the island. In their inebriated state they would make arrangements with a couple of 'grog' infected mates to meet up in Derby, where they would buy a car and head down to Perth.

Later in Derby, they'd celebrate their arrival, sleep that off, have some food, and top it up with more beer by which time more mates both known and unknown would arrive and the pattern was set.

These 'one for the road' rituals, continued until they set off many days later than planned. Each rare meeting along the Highway was cause for more celebration, as every one in the whole North West was a 'mate'.

Given the huge distances and road conditions, plus time required to recover from roadside binges, it might take several weeks before they inevitably arrived at Whim Creek, that corrugated piece of isolation next to its mountain of beer bottles in the middle of nowhere. There, finding ice-cold beer, food and the company of occasional drinking mates from up or down the highway, they were destined to continue that same endless party.

"We were on the piss the whole time!" was a saying I'd got used to, but I never really got used to the Australian North West version, which was, "We were drinking piss the whole time!"

In that bizarre fashion it was common for men to finish off their whole pile of miserably earned cash, without ever getting beyond that hotel where they immortalised themselves by adding to its giant heap of beer bottles.

Then on a final 'broke' awakening, having long ago traded or gambled the car for more booze money, they would likely cadge a lift North with new mates and commit themselves to another term at Yampi, but on a different island to avoid the shame of having blown the price of a house, with nothing to show for it.

So, this was the story that solved the mystery of that heap of beer bottles next to Whim Creek Hotel, a picture immortalised by Rigby the cartoonist, now on postcards for sale at the modern Hotel's bar. It is a place with quite a history and many stories. One being that the original enterprising Landlord, acutely aware of the scarcity of passing trade, but trusting the Australian man's overwhelming need for cold beer, had a fireman's pole fitted from his bedroom to the bar, so that when he heard an engine approaching he could slip down and have cold beers waiting on the bar, be it day or night.

Not long after our arrival on the Island the anticipated 'wet' broke producing an amazing phenomena that was preceded by fantastic electrical storms.

Standing on that lump of iron ore in the Indian Ocean, it seemed that every strike of lightening from the horizon pursued a glittering path along the surface of the ocean, literally magnetised towards our feet. According to the figures quoted later in the company's newsletter, twenty-four inches of rain was dumped on the island in under seven hours.

Stepping into that torrent, even for a few moments, brought on an immediate sense of drowning.

As every bit of land sloped down to the sea and was mostly rock, there wasn't a huge flooding problem, at least not in the community area where I was at the time, but the sheer volume of fast flowing water carried all manner of things, including not just domestic valuables, equipment and debris, but also a multitude of live creatures, including snakes, which flowed helplessly into the sea.

When the worst of the storm really hit, a wind speed of a hundred and thirty-seven miles an hour was officially logged, before a huge gust blew away the wind recording equipment. All of us that were present on that day agreed that it blew a lot harder after that when many of the substantial wooden houses were damaged, several were wrecked and one disappeared.

The noise was incredibly loud and so totally constant, that it drowned out all individual sounds so that what we experienced was a sort of soundless unreality, probably enhanced by the change in atmospheric pressure. The fact that joists of timber and sheets of corrugated iron seemed to sail through the air like cigarette papers, silently crashing into solid structures, leant the whole experience a cinema-like quality. When the wind suddenly abated to leave an eerie, muffled stillness, the contrast only perpetuated that silent film like effect. Sky didn't look like sky, while the sea behaved like oil, preferring to slop sullenly, so that even though it wasn't calm, there was no lightness of a splash.

Word got round that we were in the cyclone's eye and worse was coming. After some twenty minutes of mixed anticipation, the second onslaught slammed in. Structures that had valiantly survived the original fury just couldn't hold out against a new bombardment coming in from the opposite direction. By the end of the storm there was massive damage, yet the open-air cinema screen, standing right out in an unprotected space, was unscathed, and a young crocodile had been washed over the shark proof rails into our tidal swimming pool.

Clearing the extensive damage brought long days of double-time and double-time and a half. From then on all new wooden houses built, plus surviving older ones, were given thick steel cables lashing them to rock or deep concrete pillars as the company was keen to attract, and not put off, potential workers coming to Yampi.

The presumably 'censored' company newsletter made interesting reading. Apparently, according to it, there was some minor damage to houses, but none were wrecked. Blown away, obviously didn't mean wrecked! Nor was there mention of the company aeroplane taking off pilot-less, or of the numerous, still missing, small boats, or of the croc in our swimming pool.

But they did write in general terms about conditions in the North West, and Ernie got more animated than I'd ever seen him, when he read that, the furiously flowing river at De Grey Crossing was now estimated to be over forty-five miles wide and expanding. He went around pointing out to everyone, that we could still be stuck there, and by now possibly very much dead!

A little mixed nationality group of us had formed, mostly travellers. There was a Kiwi at the beginning of his travels, Sam the American, an Italian from Kenya, plus a Swiss guy and a German.

We found time to chat, play cards, chess, swim in the pool, and when our shift breaks coincided, go swimming at the white sandy crescent beach. Although some of the workers angrily accused us of risking our lives unnecessarily, it was in fact a low risk situation as we were watchful and the bay was uniformly transparent, with white sand beneath clear water and mostly only three to four feet deep throughout.

There was a self-styled 'Tarzan' working on the island who had been featured in one of the Australian publications wrestling with a crocodile. Having been badgered by us for some time, he finally succumbed and gave us a great day out in his boat, taking us to a contained shallow bay where we swam, dived in after fish and rode turtles. But in spite of watching out all day, we didn't see one single crocodile.

After some time, my work shifted from rock cracking to working with the 'snake men', a term used for men working alongside the dinky toy digger that we had seen from the air. It was, in fact, a massive thing that loaded a fifty-ton Euclid dumper truck in two mighty scoops taken directly from the pure metallic blue iron-ore cliffs. It was powered by electricity and had a long, three-inch thick rubber cable known as the snake.

Four or five men had the job of carrying the snake on their shoulders and followed the slow moving digger as it lumbered into each new position so the cable wouldn't overstretch. Bizarrely, as snake men, we also had to move the cable every twenty minutes during a night shift, in order to prevent termites from devouring it.

Those northern termites, generally referred to wrongly as white ants, are ferocious devourers and builders. Three times a night those little chaps would build their three-foot high pillar outside the canteen, and three times a night some creep would get a kick out of knocking their creation over, yet by the next tea break there was another three foot pillar.

A lot of that ore was so pure that roughage in the form of mullock had to be mixed with it, so the crushers could have something to crush or they would just clog up. Occasionally that iridescent blue ore, which has the consistency of block salt, has clear bright rainbows running through it, but I soon discovered that as with their celestial cousins, they are not for capturing. I tried but they simply crumbled away on contact.

The bonus of night work was having willing men with time and reason to teach me how to drive the monster trucks; and their reason was simple enough, it was so they could sleep while I practiced.

I started on one of the island's four, 50 ton, silent Euclid's that had originally been built for Alaska. Just getting aboard felt like climbing up into an aeroplane's flight deck.

They were very fast and, even when fully loaded, due to having fluid-flywheel clutch systems. Their amazing silence was helped by the exhaust being channelled through their body structure, in order to prevent loads freezing in Alaska. Those four trucks were at that time the biggest in Australia, and if one of them driven through a dust cloud had hit one of the land rovers that scurried about the quarries, it is doubtful whether the truck driver would even have felt the impact. I know, because I accidentally managed to hit one of the forty-five gallon marking drums which was full of iron ore dust, and felt nothing.

Following Euclid driving I progressed to one of those thirty-five ton, side tipping Mack trucks, with its unbelievably noisy exhaust pipe poking up just ahead of the windscreen. What a racket! Their tandem back wheels were chain driven, which made them particularly good at working through both mud and deep ore dust.

They were incredibly hard to drive, having fifteen gear shifts with no synchronisers. This made it essential to double, treble, even quadruple de-clutch, while precisely matching the cogs and two gear boxes to progressively more demanding engine revs. They were so tricky that each truck had two big iron wedges hanging behind their back wheels for instant release, should a critical gear be missed when climbing a slope with a heavy load. Very reassuring, and the only way to stop a truck rolling backwards near the quarry's edge.

There was one particularly steep hill with a bend on the edge of a drop, where I never managed to go through the final gear change without discovering that I was holding my breath, sweating and perched on the very front edge of my seat. But eventually through persistence, practice and keeping my cab door open just in case, I got it right, and was finally able to leave the island with a company driving licence in the name that I had given myself in Australia.

My decision to leave the island came after only nine weeks, when the monthly passing state ship on its way from Perth to Darwin off-loaded a group of flirtatious girls for a one-hour visit. Fit, rested, well nourished, and feeling vigorous I thought, "hmm" and promptly gave notice to coincide with the next monthly northbound ship and began to enjoy some very promising dreams.

Sure enough I was on the next ship bound for Darwin via Wyndham. But in those days no one had taught me how the 'bow wave of desperation' ensures failure. Needless to say, there wasn't one single girl on board!

I must have really sulked because I don't remember anything about that whole thousand-mile trip! Meanwhile, Ernie had very sensibly decided to remain at Yampi and save money.

CHAPTER THIRTY-FOUR
'The Old Ghan'

There seemed no reason to risk staying in Darwin even though it was tropical and seemed such an interesting place, as sooner or later I would be caught and deported, so why make it sooner? With bush hat, bedroll and water bag, I stuck out my thumb and quickly began the nine hundred odd mile hitch to Alice Springs in order to see inland Australia while I still could.

Even though the bitumen road was wide and straight, the journey seemed to take forever, due initially to getting a lot of short lifts then being stuck for days at 'Three-Ways' the junction where the north/south highway is joined from the east.

It had to be the most boring wait I've ever had, punctuated only by a bad tempered man from the junction's lone roadhouse, who came striding angrily with a gun to see me off.

"Don't want you no-good-bludgers 'angin about my property. So ya can bloody well piss off!"

Knowing full well that I couldn't go anywhere, he dictated a boundary line that I wasn't to enter.

"Step inside this bloody line why don't cha, an if ya got any brains inside that bloody pommy head, I'll blow the bastards out!"

For the whole time that I was stuck there he all but prevented me approaching for either shade or water and tried hard to deny me, on one occasion, the right to fill my water bag. The only compensation was the nights spent within arms length of an unbelievable canopy of stars.

Little else stands out from that trip down the Stuart Highway, except sharing food with an Australian family beside a pile of curious large round boulders called 'The Devils Marbles', and surprising various people that picked me up by giving them money as a way of balancing life for my good fortune.

I experienced Alice Springs as hot, dusty, dry and expensive. Merely keeping cool seemed to cost a small fortune in cold drinks, and spells in the small swimming pool that was charged for by the hour. It probably felt worse, as I didn't get to know anyone and the situation just wasn't working for me. Who knows, on another occasion in another state of mind I might have liked it.

As I had been told there was no road beyond Alice, I looked at the station for, and eventually found, a railway man to ask, "What time is the next train to Adelaide mate?"

His languid Australian reply came back as, "Ah, The Ol' Ghan should be along about Wednesday, I reckon. Only goes s'far as Augusta mate, you'll have to get another train through to Adelaide."

It was another three, hot, dry, expensive days of hanging about in that heat with flies, waiting for the Ol' Ghan to arrive.

I did ask about 'Ayers Rock' as it was close to 'The Alice,' thinking it might be worth a visit. But close turned out to be some two hundred and fifty miles cross-country and there wasn't an obvious way to visit the place. Suddenly it was just too hot to bother.

When the 'Ghan' finally did show up, she was an old relic that could have been in a cowboy movie. I heard how she regularly, in an irregular sort of fashion, plied her way back and forth along the seven hundred mile stretch between 'The Alice' and Port Augusta.

She was supposedly named after the hardy Afghan Camel Drivers who had for several decades, on their wonderful belching beasts, carried water and essentials to the gold mines and other remote projects of the region. But there is a chance that the story wasn't true, as it may have been Pakistanis and not Afghanis who drove the camels. Whatever the truth, the remnants of their journeys remain all over the centre of Australia in the form of camels running wild, and hard, green, gone-to-seed water melons that are descendents of the fruits that were scattered about in order to feed their trusty animals on route.

About to clamber onto the appealing veranda at the back of the wooden seated train, in which hung a three-foot long tubular canvas water bag, I saw that some hard drinking Aborigine guys were likely to use it up before the train even left the station. So, I went back along the platform to make damn sure that my water bag was stuffed full before we left, then chose a place well away from the drinkers, even though by then, they were all pretty much out of it.

At several stages of the journey, that old train actually came off the rails and workers appeared each time, from god knows where, to ease the train's iron wheels back onto the unsupported iron track. I began to wonder if those guys might have actually been travelling in some carriage with us.

A thin ancient Australian guy with parchment skin, who I'm sure continually puffed at an old smokeless pipe to keep his teeth in place, explained to me over an elongated period of short sentences.

"When the bloody rail people were first going to lay the track, no one, not even the Abo's, had ever seen or heard of rain in the region."

Three minutes past and I was wondering about his comment, when he continued with, "So they just went ahead and laid the bloody thing straight on the sand."

I had just got used to the idea that he would say no more when, pipe still in mouth, his voice started up again.

"Did bloody rain though."

There was a long period of me waiting for something to follow while he just stared ahead.

"Yeah, the 'ol girl's been slipping off them tracks ever since."

I relaxed, believing he might have finished. Then abruptly he was off again.

"She's right though, the 'ol girl', she'll outlive us all I reckon."

"Reckon you're right mate." I said, sitting forward to show interest, but after another ten minutes I felt I could stop waiting and relaxed into the timeless journey.

The next stop was nowhere. We just rested on a massive textured plate with nothing larger than a pebble to be seen. Our twin tracks in either direction quickly becoming one thin line, to eventually disappear towards the horizon that totally encircled us under the spotless blue sky. Then somehow, from somewhere right in the midst of that incredible nowhere, three people boarded our train.

The only explanation I could think of was that maybe they were prospectors or opal gougers who had emerged from some underground diggings, whose shallow mounds were too elusive to be visible in that gigantic terrain. I asked the guy with the pipe, and five minutes later he risked his teeth to say something that I didn't quite hear. It must have been a big risk though, because he never said anything else for the rest of the journey, nor did I ever see any smoke come out of his pipe.

I last saw him and his pipe at Port Augusta, where I was the only passenger travelling south to Adelaide. Apparently the change of trains had something to do with the fact that the hundred-odd mile track on to Adelaide was of a different gauge, and there is still some national embarrassment felt around the fact that the enormous lengths of track from Sydney in the east to Perth in the west didn't meet in the middle because, 'whoops', they too were of a different gauge!

From the moment I emerged from the wilderness into the modern town of Adelaide, I felt embarrassingly out of place and dirty in a place that reminded me of an average town in southern England.

In spite of my appearance I found a room and once washed and beard removed, I went straight to a clothes shop and gave the guy full freedom to kit me out, as I didn't have a clue. After all, the last clothes I'd chosen were the long-lost teddy boy clothes in which I'd set out for the Aldershot Palais in 1959.

Walking down the main street of Adelaide in the new outfit was a self-conscious experience of constantly adjusting shirt cuffs, either up or down, as I saw how other men wore theirs. I even found going to the cinema intimidating, as I felt so uncertain of how to behave.

I'd been away from normality for too long and there was a fear of making a fool of myself. I remember thinking that this must be what a released prisoner feels.

After a couple of days I hadn't got to know anyone, so still feeling uncomfortable I began to wonder at my attitude since Cockatoo, and quickly realised that I had been wallowing in a sort of sulk since my thwarted expectations on the state ship to Darwin.

A quick re-think and I remembered the fact that I was in Australia to see Ken. Then enthusiasm returned and it was straight off to get a plane ticket for Perth, feeling a mounting excitement at the idea of turning up to Ken and his mum so unexpectedly, and in a suit.

The Compass of Naivety

CHAPTER THIRTY-FIVE
'Reunion Achieved'

No sooner had we taken off than juice came around and, in no time at all, a menu, then coffee and before long food was being served. Ever since this first experience of sitting at however many thousand feet it might be, enjoying a meal, I've had a childish excitement about it, and I look around wondering why everyone else looks so indifferent to the miracle.

That first time was probably the best and, as there was little to see but cloud below, I sat back and enjoyed the endless attention that passengers received in those days, which included meals and endless snacks. But as we began our descent towards Perth, I was experiencing uneasy feelings about landing when it dawned on me that although I had taken off in planes many times, I'd always come down by parachute, and this would be my first landing in a proper plane. Somehow the little taxi plane to Yampi hadn't counted, as I'd felt the pilot could easily glide into somewhere safe if the power had failed. But if anything went wrong on this descent, well..! As the announcement came for us not to leave our seats, I realised just how long I'd been needing to! However, focusing on that problem took away all the nervousness of landing.

Perth airport was quiet, the toilets were free and I had no problem getting a taxi to Peppermint Grove where Ken and his mum lived in a splendid, large old timber house in Cottesloe, a posh suburb between Perth and Fremantle. Their long front lawn lead directly to a low wooden fence, where a quiet road was all that separated them from a few peppermint trees and a wide stretch of the beautiful Swan River.

When Ken's mum answered the door, she could hardly believe her eyes, and as luck would have it for some reason Ken had taken the day off work. The reunion was fantastic. They were both amazed and astounded at the way I had got to them, and totally unable to comprehend, following my brief description off passing so near, why I hadn't come straight to them when I first arrived in Oz.

1961 Clive (left) with Ken (right) in Perth.

They were, as I always knew they would be, absolutely welcoming. Mrs Brett, who didn't seem to have changed at all, immediately set about making me one of the delicious curries that I will always remember as her speciality.

We had masses to talk about and there followed a few days of them showing me around and introducing me to various friends. We went sightseeing, spent days on the beaches and Ken took me to experience a drive-in cinema.

They really lived in a special place, not only right next to the river which was swim-able with a sandy beach, but also just a short walk past Cottesloe's shops to a popular ocean beach. They were fifteen minutes drive to Perth in one direction and less than ten minutes in the opposite direction was Fremantle.

Ken's mum made absolutely sure that I knew, for however long I remained in Australia, their place would always be my second home. Soon I was basking in normality as 'Clive', and looking for a job. I found one stacking wood in a Cottesloe timber yard where, unlike jobs I had worked at in England, there were showers and lockers so that workers could leave every day clean and out of their working clothes.

While I still had some money I bought a German scooter, and enjoyed bombing around the general area of Perth, Fremantle and the surrounding hills.

Meanwhile, Ken had been so impressed with my descriptions of the work, pay and conditions at Yampi, that he quickly got himself employed and left by plane for Derby. When he wrote to his mum telling her how good everything was, I recognised that he had landed that job in the underground cabinet vibrating iron ore on 12 hour shifts onto the ship-bound conveyor belt.

I told his mum how they moved men around and that Ken had landed a job with a great sea view and, of course, like any mum she was happy.

Gradually I began to discover some of the Bohemian nightspots around Perth. There was 'The Coffee Pot', where mainly university students hung out from eight until two a.m. and another two places that stayed open even later.

Being slightly unusual, I soon had a circle of quirky friends with whom I shuffled back and forth between venues. Through one of them I was introduced to 'The 69'. A dark and secret place run by an exceptionally beautiful dark and secret Dutch Indonesian woman called Lhana, who had eyes for both men and women, and a personality that was incredibly magnetic to either.

The '69' was open from midnight till three, serving coffee, spring rolls and chocolate cake, but from three a.m. the door was closed and we, the trusted in-crowd, had our coffee cups filled with whatever appealed.

Lhana ran her business along minimal lines, utilising very light cane furniture and essentials, such as portable camping gear for making coffee or occasional heating, backed by decorative screens and candles for atmosphere. She utilised temporarily vacant property acquired through a friend that worked for an estate agent. Her personality held it together with all her customers becoming friends.

Once it became a going concern Lhana sold the good will, acquired another temporary space, got more similar equipment and started again. Her loyal customers followed. The '69' was her third coffee lounge and I helped her with setting up the fourth in Fremantle, and as I could borrow a van, this made me very useful.

With nightlife sorted, scooter and a job, plus the beaches and ocean on Sundays, I was finding life in Perth very enjoyable, and then Saturdays also fell mysteriously into place.

I had spent a couple of Saturdays painting out a summerhouse for Helga who was the mother of someone I'd met at the Coffee Pot. Over several refreshment breaks she confided about various things, which including her boredom with Australia and a fantasy she had about kidnapping a young man.

The outcome was that for a few weeks, Helga 'kidnapped' me on Saturdays as I walked along a road and whisked me off on a wine tasting tour of various vineyards around Perth. It was all very enjoyable until I realised she wanted her husband involved, and I called it off.

Although I met a lot of girls in Perth nothing much ever came of it, as they were usually involved with, getting involved with, or getting over someone, or just not interested. Something nice was starting with Lhana, but a jealous admirer spread a malicious rumour about me, which unfortunately Lhana believed and went cold on me.

Now avoiding the '69', I began exploring Fremantle which wasn't then much of a town, but had both a fishing harbour and sea port, with its fair ration of sleaze, which I was bound to run into sooner or later.

As it happened it was sooner, as one late evening I got chatting to a friendly part-Aboriginal girl at a coffee stall who liked me enough for us to wander along the quay hand in hand looking at the resting fishing boats. In that atmospheric setting we soon got closer, at which point she surprised me by urgently persuading me to come with her.

The place she lead me to was a run down building behind the shopping area, which must have been two or three flats that were no longer separated. Inside it was dark but light enough to see, as there were candles burning here and there. It quickly became obvious, as Amy led me past doorways with rooms full of couples on mattresses, that we were in a knocking shop.

Realising I was hesitant, she reassured me that I was her boyfriend and it was for love not money. Then, being intermittently passionate and firmly tugging at my hand, she made brief comments of apology as we picked our way through the array of bodies, mattresses and scattered clothing. It was clear we'd arrived when I was hauled on to a mattress.

I didn't question too much, it was clear she was a prostitute, but she never asked for money and after a couple of days spent swimming and generally enjoying each other's company, it felt like any other relationship especially as among her friends I was referred to as "Amy's boyfriend".

It all came to a sticky end when she asked me to become her pimp, telling me, while hugging and stroking, "You would only have stay in the background. When customers know there's a guy around, it's enough."

"Amy, there must be someone else." I said.

"But you're my boyfriend, everyone knows that, you won't even have to work anymore, and I'll pay you."

"No!" I said firmly, feeling very uneasy as I watched her shift from persuasiveness to ugliness as she took my reluctance for rejection.

Suddenly she was very clear.

"Do you really think my friends will let you show me up by dropping me now!"

Next day I was 'Steve' again, and was back on the Great North West Highway rapidly heading north!

As I was left to my thoughts in a noisy truck, there were questions. Had the legion affected me more than I realised? Had I really become so very different? Had Amy really liked me or had she only seen me as a good protector and set out to ensnare me and if so, why? Why did Helga have kidnap fantasies about me? Why was the beginning of my friendship with Lhana attacked so vehemently by her friends? And why couldn't I find myself an ordinary girlfriend?

When it had taken over ten days to get near Roebourne, which was only part of the distance that Bluey had taken me and Ernie on our original lift, I realised just how lucky we had been to reach Derby so quickly and trouble free. This trip was a series of short lifts and long waits with hoards of flies.

Most mornings I poked my head from under cover to find that the usual small margin of pre-sun comfort had been replaced by a 'hell' of dry, single-minded, thirsty flies that homed in on sleepy eyes to lap-up the slightest hint of moisture. These weren't your average agile quick-to-leave house type flies, oh no, these were big, dry, slow moving, easily squash-able, indifferent to their fate kind of flies.

Each persistent fly had to be individually and carefully rolled out of eye sockets firmly enough to clear them, yet light enough to not squash them. Washing away the morning sleeps didn't work as the little beggers simply followed the water. Meanwhile, some opportunists feeling 'lucky' slipped into the water bag, only to become corpses that had to be spat out later.

Rising sun saw the water bag carpeted with them, as a thick black layer settled on the shade-side of 'anything' available, unfortunately the only other 'thing' for miles around, was me. And there was another problem.

Since the original trip north with Ernie, when I discovered I'd been sleeping with something that was thick as my thumb, nearly a foot long and with a mass of legs, I'd become a lot more careful about shaking out my bedroll. The question now was how to shake out a bedroll, roll it back up, and not create a graveyard of flies.

It felt a long wait until the next lift.

....

CHAPTER THIRTY-SIX
'Ghost in a Ghost Town'

Just south of Roebourne, the trip was interrupted by a curious encounter with a very rigid middle-aged Englishman, who pulled up in an old tray-backed T-model Ford that was held together with a lot of wire, string and the like. He glared mistrustfully towards me and barked in a clipped British army officer manner.

"Ben Armitage." He shouted. "**Be quick now, climb on board, throw your kit on the back, we can't hang about all day.**"

Having thrown my bedroll on the back I stretched out a hand, but he ignored it. "**Christ you pong. Better get you back to my town for a shower and some food.**" The Ford was already turning and heading 'off road'. It wasn't like I'd asked him, or particularly wanted to go there, yet there we were heading towards the horizon.

Attempting to work out his intentions I asked, "**Is this the way to Roebourne Ben?**"

"No of course its not, I've already told you were going to my town. Its on the coast."

"**Are there many people there Ben?**" I asked loudly over the din, as I hadn't seen a town marked on any map.

"No, only me. I'm the only resident of Cossack, been there over twenty years. Got squatters rights, they don't know it yet, but I know the law. I'm English, from good stock, successful scientist in the old country, a damn good one. No time for it. Got no time for science, governments, or religion. Don't have much time for people either. No one was interested in Cossack when I first got there, it was a ghost town before I took it over."

Ben went on pouring out statements, never looking at me, just sitting bolt upright staring ahead like a man having to concentrate on a narrow road, even though we were travelling over compacted sand that was flat for miles around.

As we arrived I saw that Cossack was the remains of a complete town with several seriously built stone municipal type buildings, still very much intact. Ben had picked the best building and made it his own, so that's where we both went. Still barking in the same abrupt manner, he more or less demanded that I take a shower.

"Use these." He said, chucking some clothes towards me.

When I emerged washed and dressed, he shoved a plate towards me commanding that I eat! Ben had been knocking up eggs, toast and coffee, even while continuing his verbal delivery as I showered.

As more facts emerged I learned that he'd made all his furniture, renovated an abandoned boat and fixed up the old Ford we had arrived in.

Throughout the three days that I spent in his company, Ben never stopped talking, yet he never even asked my name or anything about me, plus I could hardly get a word in edgeways.

I did manage to ask if I could see his boat, but he answered something I didn't hear in a manner that implied 'private keep out' and followed up with, "She's alright, I keep her 'safe', she's just for fishing."

In fact Ben kept her so safe that I never even got to see the jetty.

As there were a lot of 'remittance men' in Australia at that time, men that had been provided with a pension by their families to stay away from England, I had begun to wonder if Ben might have been one of them. But the fact he so obviously prided himself on his self-sufficiency made me doubt that somehow.

I knew that a lot of men in the North West had staked 'mineral claims' somewhere, for which, as long as they worked it, they received some sort of allowance. The trick was to work it just enough to satisfy the authorities and meanwhile trade whatever amount they chose to dig up for supplies at the nearest town, a sort of black economy. I had reason to think that Ben had probably been on his way back from trading when he saw me and decided to pick me up.

For those days that I was Ben's captive audience, his insatiable need to talk made it impossible to sleep.

On the third day, I was vacantly staring out of the window, when I saw a dark haired woman pass behind one of the buildings.

"Ben," I called out, "there's a woman out there."

Abruptly, in a voice suddenly laden with anger and an expression to match, he shouted actually looking at me for once.

"You didn't see her, she's not there. Don't you ever think of talking to her, as far as we are concerned she doesn't exist. Right!"

I was taken aback by the very real anger in his eyes, as it suddenly occurred to me that we were a long way from anywhere. I decided that once Ben had calmed down, I would have to fabricate a story for him to drive me the dozen miles or so back to where he'd initially collected me and I knew he wasn't going to like it.

I wondered about the woman, she had looked real enough to me in that moment, but Ben's outburst and my lack of sleep had really thrown me and, although I looked, I never saw her again.

Later that day when I explained I had to leave, Ben agreed to take me. But I felt shoddy, knowing he hadn't believed me and it was obvious that he felt offended. He dealt with it as I guess he dealt with most things, simply ordering me to throw my stuff on the Ford.

On the journey back Ben stayed silent, unceremoniously dropping me off with my things before driving off without a word. As I watched with disturbed feelings that lonely man's shrinking cloud of dust disappearing into the haze, I was sure that the situation had played into many other examples of people letting him down.

Then two locals in a Land Rover pulled up and I was on my way again.

I mentioned nothing of Ben to the car's occupants but asked about Cossack.

Apparently it had once been called 'Tien Tsin' after the ship that brought the first settlers. Gold in the region had brought people, and the town flourished with a thriving port. Fishing led to discovery of pearls and there was a short boom before Cossack's decline and final abandonment in the early fifties.

"What about now?" I asked.

"Well a few people stayed on, but there's only an English eccentric bloke there now." "What all on his own?"

"Yeah, he's been there a long time, had a 'Sheila' there once, but she's long gone."

I found myself wondering about that 'Sheila'. Had she been a threat to Ben's 'squatters rights claim', or was she still a threat? Was she in any danger? And did she really exist? A slight shiver passed through me and I dropped the thoughts, the temperature was up in the high 90s.

Those guys took me straight through to Port Hedland where I decided to stay, as Bob the driver had told me of a likely job driving a semi-trailer out to Marble Bar.

It was early evening when we pulled up near Larson the boss, who was urinating against the wheel of a parked truck. Bob introduced me and without even having to show my BHP driving licence I got the job driving to Marble Bar that night, and all before Larson had even finished pissing.

I'd never driven a semi before, but figured I could get the hang of it by practising around trees when I was well out of town. As the truck was still being loaded, and it was to be an overnight drive, Larson suggested I kill time by watching whatever film was showing, so I got some food and took his advice.

The open-air screen was showing 'The Innocents', a classic black and white horror movie with Deborah Kerr based on 'The Turn of the Screw', a psychological thriller that wasn't quite the best thing to watch at an open-air cinema in the tropics just before heading alone way out bush on a dark night in a noisy truck.

Straight after the film the truck was ready, and I set off for Marble Bar in an over-laden noisy semi, along that same sand-fly infested causeway that I'd been stuck on with Ernie. In fact it might well have been the same truck but hopefully without explosives!

Stopping a few miles after crossing the main highway to practise reversing between trees, I found it a lot harder than I had expected, especially in the dark, even though the trees showed up white. After a while, without hitting too many, I sort of got the hang of it and continued my journey.

It was so monotonous driving hour after hour along the endless dirt road between low trees and tall scrub, with the engine's racket and vibrations inside the cab, particularly as the lights only picked out a limited area of whiteness ahead.

Two hours down the track I uneasily pulled up, no longer able to put off the job of checking the tyres, and as the engine died the world plunged into an ominous silence and I felt incredibly alone. Headlights still exposed the whiteness ahead but left everything else in darkness.

Walking back the length of both truck and trailer, armed with a feeble, failing torch to check numerous double wheels, of which there were suddenly so many, and all with my back exposed to the bush, became un-nerving. The film was preying on my mind and I couldn't get its images out of my head.

At the furthest point from security of the cab, I got myself in a right state and then had real difficulty in completing the ten-minute task of checking not just tyres but security of the load.

On completion of the job I scrambled into the cab, now grateful for the sound of that roaring engine and was once again trundling along.

Relief soon became concern as everywhere looked the same, and I wondered if I had passed the fork and taken the wrong route and if I had, how many hours of driving would there be before I could know.

What seemed like hours passed with no variation, just trees and still more bloody trees until beneath a lightness of sky I began to recognise the ups and downs and the tight bends of my earlier trip with Ernie, and Dave with his explosives.

Time to practice some real driving, but racing across the first river bed, the over-laden truck shot straight through without slowing down as I fumbled a gear change and only just stayed on the twin concrete tracks.

After all the driving in those chain-driven dinosaurs of Cockatoo Island, I still couldn't master the gears of that over-laden semi. But when the delivery place was safely reached my reversing procedures were well negotiated, and I appeared quite capable.

Unloading in the suffocating oven that is Marble Bar was slow and not pleasant. There was no access to amenities and, even at the end of the day, it was still a case of hanging around uncomfortably hot until after midnight for a wash. The only shower available comprised of a two-inch stand pipe, rising fifteen feet into the air from a deep artesian bore, allowing its water to pass down through several feet of sacking in an attempt to cool it. Yet even after midnight, the water was barely cool enough to stand under.

During the latter part of the drive to Marble Bar the truck's engine had been showing signs of over-heating, so out of necessity I rigged up a make-shift cooling system, just in case. Sure enough, on the final leg of the trip back to Port Hedland the truck over-heated.

A dried milk can on a stick was the ladle for periodically lifting water from a fifteen gallon oil drum in the cab, so that by reaching around the windscreen I could pour water on layers of sacking that were hung on the outside of the radiator to create a water bag effect. Evaporation from wet sacking did keep the truck's temperature down, as it does with Australian water bags.

By driving mindfully the truck got safely back to Port Hedland.

Unfortunately, there was no further work driving.

"If you could do a bit of welding or mechanics then maybe, otherwise sorry mate!" Said Larson.

He suggested I try a couple of his mates around town, which I did, but it was much the same story.

For a while I found myself wishing I'd taken the opportunities at Yampi to learn some welding, but in retrospect there probably weren't many, as all the tradesmen I knew were sharing skills in their free time to help each other build yachts out of 'conveniently' spare materials.

Hanging around town for the rest of the day led me to meeting and becoming friends with both a guy who, for obvious reasons, was called Bluey and his beautiful part-Aboriginal girlfriend, Amber. Bluey, barefooted and rugged with his Celtic looks, together with Amber, who in her figure-hugging dress was dusky, curvaceous and also barefooted, presented a Hollywood beachcomber image of which they were obviously very proud.

They both showed me endless photos of themselves in various desert island castaway poses and I stayed with them for quite a while, joining in with their favourite activities. One of which was going out with Bluey to drive his old, beat-up Holden, shuddering at high speed along the bitumen causeway intent on reaching a hundred m.p.h., in spite of a broken engine mounting. Another activity, that was popular throughout the northwest, was shooting kangaroo's.

Practically everyone I met up north shot kangaroos for fun, or at least condoned it. Shamefully I went along with it once, but soon sickened of the whole thing.
    Even more horrible, and equally condoned by many in some North West towns, was the practice of scaring, abusing and generally using the local Aboriginal people, who had set up their humpy-style dwellings a mile or so out of each small town.

Thankfully with Bluey it was only shooting kangaroos and seeing that Amber didn't like it either, we joined forces in distracting Bluey so the creatures could get away.

After some time, a friend of Bluey's, on his way to Perth, dropped me off at the next town south where we'd heard there might be work. There wasn't, but on the second day I struck up a friendship with an American guy called Hank, who told me that the oil exploration company he worked for needed a 'Soil Tester' and that he could easily get me in.
    "Just tell them you've done the same stuff for the Main Roads Department up in the Territory." He said, with casual expectation.
    I told him I couldn't see myself able to bluff my way through, explaining my lack of abilities with both spelling and figures, he was flabbergasted that anyone could not even know those basics. He remained encouraging, persuasive then adamant and finally angry as he realised I was serious, at which point he became scathing and dismissive.
    By the time I left, I was feeling embarrassed and angry with myself, there had been no other work and I had ended up feeling like a conspicuous idiot in that small town.

It was such a relief when I was back at the junction of the highway and once again heading for Yampi.

CHAPTER THIRTY-SEVEN
'Snakes Don't Chase?'

It was that time of year in the North West that, from a deep blue spotless sky, the relentless sun dried out the sharp spinifex grass which extended to form a circular horizon. It was also when, from a driver's perspective, the hard, corrugated sand highway no longer disappeared a few thousand yards ahead into realistic looking, but ever-moving, watery lakes.

At the junction where I waited rubbish lay scattered from vehicles whose occupants had sorted their contents before continuing their gruelling journey north, having probably decided not to waste fuel and effort on visiting yet an other small town, likely to be much the same as all the rest.

There was no shade, and it could have well turned out to be an all day wait. So, by constructing a small shelter from discarded rubbish I could lie flat on my bedroll, with my head at least protected from direct sunlight. Waiting there listening and dozing in that intense heat for the sound of an approaching vehicle for several hours, nothing happened.

Then suddenly, responding to some basic instinct, from lying horizontal I was 'elevated' and on my feet, staring in horror as the small dark head of a five foot straw coloured snake appeared to strike at the very spot on the bedroll where my face had just been. It then reared itself up to come hissing angrily towards me.

With heart pounding, too mesmerised to turn and run but picking up a stone while stumbling backwards, I desperately hurled it in the snake's direction and inadvertently slammed the reptile's head on to the concrete sand, which only resulted in making it angrier.

Three times, due to the mysteries of adrenalin, panic and luck, a stone miraculously hit that small head each time with the same result. Almost tripping backwards over a convenient length of timber, I used it to frantically bash over and over, never totally satisfied the creature was dead, as even its mangled remains continued to writhe long after I'd finished.

"Snakes don't attack unless provoked."
"Snakes don't die until after sundown."
"Snakes always have their mate nearby."

Words I had heard from my childhood repeated themselves in my head as, within a short period, I found another five similar snakes, each around the same size.

The prospect of being stranded in 'snake land' overnight became uncomfortable as did the thought of spending hours walking along the road 'snake spotting'.

It was a huge relief when I was finally picked up before dark. Then between the two occupants of the Holden and myself, we counted another eleven snakes on the road before passing out of the area.

I made up my mind to never to let myself be left in that place again.

Some time later when I met Ann, the girl I would eventually marry, she told me how she had ridden her scooter, accompanied with just her dog 'Lady' through sand and over corrugations the length of the great North West Highway from Perth to Port Hedland. It was quite a feat in those conditions, particularly with the small scooter wheels.

She also said, that before setting off some well meaning Australian guy had told her stories about The North. One of which was that there were many 'race horse goannas', big fat lizard-like creatures that when startled run up the nearest tree then try to burrow.

Ann hadn't liked the idea of those creatures anyway, but even less when the guy went on to say, "Trouble is, there's no trees in some parts so they'll probably try to run up you. Best thing you can do then is lie down quick before the bugger starts burrowing, an' with a bit of luck it'll just run away."

Ann became so horrified at the thought, that she had worn her crash helmet day and night for the whole journey, even sleeping in it just in case!

She also told me of an occasion when, in her bedroll, she had opened her eyes to see, only inches from her head, the silvery upright body of a snake, that for a long time was holding its head high and gazing at the full moon. She had watched fascinated at the spectacle, not at all frightened, but simply fell asleep when her eyes had tired.

As we shared our respective experiences and my lack of courage in the presence of snakes, we realised that both events had taken place at the same junction and that we had both heard of other people having snake experiences in that same place.

Throughout my stay in Australia, I must have slept directly on the ground in open country with only a canvas bedroll for at least fifteen months. But my experience at that junction was the only encounter I ever had with a snake.

As my latest lift was going through to Port Hedland, I went with them on the off chance that some work might have come up in my absence If not, there would at least be an opportunity to say goodbye to friends.

It was while picking up some bits at the general store that I heard a very familiar soft English voice, which swept over me like a breath of fresh air in that harsh land so far from home. Then I saw her clear blue eyes, bright lips and radiant smile. That was Ann. The feelings of familiarity increased as we discovered things we had in common - similar age, coming from nearby towns in England and both lone travellers.

As we both knew I was only passing through, we arranged to meet up with some food later to cook on the beach.

It was an exciting release for both of us and we hardly stopped talking all night. Then in the morning, before her work, she took me on her scooter, accompanied by Lady her Blue-Heeler, out to the highway junction for me to continue hitching north.

That evening, just in case I was still there, and I was, they returned bringing food, which we cooked over an open fire while the billy boiled.

Sleeping on bedrolls beneath a carpet of stars on the bare earth as I usually did on my own felt so different with someone else, and there was a whole new glow on those occasions.

Ann told me when she came out on the third night she had hoped I would still be there. I know she was quietly pleased when I told her that I'd actually turned down a lift in the hope that she might come. We enjoyed another night under the stars, and during the fourth day I accepted a lift that was going straight through to Derby.

Months later we would spend time together again and Ann told me how on the fourth evening she and Lady had come out again and, seeing that I must have got a lift, both camped the night there anyway.

I never lost fascination for that vast track, which changed totally with the seasons. For example, a flat section we had travelled months before now had a fifteen foot cliff barring the way forward, and as the first vehicle through following the 'wet' it was for us to find a way round that new feature. From then on, all traffic that followed would be guided by our tracks to become part of the highway until the next deluge a year later would re-form the landscape.

There were so many changing patterns, so many colours, and so much going on.

Of course, for a time I had enjoyed the benefit of naivety, unaware of the many dangers, until one old timer called out to me from the other side of his noisy engine, having picked me up from beside a water tank.

"Jesus mate don't you ever worry about fire out here by yourself with all this explosive tinder about?"

He was referring to the dry, highly flammable spinifex.

"Oh no." I said, in a moment of stupid arrogance. "I'd just hop in the water tank, I always make sure I am near one."

"You reckon yah'd do that, do ya mate?" He gave a contemptuous nod. "I reckon yah'd 'boil' like a five minute bloody egg in there mate, my bloody oath yah would. Yah'd be better off burning, or better still, letting the smoke get ya. My bloody oath, what a crook way to go."

It was a sobering thought, which slightly took the edge off my enjoyment of that lifestyle from then on, especially as there didn't seem to be a lot I could do about it. I pictured a wall of fire moving towards me while waiting for the inevitable.

The options I had imagined like burying myself in the sand, this old timer told me would require too much time and at least a pick-axe. And as for clearing a large enough area around a water tank as a fire break, no chance.

"**Smoke or fire would overcome ya well before completing that mate, unless ya reckon yer can outrun the bloody wind!**"

I felt foolish after that, and shut up.

An experience sometime later, really brought that reality home. It happened when I was travelling with a friend, we were among a clump of trees boiling the billy over a fire beside a dried-up riverbed, having taken great trouble to make it perfectly safe in a well-prepared space. Seemingly out of nowhere, something big and ferocious came crashing through the trees causing us to drop everything and run leaving the fire burning.

It turned out to be a cock-eye-bob creating mayhem as it spun roaring among the trees, tearing off leaves and branches, while scattering our belongings everywhere. Luckily that mini tornado missed our campfire. If it hadn't, it would have spread the fire through the surrounding sea of spinifex and surely caused a fatal disaster.

An English guy who I became friends with, called Vince, worked for an engineering company and serviced a massive area of the north west for them. He was extremely lucky to escape from a spinifex fire in his company's four-wheel drive, and then only with his canvas canopy on fire, due to the wind-born flames that pursued him.

Vince also told me of a time when driving that same truck in a ferocious wind, he had become progressively uneasy having changed right down through all the gears to find himself barely able to make headway.

CHAPTER THIRTY-EIGHT
'Good as any White Man'
and
'The Tree of Healing'

Every truck driver in that vast region either knew, or knew of, every other truck driver or even if they didn't, soon would because they automatically pulled over a 'while' whenever they met. And in those timeless spaces a 'while' was, more often than not, at least a meal together, an overnight stop, or both, which then, of course, led to a drink or two and to breakfast the following morning.

It was always a pleasurable anticipation to see either by day or night the dust trail or the appearing, disappearing and re-appearing headlights of an approaching truck that was still maybe an hour or so away, and to wonder who the driver might be. Then once close enough, it was also pleasurable to detect that tell-tale glint of flame or, if it were day, smoke, which indicated that the other driver had stopped first and was preparing at the very least a welcome billy of sweet black smoky tea and maybe even some tucker.

Whether hitching or driving, there was always ample time to share companionship and food together. Conversation was generally simple, often about obstacles or events of the journey, or encounters with other drivers, and of course time was spent recounting endless experiences similar to those of my friend Vince.

If more than two men were involved those stories often took on the nature of 'bushman's yarns', with inevitably amusing and often very hilarious endings.

I never heard of any women truck driver in the region at that time, but there was one Aboriginal driver called Snowy that everyone spoke of in fiercely protective terms. "**He can drink like a fish mate, a real dinkum fella is Snowy.**"

"**I'll 'ave nothin' crook said about the bugger, and anyone say's different about 'im they'll 'ave to bloody well deal with me!**" Shouted another.

I had imagined Snowy to be one of those fine looking older Aboriginal men with white hair, but when I eventually saw him it was not the case at all. He had black hair and certainly wasn't old. I was somewhat forcefully introduced to this smiling black fella, standing among several of his truck driver mates.

"**'Ere Steve, ya pommy bastard, shake 'ands with this black bastard. This 'ere's Snowy, we call 'im that coz he's good as any white man, ain't that right Snowy?**" In the midst of a chorus of "**Yeah!**" "**My bloody oath!**" "**Too bloody true**" and "**Right on!**".

It felt like some bizarre challenge as Snowy, who was nodding and grinning furiously while absorbing none too gentle slaps on the back, was pushed forward to meet me, 'Steve', this bloody pommy bastard all the way from England.

It was as though we were thrown at each other and, in effect, made to shake hands in front of a beer soaked jury.

"Good on ya mate, good to meet ya Snowy." I said.

"Good on you too mate." Said Snowy.

"Blood oath." I risked.

"Bloody oath." Said Snowy.

Then, to an uproar of appreciation, we were both slapped unnecessarily hard on our backs, indicating that the weird test had been passed, and like Snowy I was now part of the club.

Later on, while trying to survive by 'appearing' to actually drink the beers that I'd 'earned', I watched the jostling and joking become less good-natured. I saw how Snowy was having to grin from ear to ear and take endless slaps in order to remain acceptable.

Snowy was in a unique place and continually paying a high price as he trod a thin line for the dubious privilege of being regarded as 'good as any white man'!

God, how I hated those beer-fuelled gatherings, with all their undertones of racism, sexism, and any other 'ism'. They always produced in me an uncomfortable itch to get away, which is exactly what I did in this case.

As soon as possible I hit the open road.

Once again, as so often, I was sitting by the roadside waiting, but never bored. At the start of the 1960's it was impossible not to be taken in by the sheer beauty of what, unfortunately, nowadays many people would see as an uninteresting landscape. Speeding along, in their insulated cars with air-conditioning on and music playing, down the now unvarying, convenient, flat and mostly straight, bitumen road, they often see a barren terrain, devoid of wild life.

The new modern road follows the high ground further inland, in contrast the old track used to cross coastal land where millions of tons of water regularly created deep rifts as it rampaged across the hard, baked land during the Australian 'wet'. That phenomena sculptured a bizarre and varied landscape that was home to a world teaming with animals, reptiles, insects and birds. Being closer to the coast it also allowed views and occasional access to an untouched and beautiful coastline.

During those drawn-out periods of dreamy isolation both waiting and sleeping along that track, I continued to develop a kind of communication with life, which was part of a growing awareness. For instance, a couple of willy-willies twirling on the horizon, a bird following a particular course, combined with some sound, feeling or other observation, would alert me to look for another indicator that might complete a message.

On one particular occasion a bird's flight was interrupted by the predatory actions of another bird, as a dust spiral faded. Those things together with a familiar feeling warned me that there was some threat to watch out for. My concern was enough to take precautions, such as checking out the bedroll for insects and the immediate area for snakes or potential hazards, but I didn't find anything.

My next lift came some twenty minutes later with a Dutch driver who said he could take me, if not to Derby, then at least as far as the Broome turn-off. We were enjoying some easy conversation, when we were temporarily blinded by the dust trail of an on-coming car as it passed. We emerged out of that dust cloud heading directly for a massive goanna-type creature.

Hans did what he could to miss the brute, but at the expense of leaving the road completely with us ending upside down at the side of a sand dune, shaken but protected by the volume of soft things, including my bedroll. The car seemed okay and rolled easily upright but we would need help to get it back on the road.

As for the beast we avoided, it had long gone.

Spotting the ocean from a sand dune, we grabbed a few things for comfort and went to recover on the beach. It was beautiful, but soon became monotonous and hot, with neither of us quite having the guts to go for a swim in the warm and extremely tempting but potentially dangerous water.

The sound of a labouring engine brought us scrambling back to the car where four strapping young Aussies with big smiles to match their bodies, piled out of a Jeep. Then they went without hesitation, or even asking, manhandled the stricken beetle back on to the road, literally lifting it around the other way as Hans pointed out that we were heading north.

"No sweat guys, jump in."

Cheers went up as the engine started to the sounds of, **"Plant ya foot mate!" "Give it heaps!" "Good on ya's!"** and **"She'll be right!"** as they all pushed, while Hans part-drove, part-skated with their voices fading as we continued in the general direction of Broome.

Even inside the V.W. the noise and concentration of the journey didn't allow for discussion. Once we'd settled to the monotony of heat and Hans's mixed technique of ski-driving over endless talcum powder, there was time to ponder about why I had automatically checked my bedroll and immediate surroundings, then left it at that, when the signs had clearly warned of the forthcoming accident.

I thought back to the ship passing between those two hills in North Africa, with the bird of prey leaving its rock for freedom of the sky. I had on that occasion automatically and without further thought, taken that observation as time to leave and my part-conscious response had been appropriate. With this car accident, I recognised similarities and resolved to be much more alert.

Although I couldn't have realised it at the time, it was all part of developing skills that would become essential to my survival later in life, when I was to become unwisely entangled in a seven year struggle with what could best be described as the 'occult'. I was still musing over mysterious patterns, which included having started this journey from Aldershot in a 'hearse', when we arrived at the next turn off.

Hans dropped me to continue hitching as he'd decided to get his car safety-checked in Broome.

Both road and traffic became good and I was quickly picked up. This time by an elderly English sounding guy from a north west cattle station called John, who immediately began, and clearly enjoyed, telling me about local interest.

So, I just sat back listening as we passed the fascinating 'Alice in Wonderland' upside down trees, which he didn't seem to consider worth mentioning even though he did tell me about the world's 'second' longest cow trough! I thought there must be something really special about it, so asked.

"What's it like John?"

"Oh, just a long corrugated iron water container, like any other. The longest one's in America!"

"Can we go and see that one?" I asked, smiling.

"Not really." He replied, with no trace of a smile. "We can go and see the Australian one if you really want to?"

" Oh no thanks, not now." I said, "I'd really like to get to Derby today."

"Ah well, suit yourself. We get tourists these days that pay good money to come way up here on one of the old monthly 'Stateships' just to see these sort of things."

"Oh really!"

"Yes, they come out by Land Rover just to see the trough and then if there's time they're taken to view the old boab tree that we call 'The Prison Tree'. It's a fat, hollow, pudding-like tree, that was used once to hold prisoners, mostly Aboriginals as it was easier than running the poor wretches into Broome. It's on our way, we can stop off so you can at least take a look if you like."

"Thanks John." I said. "I'd like to."

I wondered about those tourists being taken 'out bush' just to view a corrugated iron cow trough that wasn't even the biggest in the world. That round trip would have added up to many miles and a long hot tiring day out. Obviously tourism hadn't been thought out in the North West by 1960. The locals hadn't realised the appeal of the natural beauty around them and believed that tourists had to be shown man made features.

Many years later that same prison tree, that we were about to visit, would become a Mecca to a different kind of tourist. Travellers of a new age would come seeking to stand within the tree's aura, hoping to feel or sense what the Naturopath, Ian White, had felt when he first recognised the boab tree to be a wonderful source of healing, and which later led him to create a Bush Flower Essence from the blossom. "Boab can help break the chains that have been around human consciousness for thousands of years." (Ian White, 'Australian Bush Flower Remedies', Sixth Edition.)

Interestingly, sometime later in Broome, I was told that it has long been a practice of indigenous mothers-to-be of that region to scoop out a hollow in the sand for lining with boab blossom as a protective receptacle for the birth of their child, so that the newborn being may arrive clear of undesirable influences of past generations.

I have now come to believe that the tree of imprisonment held among its captives, wise men of sufficient compassion to recognise and acknowledge the karmic plight of distant visitors to their 'custodial' land. And that their 'beings' entered the 'Dreamtime', petitioning the 'Ancients' that all future visitors be allowed to shed their inherited burdens of abusiveness, prejudice and greed. Because if not shed, those same influences from past generations would continue to be perpetuated. And so, as a consequence, the tree of imprisonment has become a tree of liberation.

Travelling nearly fifty years ago I was oblivious to all of this and only because the opportunity occurred did I visit the 'prison tree'. It was dark, smelly, fly-ridden and felt foreboding. Even had I been tempted to sit inside awhile and take in some of its atmosphere, I couldn't have, as it had been used as a lavatory.
"It's very big." I said politely to my host.
Then we continued our journey towards Derby and thankfully, no more was said about visiting 'the world's second longest cattle trough'.

CHAPTER THIRTY-NINE
'On a barge Among the Islands'

The office in Derby wasn't taking on workers for either Cockatoo or Koolan Islands, which meant hanging about waiting for the situation to change as there was no other work about. Meanwhile, I bumped into Norman, an ex-Londoner that I'd previously known and worked with on Cockatoo.

Having worked keenly for a long time with surveyors, Norm knew the complete process inside out, but wasn't good at pushing himself forward, so was still just a survey hand. He said he was waiting as part of a team to go into the remote Kimberleys, but that the Main Roads Department were holding them back until a surveyor could be found.

It seemed a perfect opportunity to put right the pathetic experience of not risking Hank's offer of the Soil Testing job.

"Tell them you've got a mate who's arrived from surveying up in the Territory and willing to start immediately if he can choose you as his assistant" I said.

Norm took this at face value and went off with the message, and quickly reported back that the office manager would be more than grateful. We went to his office as he was leaving for lunch, there was no formality, just a handshake and relief at having solved the problem.

It wasn't surprising, but it was absurd, given that I was totally inept at spelling and figures and knew nothing of surveying beyond holding up a marker. It was reminiscent of the lifesaver job I'd got in Aldershot when there'd been no water in the pool to test me.

Next morning, in a couple of Land Rovers, we followed the bitumen to the highway and turned left towards the Northern Territory. Two hours later we were off-road and heading north, deep into the Kimberly's.

Norm knew the whole setup from driving, cooking, navigating and first aid, to organising everything and everyone. On arrival at location he shot a cow, skinned it and followed the unspoken law of hanging the hide up as evidence, so that passing stockmen could include the beast in their annual stock count.

Our cook then roasted it on a big fire, as we all worked steadily on gathering wood and setting up camp. After that long hard day an incredible hunger was generated by the purposeful exercise and fresh air in those remote hills. When the time came to eat, the flour and water dough, affectionately known as 'damper' because while being cooked it can also damp down the campfire, was gritty from ash.

The meat was both smoky and gritty but tasted fantastic, especially along with endless mugs of sweet, strong, smoky tea, while sitting around a roaring fire.

Later as the fire was being raked and 'damped down' in preparation for the night, I suggested to Norm, as he sipped at his beer nightcap, that if he really wanted to upgrade himself, now was the ideal chance.

"Take over all the survey work and use me as your assistant whenever you want me, and I'll check your work over in the evenings."

Norm still wasn't aware of my inabilities so it was just the push he needed, and it worked! Because weeks later when I left the team, Norm, on my unquestioned recommendation, took up the position of Surveyor. Everyone was really pleased for him, saying he was a dinkum pom, and really deserved it.

In his curious way Norm reminded me of my legion mate, Johnny. In a similar way Norm was loyal and enduring, though nowhere near as young as Johnny, in fact, due to some bad war experience, Norm suffered shellshock.

It wasn't unusual, while walking through the bush behind his thin, ruddy figure, with oversized sweat-stained bush hat and brown band of knobbly knees suspended between khaki shorts and long white socks, to hear him screaming and angrily fighting with bushes. Yet, the rest of the time he was constantly good-natured.

When I asked him once about his habit of going to bed early he said, chuckling, "Dunno, I just like reading in bed, supping at my beer till I can't see the print anymore, then I'm a gonna."

Taking off alone in those vast Kimberley hills whenever there was a chance, felt like walking in unexplored territory. There is a wonderful 'feeling of expansion' in being that remote. I enjoyed a fanciful sense of possibly being the first person to ever stand on a particular hill.

It was probably that feeling which influenced me when, on one of those exploratory walks, I imagined finding gold and other minerals and how great it would be to discover some sort of valuable treasure. While fantasising that, a familiar sensation came and I was drawn to a configuration of features in the landscape that I understood as an invitation to participate in something.

Alert to further indicators, I took a little dust-spiral's antics as a sign that it was okay to interact. Then, using a convenient shard of rock to 'mark out' like a map, I set about duplicating the configurations of that landscape. When it was complete, a piece of fluff, that could just about be called a feather, landed on the creation.

In the eagerness of that moment, I took the feather and placed it on what I 'knew' was the most auspicious spot on my map as an intent to affect an outcome. Immediate conviction followed that I would definitely find treasure!

But during that same walk I passed through an area of heavy black sand and collected some to look at later. As everywhere in that region was so hot and dry, it was striking to enter an area that in spite of sunlight was really cold, then to notice an uncomfortable absence of bird song, insect sounds or any other noise. It felt eerie, as the sun looked the same but felt as though a dark cloud was obscuring it.

For a while I was caught up in the disturbing thought that my ritual with the feather had in some way been the wrong thing to do.

The cold feeling didn't last long as the area was quite small, but it was a comforting relief to be out of it. If it hadn't been to do with my actions, then it strongly felt that something bad had happened there, or that maybe there was some kind of radiation in the rocks.

None of my workmates expressed any particular opinion but much later, one evening at the Hotel bar in Derby, a local policeman and a bearded old timer were leaning over their beers when I heard the old timer talking about some long dead tracker fella's telling of massacres that took place in the Kimberleys.

"There's plenty of places like that out there." Said the old timer, "An' I've felt 'em."

"Well she's a bloody big area." The policeman muttered into his beer.

"My oath she's big, I'll drink to that!" Said the old timer, raising his glass.

I tried to bring in my experience of the cold place, but all I got was, "Yeah, she's a dinkum funny old place." from the cop.

Then they both turned dismissively away from me changing the subject, and that was that.

The next morning, having signed on, I flew back to Cockatoo Island where I was surprised to be given the barge-manning job, the very same job that had inspired me in the first place. Yep, out there among those beautiful islands all day on the water! It was one of the nicest jobs I've ever had.

Considering there were only two barge handlers required for the island, and over five hundred men to choose from, it was impressive that from a decision made while aboard the *'Estonia'*, not yet a free man or even in Australian waters, I should not only make it to Cockatoo Island in the first place, but actually get the very job there that I had intended.

The iron barges were mainly used for loading and offloading stores between the island's domestic jetty near the swimming pool and the monthly visiting state ships that were anchored some way out. Touring passengers were brought ashore by one of the island's boats.

The two barges also functioned as mobile work platforms for jobs such as painting structures that were only accessible from the water. We were towed around by an eight-cabin boat that provided comfortable accommodation for both its own crew-members and us barge handlers, whenever that was needed.

My job was mainly to keep adjusting ropes as the barge floated higher or lower in response to either changing loads or swift tidal variations. The job was easy enough, yet I made a classic mistake on my second day.

I had been shown the procedure while teathered to the quay on day one. As the tide went down I adjusted ropes by constantly letting out or hauling in, in order to avoid tipping the barge or snapping a rope. As the tide rose, the ropes if not continually adjusted, would allow the barge to drift dangerously away from the quay. Seems simple enough. However, when I was first tied up alongside the ship I diligently continued for some hours to ineffectually adjust the ropes.

I was not the first, nor will I be the last, to feel like an idiot when the embarrassingly obvious was pointed out. As both the barge and the ship were floating on the same tide, the relationship between them remained unchanged therefore, of course, the rope lengths were not affected by the rise and fall.

At each cyclone warning (they came frequently), the barges would be towed to a protective cove until it was deemed safe to come out. Usually it was for only a day, but on occasion several days, which was very nice for us as we got to enjoy walking the beaches, fishing and, with care, swimming in those beautiful tropical waters.

In the evenings men drank and played cards. I just enjoyed being there, but what really added cream to the cake was that throughout we were paid unbelievable rates, which quickly settled at double time and a half, contributing to some pretty hefty pay packets.

Soon, as with any holiday, it was time for a change and because I had a licence, I was able to transfer to night shift on the trucks. After being so long on the water in tropical sunshine I thought it would be a relief to work the cooler nights, although with the tropical 'wet' approaching, nowhere was going to feel cool.

Then in the midst of that all male environment, I was excited to get an unexpected telegram from Ann. She was coming to Derby for ten days and wondered if there was any chance of us seeing each other. Too damn right there was!

I pompously contacted the charter office to book the same air taxi our management used to be flown the 90 miles to Derby, where I acquired a room at the local hotel. I met Ann at the town's airstrip, looking happy but 'appropriately' dismayed, as I discreetly informed her there had been no single rooms available.

We enjoyed a smashing ten days spending most of our time in the hotel swimming pool, playing chess, or trying to keep cool in our room under a mosquito net beneath one of those beautiful old tropical ceiling fans.

The 'wet' was still holding off, as large heavy-footed flies lumbered slowly around like drunken bumble bees, bumping into everything and anyone. Cloud cover was heavy, low, brooding and swollen, compressing the kind of heat that was overwhelming and unbearable for most people. But both of us, especially together, with constant access to the pool and a fan, thoroughly enjoyed it and we still seemed to have an unlimited amount of things to talk about, which included fascinating insights into Ann's adventurous life.

All too soon, our ten days of pleasure were up and Ann was flying down to Port Headland. So not wanting it to end so suddenly I accompanied her that far, with the intention of hitching on to Perth.

Before long I was at that familiar junction outside Port Hedland, held up for a day and night with a Yugoslavian guy called Milos, who was travelling the opposite way. As we sat around that evening eating and boiling the billy, I showed him the heavy black sand sample that I was taking to the Assayer's office in Perth.

"I found a huge valley of this stuff up in the Kimberleys." I told him.

The story of where and how I'd found it enthralled him and soon led to exciting talk about gold prospecting. Fast friendships are formed under the stars around a fire, and we vowed before sleeping that if either of us should ever find gold or any other treasure we would write to each and share it.

The next morning when Milos' lift came we were still fired up and enthusiastic, but it was several hours before a guy turned up in a battered 'Ute' that was only travelling a few miles south, and by that time any thoughts of finding gold or treasure had all but left my mind.

Where he dropped me and turned off the road was an area of unusual stones that were lying about everywhere, like coconuts in heaps.

Over the next few hours, I was idly chucking a few of them around to pass time, when one split open to reveal its contents and re-kindle my interest in treasure. It was packed full of colourful crystals.

I naturally smashed another, then another and so on. As several of them revealed magical contents, I was like a kid opening Christmas presents. Most were less impressive, but occasionally one would reveal sheer beauty, and every opening was a surprise and exciting.

When I told the next driver that picked me up about them, he seemed disappointingly unimpressed, saying, "Ah those mate, they're all over the place, more of a bloody nuisance than anything."

"But what are they?" I asked.

"Oh look mate, I dunno the real scientific name for 'em, we've always called em' 'volcanic eggs, an' we've called 'em a lot of other things too, including 'bloody nuisance'. My oath if we haven't."

During the drive he explained that the eggs were caused by molten volcanic materials of varying densities, thrown high into the atmosphere, cooling and separating into molten droplets. They spun as they fell, causing crystal substances to remain in the centre as the heavier rock was spun outwards cooling and setting harder. "Why don't they all smash on landing?" I asked.

"Oh strewth mate, I dunno. I just told you what I got bloody told, it was good enough for me then, an' it'll 'av' to be bloody good enough for you now."

I couldn't think of much to say after that!

Back in Perth, Mrs. Brett welcomed me as always, eager for first-hand news about Ken and what his work at Cockatoo Island entailed.

He was still working underground operating that dusty hopper, so quite truthfully I was able to say that Ken was happily managing aspects of B.H.P's distribution and doing so well that he was required to stay on for a while.

Satisfied with that answer, she was keen to know all the general news I could give her.

Next morning I took my bag-full of black sand to the Assayer's office, where it turned out to be quite a valuable find. *"Tantalite."* They told me. It was a substance used in the process of hardening surgical steel.

After asking questions that led to talk about legally staking a claim, extracting, marketing, shipping it out of the area and that sort of thing, it all felt too complicated and I quickly lost interest. However, I did get a kick out of seeing my little symbol added to their geological wall map of Western Australia.

After a week of enjoying Perth again I was driving my scooter round a one-way system in front of a bus when my front tyre burst. I survived unharmed, but my scooter ended up on the scrap heap. I seemed to be spending a lot of money in Perth just trying to fit back in, so I had begun to think of getting a job when Ernie turned up having experienced a run of poor jobs and really needing work, which in turn spurred me into actually looking.

Still having the suit I had purchased in Adelaide, it seemed natural to look for a job that might fit a dressed up image. An advert in the local paper caught my eye. It said:

Smart, intelligent, presentable people wanted as business representatives.
No experience necessary, as full training will be given.'

High on ego, even if a bit low on evidence, I thought that sounds like me! So, along with Ernie and several other equally deluded people, I applied. Of course we were all accepted and began training straight away under the impressive tuition of Cliff, who turned out to be a brilliant American psychologist/sales trainer.

Cliff taught us a lot about the powerful psychology of 'affecting'. In particular he let us into what he called the hidden mysteries of A.I.D.A. Those four letters, Cliff explained, stood for the first letter of words, representing conditions that should always progress in that particular order through any influencing activity.

He said, "If you ever identify that you have created one of these conditions out of that order, then go back to the previous one, or you will be wasting your time."

The words represented were 'Attention, Interest, Desire and Action'. And I soon excitedly found out that they really worked.

Cliff soon had us all raring to get started, even though by the afternoon of the third day we still didn't know what the work would entail.

Only in the final hour of the three-day training did Cliff inform us that Ernie and two people plus me had been selected to work with Cliff as his chosen team, and that under his direct, personal supervision we would be travelling the wheatbelt towns east of Perth, staying and eating in hotels.

I don't remember the exact jargon that Cliff used, but by the time he had finished working A.I.D.A. on us lot, we had become electrified at the realisation that we were to sell *bread slicers door to door!* His hype had really worked. By the time we left the Perth office and were crossing the road we were all high as kites, enthusiastically impatient to get started.

I was so inspired by this new-found A.I.D.A. power, that while waiting on a traffic island of the wide, busy, road, standing next to an utterly beautiful looking dark-haired girl, I found myself without any hesitation, directing the skills of A.I.D.A. in her direction, and she bought what I sold! There and then I had sold myself to that beautiful English girl from Leeds whose name was Janice.

Cliff's exclusive team involved four of us - Ernie, myself, and a guy called John, plus a girl who got sick and dropped out at the last minute, but once I'd successfully used the A.I.D.A. process on Cliff, our team also included Janice!

We all met up early next morning and headed east towards the sprawling wheatbelt towns in Cliff's Holden. At the first town we stopped, booked into a hotel, and after a quick breakfast began work.

We were driven by car and constantly overseen by Cliff, who not only made sure we called at every house but analysed every aspect of the process - how we knocked, how we observed and how we evaluated non-responses. Soon we were successfully pumping bread slicers door-to-door, street-by-street for two or three days in each small town encouraged and enthused by Cliff, and fired up by our own hype.

I conveyed the magic on to Janice, and we both became successful very quickly, falling for all the praise that went along with being the two top reps of the company, which Cliff verified each evening when he called head office. Commission and bonuses were climbing.

Then the two of us were upgraded from selling bread slicers to selling food blenders, which had a higher commission.

Unfortunately, on one selling trip my cheeky sales patter in a 'small town' customer's house was taken as something more serious than innocent flirtation. So much so, that on returning to our hotel I was bewildered to find myself arrested on some archaic charge called 'evil designs'. Bear in mind, that this was at a time when, I'm told, Australia was still classifying its indigenous people as flora and fauna!

Later, when Cliff visited me in the nick, he was clear that it was a case of protectionism and that the town simply didn't want competition.

At the hearing I pleaded guilty to get it over with, and although I was innocent, I was acutely embarrassed as I imagined Mrs Brett reading about it in the paper and somehow the story getting back to my family in England. Also I assumed that as an illegal immigrant, a fugitive with a falsified driving licence, and using a false name, I was already a criminal and would be sentenced accordingly.

I figured I would serve time before remaining 'detained' pending deportation. The more I thought about it, being deported would be a proper recorded process and seemed to me to be the way to a safe passage home.

Once it became obvious that I wouldn't withdraw my 'guilty' plea, the judge had no choice but to fine me the minimum amount, which Cliff got the company to pay. Then to my surprise and disappointment I was free to go, having begun to assume, and even look forward to, a safe repatriation.

Without further ado I walked straight into the police section and told them the facts. "Ah well, lets take a 'sticky beak' shall we mate."

The desk Sergeant, fingered through his paperwork and soon came up with a warrant for my arrest.

"Ah it's you all right mate, now lets take a closer look."

Following a short check of some other paperwork, he concluded that the warrant had been withdrawn some months ago.

Then with a feigned look of disappointment said, "S'far as we're concerned, the case is closed mate."

"So what do I do now?" I asked, feeling confused.

"Guess that's your problem mate, good luck to ya I say." He shook his head from side-to-side grinning as he turned to his next job.

Realising I was no longer on the run which should have felt good, I wondered where the hell did that leave me? I couldn't go home, I hadn't a clue how to get a passport, or prove who I was, and I still had a false name on my driving licence, which the police seemed to take no interest in whatsoever.

Until these events I hadn't even thought of returning to England, now it felt like a slim chance of being sent home had been snatched away, which brought up feelings and thoughts that I hadn't even been considering. What I couldn't have known at that time was that these events were going to turn out very much in my favour.

That evening I mulled everything over with Cliff who, although obviously disappointed and perhaps experiencing a little disbelief at my story, was nonetheless supportive. He suggested I see Peter, a friend that he knew in Perth, and gave me an introduction letter with Peter's address.

Back at head office, not entirely without embarrassment, I gave my notice although they were still keen for me to stay on.

At first opportunity I called on Cliff's friend Peter who was fascinated with my story. He explained that, to be able to do anything for me, he would need something on paper with an address.

"The best thing you can do is purchase a name, find a farm job, or some work with accommodation. That will provide an address from which I can receive a letter. Then I will have something on paper for approaching authorities. Also they are likely to be more amenable if you are working in the country, rather than hanging around the city."

I hadn't been able to think quickly enough to choose another name, so I bought the adopted name I had become used to for two pounds! I then left Peter with the promise that I would follow his advice.

How strange I thought as I exited the building, that a 'nobody' can become a 'somebody' just by choosing a name and writing a letter!

....

CHAPTER FORTY
'Nip of the Red-back'

Travelling through the wheatbelt region, there'd been plenty of adverts for tractor drivers so, after talking my intentions over with Janice, there seemed little point in waiting. Early next day, after Mrs Brett had packed some sandwiches and handed me a letter, I caught a bus out of town to begin hitching in the general direction of the potential work areas East of Perth.

By sunset I had a live-in farm job somewhere west of Southern Cross, which is a town on the road to the famous gold mines of Kalgoolie.

I arranged with Lem, my new boss, that I was able to start in the morning providing he could post a letter for me, which was of course my important letter to Peter. He agreed, saying he would call me before sunrise and then said, "Meanwhile, the wife can sort you out some tucker."

She did. In the form of a vegemite sandwich, which arrived on the kitchen table, and before I could say anything she'd left.

Hunger woke me next morning and while waiting for Lem, I discovered in my pocket the letter that Mrs Brett had handed me before leaving and tore it open. With great difficulty in limited light, I managed to pick out eight words that were written in big letters.

"I've struck gold mate an she's half yours!"

I knew it just had to be Milos, but I couldn't see the rest so I would have to read it later.

After polishing off the solitary egg on toast and cup of tea that had been left on the kitchen table, Lem drove me out to the lone Caterpillar that I was to drive all day following a straight line at walking pace.

He showed me the ropes, told me what I needed to know then, before driving off he placed a bag beside me on the already moving tractor calling out above the noise, **"It's ya tucker, an' a drink."**

No sooner was his dust cloud out of sight than I stopped the tractor to hungrily open the bag and eat, while I read Milos' letter, only to find a lone cheese sandwich and thermos of tea. I knew it would be a long day but I was famished, so completely devoured it there and then.

'Yes' the letter really was from Milos, and 'yes' he had found gold. Milos was keeping his fireside promise by including me! The letter went on describing in miner's terms, things like, extracting pennyweights of gold from tons of rock, which I gathered would only happen after a lot of preparation.

Milos didn't say exactly where the claim was but I knew it was up in the Northern Territory, somewhere very hot and very dry.

Somehow sitting reading with the early morning sun already beating down in that dry, flat, featureless terrain, made gold mining dreams seem a long way off. Even though I realised it was a rich find, the thought of commitment to shovelling through tons of rock to find mere pennyweights of gold in the middle of nowhere just conjured up thoughts of long, hot, hard, boring work.

Anyway there was nothing I could do about it there and then, and by the time I was somewhere else other things took over and it was out of my mind. Thoughtlessly or carelessly, certainly rudely, I never followed up Milos' generous invitation, eventually losing both his letter and mail box number so never contacting him again. But there is one thing I'm sure of. That Kimberley ritual worked! Indirectly, through Milos, I found treasure.

I had joked to Lem about driving in the dark when he showed me how to work the lights but, long before he collected me that evening, the joke had lost its point. It was dark and I was still following that endless line with lights full on.

Back at the farmhouse, his wife dished up a mean little meal that I ate, while she practiced golf swings beside my table. I didn't see where Lem ate but I bet he got more than I did.

The following night I was sitting on the collapsing bed, with a grimy old paraffin lamp giving off an inadequate light, when I was aware of a wispy sensation down my leg towards the inner ankle. It felt like one of the abundant cobwebs. As the other foot automatically came up to brush it off something rolled away, immediately accompanied by a burning sensation. I grabbed the lantern to see what had been squashed.

Close light revealed a very small spider, which to my colour-blind vision in that poor light was impossible to identify, but there was a nasty feeling that the little patch on its back might just be red.

I took it for Lem to identify, knowing that red-back bites can be serious. Under the stronger light of the farmhouse tilly-lamp, Lem, his wife and Lem's old shaky grandfather, all in their night attire, gazed at it nodding. The general consensus was yes, it definitely was a poisonous red-back spider and their abnormally casual attitude implied they were worried.

Having heard red-backs could kill I suggested that maybe I should cut the wound to let out some blood, at which they all became enthusiastic, quickly found a razor blade, then gathered closely to watch me heroically slice my own ankle. After a lot of breath holding I only managed a pathetic little nick, then had to work hard just to squeeze out the minute-ist drop of blood.

Despite their feigned, casual attitude, they weren't about to let me go, so we all stayed up, with them continually asking how I felt. After enough time had passed with no symptoms, they agreed that it would be okay for me to go to bed. In that same spider infested, tumbledown shed!

Sometime during the night, in that dust and web-ridden place, I woke to find the old, trembling, white-haired, white-bearded, pale, grandfather who, by the dim light of his hurricane lantern, was leaning over with his ear to my chest, tentatively listening for a heartbeat.

The next couple of days involved alternate sweating and shaking with symptoms that felt like flu. Lem was obviously disappointed at their tractor driver being bed-ridden, but I bet it really irritated his golf club swinging wife.

There is an interesting sequel to this. Aged about thirty-five in England, I experienced some nerve related problem, so I went to see a haughty eighty-year old, Charles de Gaul look-a-like Homeopath who was recommended to me. He was a Frenchman with the lovely name of Pigache.

After doing all the talking, and observing me for about half an hour, Monsieur Pigache prescribed me a specific remedy, saying, "You have been bitten by...." he gave some Latin name. "...and the poison is still circulating in your lymphatic system."

When I asked him what the English word was for the Latin name he had used, he replied in his thick French accent, " Ehh, it iz 'ow you say, ze spider, Red-back."!! (As a matter of interest, my nerve problem disappeared very quickly.)

Whenever I was way up north it was 'out of sight, out of mind,' and I preferred it that way. But on the wheat farm, although Perth was a long way off, it was tantalisingly accessible and a constant magnet, as of course was Janice.

I wouldn't get paid till the end of the job, but I still had some money with me. So, once I felt better I headed back to Perth on what turned out to be a particularly cold night. I asked my first lift to drop me at the halfway house.

Having had ample time for looking forward to a big mixed grill, feeling very hungry and calculating that I had enough money, I was more than disappointed to find I had covered the whole meal with sugar. Never having seen one of the new-style sugar shakers I had assumed it was salt. I looked hopefully towards the boss but one look at his face assured me there would be no redress.

So, being cold and hungry, I scraped off as much sugar as I could and ate the meal that was, by then, cold. But I can't say I enjoyed it.

Once back in Perth and with Janice, I just couldn't face the idea of returning to that mean environment and figured that my unpaid hard work could pay off their disappointment. I chose to stay with Janice. Then Ernie turned up, having bought an old Morris Ute. So, the three of us crammed into the front and went to explore some of the outlying areas around Perth.

After a couple of days into the journey Janice called her mother and discovered she had apparently 'fallen sick'. So Ernie brought us back to Perth.

Once I'd secured work at the original timber yard, I rented a small room for Janice to be close to her mother. Gradually, Janice's mother found a variety of reasons for keeping her at home.

Ernie wanted us to set off on the journey that we'd all planned earlier, but I told him I needed to stay near Janice while her mum was unwell. Although we did manage to spend short periods together, our relationship was soon to be over.

The reality was that her parents were blocking their daughter from having a relationship with a drifter to such an extent that, a month later, they took her back to Leeds. Her dad got a lot of pleasure in telling me that the man she truly loved was waiting in Leeds, and made a point of saying that he was very rich and 'right' for her. Janice told me, with a lot of tears, how it wasn't true, and that she hadn't wanted to go, but they were taking her much-loved six-year old brother and, now that her mum was ill, she felt she had no choice.

Her dad intentionally lied to both of us as they left the day before they had said they would, so we never even had a chance to say goodbye.

As there seemed little point in continuing to pay rent on a room that I wasn't using, I moved back into Mrs. Brett's house and continued working. But Perth without Janice, Ernie or even a scooter just wasn't the same. Even the popular beach at Cottesloe felt boring on my own, and I was still a bit wary of Amy's friends so kept clear of Fremantle.

I wasn't a traveller anymore, I wasn't clear what or who I was, and on top of that didn't even have a passport.

Then one day on returning from work I was amazed to find Ann, with her bright radiant smile, waiting outside Mrs Brett's house, obviously very relieved to find me. As soon as a respectable length of time had been spent introducing Ann to Mrs Brett, we went for a walk to be on our own and talk about everything. It was wonderful seeing her so unexpectedly, even though she was upset, scared and feeling very alone.

Ann was pregnant and told me how she really didn't want to have her baby in Perth and was really frightened of having it by herself. I told her there was no chance of me letting that happen and that I would definitely be there for them.

Once she felt reassured we spent considerable time discussing where we would like to live. Broome came up as the place that we had both experienced good feelings about. In fact so much so, that by the time we had got back from our walk, we were already looking forward to being there and lost no time in making arrangements. I found someone who agreed to ship her scooter up there just as soon she was ready to receive it.

I explained the position to Mrs Brett, and just one day after deciding our immediate future, the four of us – Ann, her tummy, her dog Lady and myself – were once again back on the Great North West Highway heading specifically for Broome.

It was incredible how much easier the hitching was when we were together. The journey just flowed and we got to Broome in three substantial lifts spread over a comparatively short period, and that included a day spent in one small town.

One lift stands out with a story. It was in an overloaded small truck and trailer belonging to an all-Australian family who were travelling up from some small bush town in the southeast of the state in order to start up a new life in one of the northwest towns.

The very tall father, his wife, their two daughters who were six and seven and three sons who were nine, eleven and twelve respectively, all shared that same enthusiastic unruly quality that many of the Irish travellers have that are so familiar in England. They couldn't have been more welcoming, generous or friendly towards us and right from the start included us in their on-going life and sense of fun.

When we arrived at their target town we joined in with the unloading, as the whole family carted everything into the wooden home that they must have organised for themselves before setting off. Following a plate of egg and beans, Ann and I bedded down in the empty truck and slept very well.

The next morning was a Sunday and I was amused to see this blatantly unruly family all scrubbed and dressed up ready for Church. Ned, the dad, dressed in his Sunday suit told me he couldn't give a flamin' toss about religion, but becoming part of the community was the first step towards establishing themselves. Ned had obviously planned just how to go about setting themselves up, and going to Church was the quickest way to get known.

When they all got back we had some bread and sausages. Then Ned, speaking gently to Ann and his wife said, "Now you two ladies best stay'n rest up a bit. Kids can clear up, while we blokes'll go'n take the truck out for a wee sticky beak around the place."

Once in the truck, Ned winked giving a tooth-deficient grin, while exposing the label on a bottle of whisky.

"Reckon we deserve t'go 'ave ourselves some fun mate, I reckon we've earned it, don't you?"

I grinned back as best I could, awkwardly reluctant to immediately spoil Ned's fun, by telling him that I didn't really drink.

"Too right." I said, trying to fit in, while wondering uneasily just what Ned had in mind.

He drove out of town along the same bitumen we'd come in on the day before, turning off after a mile towards an Aboriginal camp, with the light truck bouncing easily on the sandy track now that its huge load was off.

When we got to the camp it was half a dozen make-shift 'humpies', set apart from each other and constructed from a mixture of town rubbish, corrugated iron and bits of timber, plus branches, paper bark and what looked like, and probably were, rags.

"C'mon mate ya like darkies don't ya?" Ned called, jumping out of the cab in his best Sunday suit, with the whisky bottle in his hand. **"Its party time mate, dunno 'bout you, but I'm gonna get me a bloody good root!"**

He was already off and running towards one of the humpies, where he pulled back a rag curtain and greeted the women inside while thrusting forward his bottle of whisky. **"C'mon mate, they want us to sit with 'em."**

The two women sat expressionless as we made ourselves comfortable, though comfortable was hardly what I felt as whisky was passed around between the three mouths that were already sharing it.

"Hey mate, easy on, if ya not gonna drink, fer pete's sake at least cuddle up to yer sheila a bit. You'll make mine feel bad, an' yours'll think ya don't like her an' she'll lose face mate. Ya don't wanna hurt her feelin's do ya? We're okay here mate."

The bottle was passed back to me and in a moment of uncertainty I put my mouth to it, 'acting out' a good swig.

"Good on ya pom, fer a new Australian you're not that bad." Ned called out. Simultaneously his adopted woman gave me a toothless smile while placing her hand where Ned's flies literally flew apart.

It was a weird situation, as various feelings conflicted. Indebtedness and consequent loyalty to Ned for having been so generous to us, coupled with a lack of clarity that had got me this far, plus the realisation that I didn't know how to handle it.

I began to realise that it was not this particular humpy that had appeared to be so familiar to Ned, it was the whole process, any humpy would have been familiar to Ned. This was a particular type of white male established 'help yourself to sex' society.

This 'acceptable' game was probably being played out by men like Ned throughout many of the bush towns of Australia. Similar men of Ned's mind-set probably wouldn't have thought they were harming anyone, as appeared to be the case when I brought the question up with other men at a later date.

"Ah those jinn's are fair go mate, they don't mind so long as there's grog in it for 'em." or "Yeah they're not a bad root, some of 'em." were typical responses.

Right now for me, the dilemma was how to get out of the situation.

'My' woman was already drunk and making all the right overtures to support what must have been for her, my inevitable expectations. I realised that, if I simply walked out without a believable excuse, she would have felt hurt and lost face in front of her friend, and it would have been for all the wrong reasons.

The outcome was a long period of pretend drinking, with a little bit of appreciative cuddling in the presence of Ned who was repeatedly humping his chosen woman. While 'mine', who was benefiting from both my and her portion of grog, had slipped into something close to unconsciousness.

I realised all my attempts to be a decent human were utterly wasted as we left, when Ned having gone back for something, called out as he climbed back into the cab, **"Thought I'd better give yours 'one' mate! Like I said, can't 'ave her losing face, can we?"**

Travelling back along the tarmac, with Ned still drunk in his crumpled suit with stains on his Sunday church trousers, I felt dirty from just having been there. The whole affair had been so disgustingly sordid that I was eager to get Ann, Lady and our gear on the move towards Broome as soon as possible.

....

CHAPTER FORTY-ONE
'Pearl Shells and Testicles'

It was late evening when we arrived in that hot, sultry, mangrove-stinking mosquito ridden backwater, that in a sense both was and wasn't Australia, straight into a sand-fly plague.

Knowing no one in Broome, we spent our first desperate night suffering their incessant onslaught on the mangrove-lined strip of white sand that surrounded the old pearling sheds. Thanks to the liberal amount of washed up smelly driftwood, we were able to keep a fire smoking densely throughout the night in order not to be driven mad by their onslaught.

We suffered burning eyes and lungs by wrapping ourselves and Lady in the thick smoke to avoid them, but unfortunately throughout the long night unprotected dashes had to be made for the driftwood fuel that was becoming progressively more distant.

Apparently indigenous peoples in mangrove country deal with the sand-fly problem by coating their skin with a protective layer of mud. I've since been told some years later that the little buggers don't bite anyway and that the stinging sensation comes from an acid they piss on skin, and apparently a simple coating of baby oil could have done the trick.

Following that long torturous night, which had to be so much worse for Ann being pregnant, although typically she never once complained, came the discovery that we had spent the night next to an interesting looking empty house which stood alone among the pearling sheds.

During the half-light dawn before Broome awoke, we looked around the empty corrugated iron clad single storey building and loved it straight away. Beside the pearling sheds it stood oddly tall, which was exaggerated by a seemingly unsupported balcony that protruded curiously above its front veranda.

From one of the two upstairs rear-facing windows, of what we were already calling 'our house', we could see the tide had risen and that our twenty-foot width of white sand had disappeared, leaving only a slender strip of beach with an increasing area of water between it and the mysterious darkness of the mangrove roots.

Having focused all night on evading sandflies, neither of us had noticed the timbered hulks of the two pearling luggers, now half submerged, that Dev, the old Torres Straits Islander, had pointed out when I was last in Broome.

From our left window could be seen that same low, narrow wooden jetty extending seawards, and now with a pearling lugger tied up alongside. With the benefit of height we could see how the channel was cut through the mangrove swamps for access to the creek and bay, then the Indian Ocean beyond. As the day brightened, both windows shared the vivid colours of sky and sea across the rich green foliage of the lush mangroves, around which the water now began to appear pale blue.

To the front of our house, across a sand road, was the earlier mentioned dirt square, containing a few small tin roofed dwellings, behind which 'Tang Wey's' café, Broome's open-air Cinema, and the higgledy-piggledy houses and shops of Chinatown formed a long and fascinating backdrop. A general stores and hotel/pub made up the right side of the square. It all looked so familiar because our house stood only yards from where Dev had previously shown and told me so much about the place.

'Pearl Shells and Testicles'

Our house among the mangroves on its strip of white sand in Broome.

What made our house so appealing, besides its quaintness standing high among the pearling sheds, was its little stone mushroom feet and its lopsidedness created by that odd balcony. It had clearly been empty a long time so we set about finding out if we could rent it.

We started asking around and found that no one seemed to know what had happened to the owner, other than the last lady we asked in the general stores who told us, "As far as I remember, must 'ave been ten years ago, the bloke who lived there just took off, I don't know anyone who's seen or heard of him since."

So, we decided to consider the idea of just moving in.

A view of old hulks, mangroves and the indian Ocean from our window.

Following our tiring hitch north, the arduous night of smoke and sandflies, and the morning spent asking around, we returned to the coolness of the house to rest through the afternoon heat.

Inevitably excitement prevented sleep and all our talk was about renting the house until light faded, at which point we realised sandflies were again on the rampage. Noticing that the upstairs height and breeze deterred the little buggers, we took it as a sign to stay put.

That evening we calculated a fair rent to place weekly in a tin in case the owner should return. When and if he did, we figured we might be able to come to some arrangement.

That night we slept untroubled, only our second night in Broome and we had a home!

The next couple of industrious days were spent rummaging around the abandoned pearling sheds and immediate beach area.

Following the surprise discovery of a nearby water supply, we found an old iron water pipe and some abandoned diving hose, which between them extended all the way upstairs to where we decided to have our kitchen.

Water only dribbled from the narrow bore, but the next day we acquired and rigged up an old fifteen-gallon drum to collect and hold the dripping water. It even had its own tap.

A cast iron drainpipe from the beach was long enough to pass up through a hole made in the roof and then be lowered down through both floors to provide a perfect tidal soak away. I shaped a piece of tin to wedge into its upper end, but later Ann found a big square funnel which became our permanent sink. Within a couple of days we were all set up to begin some serious cleaning.

There was a corrugated lean-to against the house where we found that by setting fire to brushwood along the length of the incoming pipe we could get a nice warm shower.

Then a supportive local Greek bloke, impressed by our efforts, took it upon himself to hook us up to a passing electricity cable. That night, as every other night thereafter, we watched our single electric light bulb brighten and dim in harmony with all the other residents of Broome's fickle power supply.

Our outside dunny was a corrugated structure containing a wooden plank suspended over sand, open as it's three sides for the tide to do its job once the user had completed theirs. Situated around forty feet from the house, it was out of reach when the daily tide came in. So for a few hours of each day a bucket, or even a back window, were the most convenient options.

Many pit toilets in Australia buzz with big flies affectionately known as 'dunny budgies'. We didn't have any of those, but what made our dunny really special was the ever-present possibility of vulnerable exposure to one of the black and yellow ringed snakes that inhabited our mangroves, or the snappy great claws of a mangrove crab.

As for mozzies and sand-flies, they were just a fact of Broome life.

Monthly high tides covered our downstairs floor with several inches of water, which left hermit crabs scurrying about making an incredible racket as they sought to utilise anything the right size as a mobile home.

That same Indian Ocean tide flowed stealthily across the square and along 'The Sun Cinema's' floor beneath an audience that sat indifferent to it on the stadium style seats at the back, or the deck chairs up front. By the time the film was over and the audience had left, so too had the tide, hopefully carrying all the creatures, friendly or otherwise, that had come in with it.

We were very quickly accepted into the small community.

A few days after our arrival a man and woman we spoke to in the street asked us how we were getting on with the old house.

"Well, great," I replied, "but we've got a fair old job trying to get rid of the rubbish that the tide's brought in."

"No worries mate," the man chipped in, "I'll send some blokes over, an' they'll sort it!"

"Oh thanks mate." I said, not at all sure what he meant.

We were puzzled the following morning to find half a dozen men raking away at the rubbish. A few questions revealed them to be inmates from our local jail.

Sam, the guy I realised was in charge, in an unfathomable accent informed me that I was expected to bring these blokes in for shade, coffee, tea, water or coke, but definitely no alcohol.

"If you like, you can give 'em some smoke's." He added. "S'up to you."

They'd soon cleared most of the rubbish but then, at Sam's request, we stretched the job out for a couple of days to give them a longer break from their confinement. Between raking and burning they sat around in the cool of our house chatting and rolling the tobacco we'd provided, as I tried to recognise bits of the pidgin English they all spoke together.

Four of them seemed to be of mixed race, and two looked Aboriginal. I couldn't make Sam out, particularly as he spoke pidgin when not talking to me. But he certainly didn't look like most of the white Australians I'd encountered.

The arrangement of inmates working out of prison seemed to work well in Broome as the authorities thought it safe enough, there being nowhere for a man to run. And if a prisoner did escape, an Aboriginal tracker would find him in no time.

Broome, separated from Derby by well over a hundred miles of corrugations, was like a 'down town' cousin.

Broome had the jail, the smelly mangroves, the meat works and the infamous Roebuck Bay Hotel. Plus, as we often noticed, many of Broome's men wore battered bush hats, flip-flops, grubby singlets, and shorts so skimpy that they regularly, whilst swatting flies, exposed at least one testicle, or worse, as they sat on hitching rails 'drinking piss' outside the Roebuck.

Derby, on the other hand, had all the major municipal offices for the Northwest and was the town for smart bush hats, shoes, long shorts, long socks and discreet knees.

It was a wonderful sight in Broome from our balcony to see drovers, both black and white, attach their horses to those same hitching rails while they purchased requirements from the general store. Then to see the white drovers enter the front of the hotel while directing their Aboriginal mates 'out back' where, I was told, they could enjoy a 'drovers work break' in the form of a quiet drink, while their white mates drank openly either in, or outside, the front of the hotel.

These were the men who drove mobs of cattle to the Broome meat works across hundreds of miles of Australia's harsh dusty north. Men who shared tough lives and dependent companionship, who intimately understood the land and cattle and who now, on entering town with their 'mates', must pay homage to the rules of segregation.

After a while we watched those noble black and white drovers leave with their horses as quietly as they had come, almost as though melting into their own familiar world.

Also from our balcony it was amusing to watch, as daylight faded, small groups of people below us begin the twilight dance of endless slapping, stamping and kicking in vain attempts to deal with the persistent attacks of kamikaze mosquitoes or sandflies.

Those events were a world away from the rowdy wild-west style scenes that we also had front row viewing of. They were an orgy of chaos, shouting, punch-ups and bodies catapulted from the pub door.

Before that nightly entertainment, we sometimes ate at 'Tang Wey's', the basic three table dining room close to the open air cinema.

There the choice was 'short-long soup' or 'long-long soup' which was convenient marketing. It was also a brilliant strategy, because it clarified things for those who complained about the size of their helping, while also limiting the use of language.

It gave Tang a 'no games' way of dealing with some of the racist remarks like; **"What's this bloody crap, Chink?"**

"Aah, you got short-long soup."

"Bloody oath I 'ave, this is crap 'slit eyes', there's not enough 'ere to feed a bloody rabbit."

"Aah, you wan' long-long soup, I get fo' you."

Then Tang would head off nodding and grinning towards the kitchen. Luckily, for every ignorant person there was usually a reasonable type to ease the situation.

Whether or not Tang spoke English I don't know, but he would have probably heard enough ignorant comments to not speak the language out of self-protection, and from what we saw he managed pretty well.

Whenever the monthly Stateship arrived, Tang closed his restaurant to join many of the town's residents, including me, in becoming casual dockworkers.

When 'working the ships' we were paid at union rates, even though Broome was geographically well above the union's jurisdiction. Consequently, although we weren't members, most of us earned more money over two or three days than we might have earned in four or five weeks!

However, a day's work did mean twenty-four hours on location, even though the period was peppered with breaks.

To keep awake I filled a flask with strong, sweet, brandy-laced black coffee, which Ann sometimes came by on her scooter to top up. It was important to be fully alert for operating the motor winch that swung heavy forty-five gallon drums of stinking by-products from the meat works, over the heads of men deep down in the hold.

An additional reason for our big pay packets was the tide, where any small delay in loading meant the ship sitting on the mud for another tide. This was both costly and inconvenient to the shipping line, but highly beneficial to us as it automatically pushed our rate forward to double time and a half, and I'm pretty sure a lot of our 'hold ups' were created by the old timers in our own interests.

As well as working the Stateships, many of the men had other enterprising ways of earning cash.

For example 'Freddie the Fin' lived a mile along the beach in a tin shack with several native women and a large number of kids. He simply stuck netted posts in the sand to trap fish. As the tide went out, he collected stranded fish and threw them flapping into his old wreck of a land rover, then just before closing time arrived to sell them outside the pub.

Some people prowled the mangroves at night catching mud crabs using lamps attached to old car batteries. Others went to sea after turtles or crocodiles, although by the 60's most of the saltwater crocs had fled further north. And even we had a scam.

Once Ann's scooter had arrived from Perth, we took packed lunches and spent days at the town's rubbish dump, a place totally separate from the refuse tip and more like a scrap yard. We found all sorts of useful items, which we either used for ourselves or traded.

A local Timor guy showed us we could rejuvenate a refrigerator by simply standing it upside down for twenty-four hours to revitalise its circulation. Most people in Broome knew the trick, but we still sold a couple and of course gained a model for our own use which never let us down.

Years later I did quite well back in London with this knowledge, as I worked a while for a retail chain and was able to get hold of traded-in fridges for nothing, revitalise them, and then sell them on.

Many years before we arrived in Broome, an elderly Aboriginal guy was found close to dying in the desert somewhere east of the town. He was brought back to the hospital for treatment where he stayed for a time recovering but then disappeared. Locals thought he'd gone back to his own people or maybe on 'walkabout', but he returned sometime later bringing with him some reddish-brown stones which he immediately set about grinding down with water into a paste.

Over a long period he etched, in outline drawings, a 'Dreaming' which took the form of humans, animals and snakes set out in circular format on four pearl shells. He highlighted every figure by working the red paste into each fine line.

Although the method that old man used was similar to the 'scrimshaw' that old time Whalers worked on bone, the artistry was very different and the materials used totally indigenous. Unfortunately the artist's eyesight was failing and he managed no more than those four shells. I was shown these wonderful objects when I gave a shell I'd found to a local guy who collected them and who, as it happened was Dev, the same man that had told me about Broome on my first visit.

What I found particularly exciting about the four shells was the change that took place as the work had progressed. Not a deterioration of quality, as might have been expected from his developing blindness, but a definite shift from the free flowing figures on the first shell, through to a rigidity of animation on the fourth. It seemed to reflect a gradual stiffening in response to the influence of our rigid culture, even in a relaxed backwater such as Broome.

With the airstrip only yards away, low planes flew directly over our house and we watched passengers, mostly locals, officials and contract workers for the meat-works who sometimes strolled up to the hotel for a drink.

Seasonally, planes ferried kids to and from their schools in the city and when sand-flies, mosquitoes, heavy footed flies and other harbingers of the 'wet' approached, many of the women and younger children were flown south to avoid those discomforts, along with intense humidity and the very real threat of destructive cyclones.

The Compass of Naivety

At the height of the northwest tourist season, a car a month might turn up in town with three or four occupants, maybe even two cars! Broome was one journey too far for many who had experienced the sameness of other towns on the way up to face that short diversion from the highway. So, they missed a gem, continuing instead along the dusty track another thousand miles northeast towards Darwin via Fitzroy Crossing and Wyndham, probably wishing their monotonous ordeal to be over.

The few monthly Stateship's passengers visited the Japanese cemetery, looked at the pearling sheds, our house and the corpses of pearling luggers, then 'penguined' around town for twenty minutes or so, before being trundled 'out bush' in a Land Rover, to photograph the prison tree and the world's second longest cow trough!

By the time they got back, most were eager to board ship, shower, change, eat and get drinking, even though the ship would probably sit overnight on the mud for another tide.

Few short-term visitors would be lucky enough to catch one of those monthly nights when a visual phenomena called 'the golden staircase' appeared. It took place to some degree during most dry months, but was truly spectacular on those rare annual occasions when conditions were perfect, and it must have been an absolute 'one off' that Ann and I were lucky enough to catch.

Although everyone in Broome knew the display was due, and someone had told us that it was best seen from the town's main jetty, when we expectantly arrived, there was no one but us waiting for it. They had said we should look left, which actually meant looking back across open water towards the reddened atmosphere above Australia's deserts.

Having arrived early we were chatting away as usual, when a startled look on Ann's face caused me to glance behind. A big oval, red body was silently hovering at eye level, seemingly a few yards away.

I was taken aback before realising it was the moon, distorted, magnified and coloured by thousands of miles of red Australian dust in the atmosphere, although we were seeing it through a lens of clear air, cleaned by the expanse of reflective ocean. As the moon rose, it became marginally smaller, copper coloured and round and its distance became normal. Beneath, the waters reflected a gradually developing golden ladder, which extended towards our feet.

Wow, so this is 'the golden staircase' I thought. But, as that disk rose still further, although less magnified, copper was steadily becoming gold and it was at that point the amazing phenomena occurred.

Over what I would guess was no more than fifteen minutes, a miraculous transformation converted that already impressive golden ladder into a perfect golden stairway, complete with curving banisters. It was truly an amazing and spectacular event.

As Ann's pregnancy developed, I took work on a 'Main Roads camp' coming home nightly on her somewhat tired scooter which had taken a battering when I'd raced the Stateship to Derby in the hope of more work, but given up when the spark plug kept vibrating its way out. As the work camp moved further from Broome we bought an old Land Rover, so that weekends and at least some nights could be spent at home.

'Main Roads department' provided useful fall-back employment. Hot, dry and dusty but rarely hard. It mostly involved on-going survey work, bush clearing, plus directing contract drivers where to tip their gravel for the waiting bulldozers to level or the graders to camber. The set up consisted of living with a small number of men just off the highway sleeping on iron beds over dirt, under canvas. A water tower served our kitchen and a Chinese cook, while also supplying our showers.

I have a nasty memory of the water running out just as I had soaped myself from head to toe, then having to wait for the next water truck while the soap dried in that intense heat. By the time water came I was a tortured, cracking, cake of soap!

When I was first allocated the job of directing drivers where to tip their gravel, I was kept busy with trucks arriving one after the other all day long, but over several days the distances grew and the eager, younger, less experienced drivers began dropping out as they damaged their trucks.

Eventually I ended up with only 'Jake the brake', a wily old truck driver, turning up twice a day for me to sign his form and point where to tip. The 'lead' had become too long and torturous for the young bucks, but 'Jake the brake', by maintaining his truck and driving wisely over rough terrain, had become the old tortoise that beat the young hares!

Jake always made his second drop just after my 'normal' working day had finished, which pleased me as it provided me with some steady overtime.

I was lucky enough to be in Broome when Elizabeth was born and, in retrospect, much too soon after, we drove the corrugated dusty road to Derby and back, as we were eager to show off our lovely baby girl to Ann's friends. The drive wasn't bad, but it took a week to get the red dust out of the poor little mite's skin. And as if that wasn't enough, while still celebrating the birth late one night in Broome with our friend Vince, and having drunk far too much, on a whim we decided to drive to Lighthouse point, as we'd never been there. A whim that could have proved fatal as it turned out.

On the way it must have rained somewhere far away, because we found ourselves with water rising all around. Once it reached above floor level, Vince, even though he was pissed, managed with some difficulty to re-route the exhaust pipe to exit above water level, but during his efforts the flood rose further.

All this happened in darkness and it was unlikely there'd be anyone on the road that night, so realising we were just a few miles from Broome, Vince and Ann fearing things might get worse, decided the best thing, rather than to wait, would be to carry Lizzie and wade home through the rising water before it was too late.

Still not used to drinking, I was too far gone for anything but sleep, which I did exceedingly well.

Ironically, when I woke in the morning everything was completely dry and a simple turn of the key started the engine at first attempt. I was able to drive, though somewhat hung over, on hard dry sand straight back to Broome and thump harder than usual into our veranda. It did little for my hangover but it really amused Ann and Vince, who thankfully had made it back with Lizzie safe and sound.

We'd long had plans about travelling up through Malaysia and Thailand in that old land rover, but as I had no passport they were just hopeful fantasies. In the meantime, I was always making abortive attempts to fix things on the old beast. Unfortunately, some of the ineffectual results meant that many bits that came off never went back on.

For weeks she was driven about with no silencer, no number plates and no driver's door, on top of which, in spite of having followed some local's advice, the brakes weren't working.

"Ah mate, just fill the ol' cylinder up with soapy water, that should do the job. She'll be right so long as ya don't take her down south mate, could freeze up in those cold places I reckon."

As my adviser hadn't said anything about bleeding the brakes, and I didn't know any better, just soapy water, made no difference.

It wasn't a problem though. As Broome had sand lying everywhere, stopping just meant rolling into some. In fact Ann found the familiar thump of bumper meeting veranda reassuring whenever I arrived home and misjudged the sand's depth.

One day, the town's copper came by.

"G'day mate. D'ya think you could do me a favour an' tidy up the ol'girl a bit? Maybe sort the exhaust an' stick some number plates up. Only my boss from down south is pay'n us a visit next week, oh yeah an' another thing…"

He led me aside to discreetly point out a reference on some official form, "Does this apply to you mate?"

It was a reference to my embarrassing incident at the court case down south.

"Ah, yeah." I said, feeling distinctly flushed and wondered what might be coming next.

Then, to my surprise, he stood back saying, "Put your right hand up mate will ya. Now, just repeat these words after me."

Suddenly, right there and then, in my own name, while swearing an oath of allegiance to the Queen and Australia, I was becoming an Australian Citizen!

With a grin he passed me some paperwork.

"Congratulations mate! Ya better decide what name you're gonna use from now on, ay?"

He ambled off calling back over his shoulder, "Don't forget to sort the car out will ya, maybe you can do something about the door while you're at it!"

I was still reeling and could only call back, "Yes, of course I will, thanks a lot!"

Looking through the paperwork I discovered that, not only was I now an Australian Citizen, I was also eligible for an Australian passport and could apply for an English passport if I wanted, all in my proper name. Just like that. Technically, in Australia at least, I had become a free man. Broome really was a great place!

Later, sharing the enormity implied by the whole event threw both Ann and me into such an intoxicated state, that neither of us even questioned how it had all come about.

Only much later did it occur to me that Cliff's friend, Peter, must have really put himself out for me, to have achieved such a fantastic outcome. By then, unfortunately, I was unable to personally thank him.

Life, which had already felt good, felt even better now that my passport was within reach. Meanwhile, Lizzie was growing from strength to strength, and everyone found her a delight to watch as she enjoyed splashing around in a natural sea water pool behind our house, clutching one of the lugger ropes. We were all healthy and the time seemed right for us to start seriously considering turning our dreamed of Asian adventure into a reality.

....

CHAPTER FORTY-TWO
'The Rot Sets In'

For most Australians at that time, Broome was a place up in a distant corner of their massive island where the first under-sea telegraph line had come in from the outside world at Cable Beach. We never saw it, or even thought of looking for it, as there was no reason.

Broome to us was the square mile that encompassed Tang Wey's eating place, China town, Sun Picture House, the hotel and general stores, plus the mud flats, where noisy passenger planes skimmed across the open air cinema disturbing the show before landing.

Beyond was an area of detached houses where 'respectable' people lived. There was also the town jetty, a meat works and a dairy. Then there was, of course, the rubbish tip, and that was about it.

As much as we loved the place, things around us were about to change. I no longer remember the order of events but it all seemed to start when a pretty girl from Broome, who was at the time living in the city, became runner-up in an Australian beauty contest. I was told by a couple of locals that a lady journalist came up from the city to do a cover story with pictures for a popular magazine.

In her article the girl's family were exposed in a really bad light, emphasising the racial mix and large numbers in her colourful family with their relationship to each other. It made issue of the shocking conditions under which she claimed they all lived. *'Chicken and pigs were wandering in and out of the living room as I interviewed her.'* Etc.

Broome was also portrayed as a dirty town of decadence with comments like, *'I was barely able to find a legitimately married couple in the whole town.'* A picture of the road to the town's rubbish tip, was published and titled *'The sight that awaits the visitor on the road to Broome'.*

It was nowhere near the road to Broome. It was the track to the rubbish dump!

Unfortunately the tactic worked, shocking her target readers who were told how they, as proud Australians, should be 'outraged'. The truth was that the existence of a multi-cultural town, even a small one tucked away in the far remote North West corner of the country, was unpalatable to many white Australians in the early sixties. It was a time when even southern Europeans seemed barely tolerated.

Then those same locals went on to tell me how that particular 'scandal' was supported by another upset, which followed the 'Royals visit'.

When the town had begun to prepare itself, the Aborigines' paper-bark, corrugated iron and canvass humpy camp out at 'one mile' (i.e. one mile out of town) was suddenly perceived as an eyesore and threat to the town's respectability. Even though a nearby humpy camp had suited most towns along the coast, including Broome for many years. Most towns seem to find it a convenient arrangement for keeping the Aboriginals at arms length, while still bringing in their appreciated revenue.

Each week, families from the humpy camps rented taxis into the towns to collect their pensions (i.e. state benefits) for spending at the long established privately owned stores who, in some cases, sold them inferior stock, short changed them or both. And although not legally allowed inside the hotels, a discreet corner was often created to ensure that their money was spent in town and not given to the illicit 'grog peddlers' who might go out to visit them at their humpy camps.

I was told of how, in order to appease a distant public and their bosses in the city who were concerned at what the Royals might think, authorities had the camp demolished and replaced with nice modern houses, completely fitted out and furnished for the humpy camp dwellers. The Queen was duly shown the nice houses, and no doubt given the impression that all indigenous peoples were similarly cared for.

The visit went down fairly well, but some time later dignitaries from Perth were sent up to admire the houses that had been built for the Aborigines, only to discover that they had all been torn apart and used by the humpy dwellers as firewood. The Aborigines were happily back in their humpies.

It is almost certain that nobody had bothered to ask the Aborigines if they had wanted the houses in the first place.

Yet those bare facts would have served to strengthen some of those attitudes such as, "See, those ungrateful buggers, they can't take care of property even when it's given 'em on a plate." And it was common to hear, "Those lazy bludgers have been 'ere over forty thousand bloody years an' done nothing with the place an' look what we've achieved in the short time we've been 'ere!"

At the time of that Royal visit I was back working on Cockatoo Island. According to Ann, Prince Philip chose to break away from the entourage and stroll among the pearl sheds and Streeters Jetty, viewing the fading old corrugated iron buildings, including our house, which he found so interesting that he photographed it with Ann standing on that quirky balcony with Lizzie held in her arms.

Both those issues, *the town of sin* and *the money wasted on ungrateful Aboriginals* upset 'the powers that be', so much that even though Broome was tucked away and isolated, officials were sent to clean up the scandalous town.

One immediate outcome was the posting of eviction orders on every offending house, which seemed to be any house of interest, including ours, the same house that Prince Philip had thought worthy of photographing.

There was no question of negotiation. 'One months notice, with the fine set to double for each additional day of occupation thereafter.' Naturally we were stunned and had no idea what to do next.

Even though we had originally moved into the house 'for the time being', it had over the year become very much our home. We had often discussed what might happen if the original owner ever came back, and so continued to put rent aside just in case. But as time passed it became even more likely that the house had simply been abandoned.

Now our much-loved house and others like it were to be demolished, just because they offended the taste buds of some unimaginative officials from Perth!

....

CHAPTER FORTY-THREE
'End of an Era'

Then, with perfect timing the compass swung again. One door was closing, another opening in the form of a bottle-laden visit from our friendly pig farmer friends.

Jed and Di who lived several miles out of Broome and spent too long renovating an old pearling lugger, had become really restless and desperate to set off on their planned crocodile hunting expedition before the weather could seriously delay them. Having heard of our housing predicament, Di believed she had come up with the perfect solution for all of us.

"Why not," she said, enthusiastically, "simply take over our land, buildings, tractor and equipment and pay for it by selling our pigs in three weeks time and putting the sale proceeds into our bank. We could sign the whole farm over to you once the money has been cleared with no strings attached! It would solve all of our problems in one go perfectly, and we'd all get what we want." Di was keen.

"What do you say?" She asked, holding her hands open expectantly.

I looked at Ann, we both realised it wasn't the moment to say no. I think because Di's Viking blood was already out among the islands hunting crocodiles, she heard a yes.

The conversation, with a few drinks and loads of enthusiasm, quickly became heady. They'd had it with farming and wanted freedom to pursue their dreams. Throughout the evening, on waves of excitement, we all raised glasses to plans, dreams and intentions several times.

By the time they'd both left in the early hours we felt like we already had a farm and, there was little sleep as we fantasised about all possible outcomes while eagerly looking forward to seeing our new home later that day.

Although their property was only a few miles away, we'd never been there before and on arrival it could have been anywhere! Both our hearts sank, although we responded initially with typical humour and optimism. But the day progressing only lowered our spirits further, as we experienced a real sense of desolation in that flat, unyielding monotony of burning brittleness.

It was a land of sparsely covered hard-baked dirt, skimpily dotted with small coarse textured trees and clumps of shrub, and it was a scene that I knew went on for hundreds of miles in several directions. We knew that Broome was somewhere near and the Indian Ocean even closer, but so what!

How different it all felt now from the heady night before to consider living and working in this desolate place.

It took no time for both of us to realise that, not only did we know nothing about farming, we weren't remotely interested in farming and couldn't begin to see ourselves as farmers. In fact we couldn't even think of spending another night in that dreary place.

Warily we apologised to Jed and Di, who surprised us by not being at all disappointed. Then they explained how some other friends, who really did want to farm, had asked for second option should we change our minds. So, we wouldn't be delaying their adventure after all.

In fact only two weeks later, we saw them off on the first leg of their journey towards the Buccaneer Archipelago and, sure enough, we heard later that all their pigs had been sold.

Back in our condemned house, we watched Broome continue through more disappointing changes and it became apparent that our own lives were unravelling. Ann's close friends in Derby suddenly moved to Perth, Vince announced his imminent return to England, and I received a letter saying that Ernie was off

'End of an Era'

to New Zealand to meet his new girlfriend's family, and possibly get married.

While uncertainty built up for us in Broome, major events were happening for Ann's family back home and she began to feel homesick. Also, our broken down Land Rover had been sold for very little as money was running out fast.

One night, as I lay thinking about the situation, it dawned on me that what was really preventing Ann and Lizzie from going home was that she came from the kind of family that could not welcome their daughter back with a child, and still unmarried.

So I got up, while still thinking, and made us both a drink, then woke her, saying, "Tomorrow we'll get married, then you and Lizzie can go straight to England, while I'll go to Cockatoo Island and get some money together so I can follow you both, and be home for Christmas."

She was delighted and by the following evening everything was arranged, which was possible in a place like Broome in those days.

By midnight we were married, had celebrated with a few friends and I was standing on the town jetty waving goodbye to Ann. She was seated in an open boat waving, with Lizzie asleep in her arms, while being taken to board the southward bound state ship.

They would be in Perth in a few days where Ann could arrange their passages back to England.

Having watched the ship leave, I had a hollow feeling as I returned in darkness without Ann and Lizzie to our much loved, condemned, empty house for one last lonely night, with only Ann's dog for company. It was doubly sad, as I knew that the following day I would have to watch her being put down.

It was a great shame, but Lady was a Blue Heeler, a one-person dog that just couldn't be handed over to someone else. Left to her own devices, she would have gravitated towards the pack that ran wild around town, only to be eventually 'culled', as there was a great, although possibly unfounded, fear of stray dogs mating with Dingos.

Lady didn't like me much, probably because one day another dog had mysteriously turned up on our veranda and chosen to befriend me. I called him Pooch and we stayed friends for over six months.

Each morning that I was at home I would find Pooch on the veranda waiting. He would casually get to his feet, wander over, exchange a nuzzle for a pat on the head and then remain with me until around midday. Then he would nuzzle again, I would pat again, and Pooch would go off about his own doggy business. But he would always be back waiting on our veranda the following day.

Towards the end of our relationship, Pooch had taken to riding between my legs on the platform of Ann's scooter. Worryingly, he felt it his right to take on the town pack, which by then had become quite numerous. Consequently, as I was driving, a battle of threatening teeth often raged beneath my safely crossed and withdrawn legs.

Then, one morning Pooch wasn't waiting for me on the veranda, I never saw him again. A few days later I realised there was no longer a dog pack.

The morning after Ann and Lizzie left began with a fire on the beach for burning the remnants of our accumulated belongings as I put off the inevitable decision. But it was soon obvious that Lady was already pining.

So, pulling myself together, I went and asked Doug, our local policeman, to come and put her down. It was a moving moment that brought to mind the occasion when I was eleven and had to take our much beloved Alsatian to the vet for 'putting down'.

On both occasions I held them close, and on both occasions received an understanding look, a gentle lick of acceptance and they were gone.

Doug, a tough policeman, was gentle throughout, even offering to bury Lady. I said it felt only right for me to do it. He nodded, placing an acknowledging hand on my shoulder as he left.

Relieved to be on my own, I dug a grave in a raised sandy spot among some vegetation near the house. Once the burial was complete, I re-awakened the fire to sit with it for a while before finally raking the ashes, damping it down and heading for the airport.

A couple of hours later I was looking down at the whole scene as I flew North towards Derby and the BHP office.

There was no trouble acquiring work back on the islands but, as with Broome, times had changed and the big money days were over. In the end I got very little together before being forcefully and unpleasantly evicted from the island.

My normal, 'happy go lucky' attitude of enjoying work didn't go down too well with the latest, more politically serious minded workers that I seemed to irritate and inevitably fell foul of. They reacted negatively to my dismissive attitude towards their work grievances, and I couldn't see why they were whingeing.

I think, at the time, I arrogantly saw it as a clash of lifestyles. Anyway, the outcome for me was being hauled up before an ugly group of angry men to be wrongly accused of putting other men's lives at risk, by playing 'chickie run'.

What irony that, with my massive fear of heights, I should be accused of challenging fellow drivers to duels in fifty-ton trucks along the sheer drops of the open quarry! It was a set up.

"If you're not with us, then you're against us!" someone had said.

I'd been cornered like that before and it was scary, as was the kangaroo court that involved me being addressed as 'the accused' before a wall of snarling, angry faces that were being manipulated by a couple of skilled, hostile, whingeing trouble makers.

I didn't see one supportive face among them and, as none of my friends or original men that I had known were on shift, or even on the island for all I knew, I was without an ally and there was nothing I could say.

They pronounced me guilty and told me to leave the island on a plane that was on its way to collect me and, "Never come back."

It all felt very strange and lonely but I wasn't bothered about leaving, as there was no point in being around people like that.

Luckily, the pilot who had flown in to collect me was friendly and not at all impressed with the new breed of workers saying, "Those whingeing poms are trying to control the whole thing mate, that's for sure. They've already messed up the flamin' place an' they'll just end up killin' the goose, you see if they don't, serve the bludgers right I reckon, my oath if it won't!"

Then with a big grin he turned to me and said, "Well mate, I've got no instruction other than to collect ya, so you might as well say where you want to go, and let those bludgers collect the bill, eh!"

I said "Broome please."

"Good on yer mate, have the last bloomin' laugh why don't ya."

He ended up flying me, not the 90 miles to Derby, but the longer scenic route all down the coast to Broome and, my oath, that felt bloody good!

In Broome I deliberately avoided where our house had been, feeling alienated in a place that had felt so wonderful. In spite of that, I found myself waiting about. It was partly procrastination as I wasn't looking forward to a long unpredictable hitch to Perth, but also I wanted to see a familiar face and get a chance to say good-bye to any locals that I might run into.

Waiting always feels better near water, especially when there's a view of the sea, so I ambled down to the same jetty from which Ann and Lizzie had recently set off. A couple of locals I recognised, Darg who was part Aboriginal, and Bruno who in spite of the unlikely name was Malaysian, looked at me and grinned. They were both dangling lines and a few reasonable sized fish were flapping about in a damp sheet of canvas.

The lush, green, leafy tops of the mangroves swaying in the current indicated that, although the tide was high, it still had a little way to go.

Three fishing boats had tied up alongside with their crews still on board. Darg said they were Italians who had been exploring new fishing grounds in the Gulf of Carpentaria.

"Must have been some bloody journey." He said, nodding. "Well over two thousand miles they reckon!"

"That's up near my country." Piped up Bruno proudly.

"Well it's the right direction." I said. "What are these guys in Broome for?"

"Ah, they're headin' for 'Freo' and lookin' to pick up an extra hand, how d'ya fancy that mate? You'll be near the big smoke there!" Darg's eyes were giving me a mock challenge.

"Oh yeah I reckon the timing's perfect." I said.

Both guys were obviously taken aback when, minutes later, the boats put out to sea and I was aboard one of them working my passage to Fremantle, some twelve hundred miles south!

The three crewmen on the half open boat didn't like me, and made it clear from the start. They were close-knit, hardy Italian fishermen on the last leg of a truly marathon journey and saw me as an outsider, a foreigner and probably a useless land-lubber. Unfortunately it didn't take me long to prove them more or less right.

Once out of the mangrove-waving tranquil waters of the bay and into deep waters for starting the long journey south, endless ocean rollers ensured a nauseous rolling and pitching movement for the rest of the journey. I love the sea, but I've never overcome seasickness.

By the time I had eaten the first of our standard oily pasta-and-fish meals then leaned over the rising and dipping side of the boat, dunking and scouring the oily pans and dishes in a solution of sea water and industrial detergent, I was already feeling rough enough for it to demand willpower just to get into that horizontal position where stomach muscles could be locked-up for the night.

Then first thing in the morning, after preparing a breakfast from an ugly, black-fleshed fish, I used every trick available to disguise that I was intermittently throwing up as I hung determinedly, stomach jammed to the side, making desperate attempts to scour away the lingering smell, while sharing my awful secret with the pounding waves... only afterwards to be tossed about as I lay wet, miserable and struggling to prevent what I hadn't even eaten from coming up!

Helping haul in the heavy fishing lines whenever I was called to do so was a fiasco. I was just too weak to respond to the loud shouted demands for the powerful enthusiasm that was so obviously expected.

I was so weak after the second day of throwing up and not eating that I was rendered practically helpless for the remainder of that long, drawn out trip. I was still, quite rightly, expected to do my allocated work even though my pathetic input at hauling the ropes wasn't much help.

The already frustrated crew, having endured their unsuccessful journey, constantly expressed their anger towards me and I certainly didn't feel good about my lack of self-discipline.

So for me the trip was a hell of an ordeal.

CHAPTER FORTY-FOUR
'France too close for Comfort!'

Back in Fremantle, I was sick in more ways than one. I felt disgusting and knew that I looked it, while the total absence of handshakes, goodbyes, or even of an understanding wave from my fellow crew-members confirmed what I then believed, I was disgusting!

Nauseous and stunned, I lurched about on dry land with clothes filthy and stiff from endless wind spray, seawater, fish oil, olive oil, industrial detergent, diesel and vomit. To make matters worse, the luxurious beard I'd once been proud of when it was long, lush and red, had now shrunk to what felt, and probably looked like, a matted yellow clump of shredded wheat.

Acutely embarrassed, head down and desperately not wanting to be seen, I made a beeline for Mrs Brett's house where, as soon as she opened the door, I tried to spare her the offending vision by dashing desperately for the bathroom to scrub, wash, clean up and remove that abhorrent mess from my face.

Only after changing into the clean clothes that were kept for my visits to Perth, did it feel acceptable to come out and be seen by a somewhat surprised Mrs Brett.

Unfortunately, it was the wrong move as I'd been too blinded by my acute embarrassment to realise that she hadn't recognised the manic image that had rushed into her home, but even worse, she hadn't instantly recognised the

'France too close for Comfort!'

clean-shaven person that came out, which confused her even more.

Following profuse apologies and a whole lot of laughter, we both recovered and spent a long time enjoying the funny side of it all, after which she kindly knocked me up some of her delicious, finely cut spring onion sandwiches which on that occasion were just the right post-seasick food.

I told her all about my messy journey down the coast and tried to explain my bizarre antics. Typically, she wanted to know everything that had been happening... what I had been up to, and of course what news I had of Ken.

As the sandwiches filled my hunger, so I satisfied her mind with the most recent I had of her son's latest activities at Cockatoo Island. It all went down very well and by noon we had caught up with each other's news, including the fact that I was heading back to the U.K.

With the help of several cups of tea, I began to feel recovered enough for a trip into Perth in order to arrange myself a suitable passage.

I was still staggering from the roll of the fishing boat, and remembered how I'd seen divers fresh from the pearling luggers similarly wavering as they walked about Broome.

On telling the lady in the travel office of my desire to avoid French territory, I found there was no guarantee.

She said, "As all our ships pass through the Mediterranean there's always the small risk of a ship calling into a port somewhere, but a French port is fairly unlikely. Our Italian ship, the 'Blue Sky' is a little more expensive but since I've worked here she has never called into anywhere French! Why not try her she is sailing tomorrow."

Pleased, even if somewhat wary, I paid the unwelcome extra and the following day, with Mrs Brett waving goodbye, I was sailing out of Fremantle totally oblivious of that shipping line's forthcoming scam.

Feeling slightly estranged among the somewhat dressed up, mostly English passengers, who watched the Australian coast disappearing, I focused on the news announcements coming from an Australian radio station.

The first was of a family that had returned from holiday to find that their whole house complete with garage, garden fence, sheds, barbie and garden plants had been stolen! In that light-hearted, cruising home mood, it seemed

[303]

to all of us that 'it could only happen in Australia!'

Some laughter brought more attention to the next announcement, which referred to sighting a previously undiscovered group of Aboriginals running naked in the western desert. It all sounded interesting until the announcer went on to say that clothes had been urgently dropped to them in order to avoid 'contact embarrassment'.

Now everyone was already laughing when a serious voice announced, "There is growing concern here, that these natives might just be using the clothes as head decorations!" As even louder laughter interrupted, I wondered what those moral guardians would have made of the white men we had seen sitting on hitching rails in Broome's main square with their balls hanging out.

As we settled in for the long journey home, many passengers quickly formed new friendships and I was lucky enough to make friends with a casually dressed, like-minded girl, who was Australian but with untypical looks having short dark hair, dark eyes, with the slightest hint of an accent.

She told me she was travelling to Europe in order to join her Sicilian physicist boyfriend who, having been unable to fit in socially in any of the three places in the world where apparently his qualifications were of use, was now living and teaching English to secondary school children in Turkey. Her name was Kristen.

Hanging about in our casual clothes, we must have looked drab among the rest of the passengers who were enthusiastically looking their best at all times. We mostly swam in the pool, lounged about and chatted, until she introduced me to drinking gin and orange in the heat. Then we mostly lounged about and chatted with the occasional swim.

At her suggestion, as the ship moved into cooler climes, we moved on to drinking Cointreau and stopped swimming altogether.

Then came the night of the ship's ball, and I got an incredible surprise. I was sitting at the edge of the dance floor when a woman with short blue/black urchin-style hair, wearing a red silk, slit-to-the-waist, *cheong-sam* walked confidently bare-footed across the dance floor towards me, with all eyes on her. She looked absolutely amazing, and I could hardly believe, until she sat beside me, that it was Kristen.

It was only then that it occurred to me that Kristen must have had some oriental background.

Ocean voyages by their nature are romantic, as everything conspires to make it so and, even though we had our respective partners to meet, by the time we got to the end of our journey there was some sadness in saying our good-byes.

But a new problem had arisen. Once the 'Blue Sky' was close to Genoa, came the scam. An unexpected but inevitable announcement to all passengers was made.

"Unfortunately we have been experiencing some engine difficulties, but passengers need not worry as we will shortly be docking at Genoa, where provision has already been made, at no additional cost, for all passengers to complete their respective journeys by train."

There were mutterings of course, but on the whole everyone seemed to accept it, even though word was going round that it was a regular event. But, for me it posed a particular problem, as all U.K. passengers were being sent across France, meaning I would have to find and pay for another route home.

I talked to a passenger about hitch hiking in some way that would avoid France, but he strongly advised me against doing it in winter. Although, he was certain I could get a train that would only 'border' France.

"Should be safe enough, if you sit on the right hand side!" He'd said, grinning.

Having spent more than I intended on drinks aboard ship, it was a relief, after forking out for a ticket that included the ferry crossing to Harwich, to discover I still had enough money to contact Ann and inform her of this change of plan. We enthusiastically agreed that she would meet me at Harwich on my arrival.

CHAPTER FORTY-FIVE
'The Compass Flickers'

On the train I found myself sitting next to Brandt, a young German guy who was returning from Australia, very enthusiastic about having come straight from, what he called, 'noodling' in the Opal fields of Coober Pedy.

As we exchanged stories he described the thrilling, unmistakable sound of his pick crunching into milky white, glass-like potch, with its tantalising promise of imprisoned beauty. He said there would nearly always be a hint of colour, and probably something of small financial value. But always there was a possibility of real treasure and, whatever the outcome, the treasure of anticipation was guaranteed.

He explained to me how opal mining involved firstly some hard digging, followed by breaking through rock and then channelling along beneath a stone ceiling, which meant there was no need for shoring-up as in normal tunnelling.

"In fact many people actually live down there, making really nice homes for themselves." He enthused.

He sensed we were both getting fired up, at which stage he rummaged through his bag to bring out a grubby looking notebook.

"My log." He said, in a tone of exaggerated pride, moving across to sit next to me.

As he opened the little book it turned out to be an exciting journal of discoveries which I could see would make fascinating reading, but it was the back page entries that grabbed my enthusiasm and got me really excited at the prospect of heading for Coober Pedy as soon as Ann could be ready.

Those entries were a list of 'finds', showing some finds everyday, then whole weeks passing with nothing found at all, then several in one day.

The excitement was infectious and we were soon exchanging addresses in readiness for our imminent trip back to Australia. Feeling the decision was now made, we chatted about other things, including Broome, which he found fascinating.

When he asked me about going back to England, I mentioned that with recent financial mess-ups and sudden changes of plan, I was feeling bad at not having got a present for Ann.

"But the present will be to take her noodling!" He said, laughing.

I sat back imagining what Ann would say when I told her we are going straight back with a new friend to 'noodle' in the opal fields of Australia.

I was brought out of my dream when Brandt touched my arm.

"My stop is soon and I want to show you something, I think it is safe enough now." He had pulled his bag over to put his notebook and address book away and now from amongst his clothing produced a jam jar, and I noticed he was trembling slightly as he passed it to me.

"Did you ever see such beauty?"

I was enthralled.

"I've never seen opals before." I said. "They're beautiful."

I was turning the jar to catch the light.

"Let me show you."

He took the jar and tipped some out carefully, as several colourful bits were very small.

"I think," he said handing me a stone, "as we will soon be work mates, you should have this very colourful opal. Maybe it will help you to encourage your lady to come to Coober Pedy.

I will see you soon my friend. Have a good Christmas."

Once Brandt had left the train, I spent a long time looking into the translucent colours, dreaming about various things, including Brandt's spontaneous generosity. I also dreamed about opals and noodling, and how Ann would react on receiving a real gem straight from the opal fields of Coober Pedy.

Apart from looking forward to seeing both Ann and Lizzie, and wondering how much Lizzie may have changed, there's little I remember about the rest of the journey except that when we docked at Harwich it was, of course, to typical grey English drizzle.

Nearly five years had passed since I had set off to meet friends at Mick's café for going jiving at the Aldershot Palais.

I had intended bringing back the six eggs for my mum had I got back early enough, which of course I didn't! Instead, I spontaneously chose to keep that schoolboy promise and visit Ken in Australia.

From the moment of that decision, the 'compass of naivety' guided me through curious adventures and helped me live out some wonderful boyhood fantasies.

What with the opal for Ann, the delicate child's seed pearl necklace I had acquired earlier for Lizzie, my passports, Australian licenses and citizenship papers, the possessions I carried back were definitely more than when I left.

Of course I was no longer wearing the Teddy boy outfit but nonetheless, like then, I pretty much only had the clothes I stood in, plus enough money to perhaps haggle for a light breakfast, or maybe even to buy six eggs!

....

THE END

Printed in Great
Britain
by Amazon